THE CREATED SELF

THE
CREATED
SELF

REINVENTING BODY,

PERSONA, AND SPIRIT

Robert J. Weber

W. W. NORTON & COMPANY

New York   London

For information about permission to reproduce selections from this
book, write to Permissions, W. W. Norton & Company, Inc., 500 Fifth
Avenue, New York, NY 10110

The text of this book is composed in New Baskerville
with the display set in Eurostyle
Composition and layout by Gina Webster
Manufacturing by Maple-Vail
Book design by BTDnyc

LIBRARY OF CONGRESS CATALOGING-IN-PUBLICATION DATA

Weber, Robert J. (Robert John), 1936–
     The created self : reinventing body, persona, spirit / Robert J.
  Weber
            p.   cm.
     Includes bibliographical references and index.
     ISBN 0-393-04833-0
     1. Self-presentation. 2. Change (Psychology) I. Title.
  BF697.5.S44W43   2000
  155.2—dc21   99-37480
                                                         CIP

W. W. Norton & Company, Inc., 500 Fifth Avenue, New York, N.Y. 10110
www.wwnorton.com

W. W. Norton & Company Ltd., 10 Coptic Street, London WC1A 1PU

1 2 3 4 5 6 7 8 9 0

For G — a Changing Self

CONTENTS

PREFACE

I CELEBRATE myself, and sing myself,
And what I assume you shall assume,
For every atom belonging to me as good belongs to you. . . .
Why even I myself I often think know little or nothing of
        my real life,
Only a few hints, a few diffused faint clews and indirections
I seek for my own use to trace out here.
One world is aware and by far the largest to me,
        and that is myself. . . .

—WALT WHITMAN, *Leaves of Grass*

Famous people come and go, great events recede into insignificance. But one player is constantly on the stage of our attention. One player offers endless nuance, fascination, romance, and turns of story. That player is the self.

Why the ever-present interest in the self and its workings? Why does this player—who struts with vanity, cowers with shyness, and reaches for the infinite—have such hold on attention's platform? *The Created Self* provides a spyglass for a close examination of the player, viewing her outward and inward manifestations, her loving and hopeful face, her smirks and grimaces, her motives and emotions, as she stretches, extends, and explores the most distant and obscure corners of life's stage.

A common purpose guides our viewing: to provide a better

understanding of why and how one deliberately transforms the self through conscious intention. Although some forms of self-change are ageless—cosmetics, body painting, tattooing—their uses or meanings are often new. Other changes—surgically enhancing appearance, becoming a surrogate mother—are radically new.

As the workings of ancient processes of mind—involving unity, interpretation, and empathy—make their way into consciousness, they become powerful modes of self-creation. Also new are the personas that people now invent. One may craft a new identity by deliberately trying on roles and masks and connecting with an admired other. Additional changes are more spiritual. People seek out, mix together, and create elements of faith in order to replace traditional beliefs. In the process, they find or design their own faith, their own gods. Why do people make these choices? What is the nature of the mind that directs these changes? These are some of the issues addressed by *The Created Self*.

The issues are examined from the perspective of William James and from current thinking about evolutionary psychology and philosophy. Walt Whitman's poems of self introduce each chapter and provide atmosphere. The perspective offered thus differs from that of most work on the nature of the self: Sigmund Freud and the unconscious, Carl Jung with his archetypes and myth, and the postmodern emphasis on culture.[1]

I agree with Freud and Jung that there is a human nature, but the approach here is not concerned with the unconscious so much as with uncovering processes that allow for the deliberate change of the self, processes that build on our evolutionary past. My view differs from the postmodernists in that it denies that the construction of the self is primarily a cultural rather than an individual matter. While culture is important in the formation of self, it is not the only factor, and I want to emphasize here the other influences: evolutionary biology and what most people would call choice.

Without any doubt, this is a high wire to walk, secured at one end by evolution and at the other by the choices that confront us.

For guidance I draw on an earlier student of the self, William James (1842–1910), an advocate of both evolution and choice. James was the first American psychologist and a founder of the most original American philosophy, pragmatism. By training he was a physician, but he gravitated to psychology, philosophy, and religion. In all of these areas he thought broadly and deeply about the self. His thoughts form our first viewing lens for examination of the self.[2] Because his ideas changed from time to time, and many of the topics considered here were not his own, his thoughts provide us with a springboard rather than a complete foundation. Were he alive today, I am sure his fascination would be evident for the subjects covered: makeovers, tattooing, piercing, and cosmetic surgery to modify the body; identity loss, masks, and empathic constructions to build the persona; and spiritual belief, the quest for purpose, the sense of the sacred, the construction of deities and an afterself—all of which may serve to craft a created self.

Contemporary evolutionary psychology offers a second useful lens for exploring the details of the self. Our present anatomy and mind are the result of ancient adaptive forces that were at work in hunter-gatherer times. Some of those forces produced new mental capabilities, or modules as they are sometimes called, and other forces tied them together in new integrations, with their own tensions and harmonies. One of the most heterogeneous and complex of such modules is that difficult to describe and analyze entity that we call the *self*.

Within the framework provided by William James and evolutionary psychology, *The Created Self* is about personal transformation that is usually of a chosen or voluntary sort. Starting with the evolution of self-awareness, we identify capacities of self for individual creation in a new and constantly shifting environment.

What, then, is this thing called *self* and why is it important? The self is a three-part system in which the components sometimes work separately and other times together: The *body* is nominally biological, but to the question "What am I?" an answer requires something more than biology because of the changes and perfection sought for that body. The *persona* is how we think of ourselves, how we present self to others, and how we are connected to them. It is concerned with the questions "Who am I?" and "What should I be?" It, too, is based on evolutionary constructions, but it transcends that prehistory through new masks and identifications. The *spirit* is the sense of the sacred that places us in the universe with origin stories, the set of beliefs we hold, and the actions we engage in to understand and cope with the eternal questions "Why am I here?" and "Where am I going?" The answers to these questions lead to the great religious abstractions of what is sacred, where we fit in the universe, and how we construct our gods.

Because of questions like these, we cannot confine ourselves to a scientific treatment of the self. While the facts and concepts of science are used where appropriate, the approach taken is frankly interpretive and speculative. That is as it should be because answers to the deep questions involve not only science but also the storytelling capabilities of mind, where meaning is interpreted or imposed on experience.[3] More than a thinking machine, the brain is a story-making organ. But not all stories are equally meaningful. The ones that compel are based on the built-in structures and tendencies of the mind.

Why now raise the issue of creating the self? Haven't we always done that? Yes, but usually at a nonconscious level, forced by hunger or fear or perhaps stimulated by immediate lust or greed. What is different now is the deliberate, intentional creation of self in the absence of a single overarching culture. Older notions of a constant identity lose force as we acquire the freedom to sample from many cultures. New ideas about the nature of our evolution and past confront us. New options from technology enhance our ability to change. We increasingly think of the self as an art form to be created, a material to be sculpted.

As more people engage in a conscious and deliberate effort to create a new identity—whether for an hour, a weekend, or a lifetime—we want to see how and why it is done, the directions pointed to, the underlying nature of self. In the process, previously separate planes of self-creation are undergoing accelerated change and coming together in new mixes. As more of us engage in a conscious and deliberate effort to create a new self, we want to know where we are in our own process of creation and what this new freedom does for us—or to us.

We will examine a wide range of self-change, although another author might well have selected a different set of topics. And certain seemingly relevant topics have been deliberately left out to make the task manageable and coherent: We will not consider pathology such as schizophrenia and mood disorder or cerebral accidents such as tumor and stroke. Nor are multiple personality or split-brain phenomena examined. The synthetic life and presentation of self on the Internet is touched on only in passing. The influence of culture on self is not emphasized. All of these have their own fascination, but others have covered them extensively, and for the most part they are not of deliberate action, a consciously willed crafting of self.

One other caveat is in order. I have sought to emphasize equally women and men in this portrait of changing self. Rather than resort to barbarisms like "he/she" or "she/he," I frequently wrote an entire section from either a male or female point of view, with the hope that overall there is an approximate balance.

Come, now; let us enter together the theater and world of the changing self.

ROBERT J. WEBER
Albuquerque, New Mexico
December 1998

ACKNOWLEDGMENTS

A book is the work of many people and institutions—even a book about the self. Some of those people who have aided me but are not responsible for my excesses include:

David Hendin, my agent, and Angela von der Lippe, my editor, both of whom saw promise in this enterprise long before I could clearly articulate it.

The School of Law, University of New Mexico, which provided me most recently with an intellectual home as a visiting research professor, even though I am a psychologist by training. I am most grateful to then dean Leo Romero and research librarian Mary Custy.

Many others contributed or read parts of the manuscript: Joe Boroughs, Subrata Dasgupta, Hana Norton, Jay Van Wyc. My critique group: Nancy Shelton, Gail Rubin, Sheri Burr, Jeanne Jensen, Kay Lamb, Susan Wyatt, April Kopp, Carolee Dean.

Also: Gloria Valencia-Weber, Tom LaMarre, Francis Laws, Marlene Keller, Carol Cox-Smith, Carol Cassell, Earl Mitchell, Jr., Dawn Bradley Berry, Beverly Brown, Matt Brown, June Skinner, Madge Harah, Gwen Spencer, Holly Ewing, Margaret Ewing. Finally, a number of anonymous and kindly individuals have also contributed in many ways.

THE CREATED SELF

INTRODUCTION

Transport yourself back thirty thousand years. Changing Self is approaching a cave. He wears skins, and wrapped around him is a belt with dangling leather pouches. At the cave entrance he retrieves a stone lamp he previously made—a hand-sized rock with a central depression—and fills it with a fatty oil. Now he places a wick in the center. From one pouch he removes flint and a bundle of dried grass. He strikes the flint and fans a spark into the dried grass. The spark flickers and turns into flame. He reaches out and touches the flaming grass to the lamp's wick.

Now Changing Self lifts the lamp and walks into the dark confines of the cave. He places the lamp on a boulder, where it illuminates the stone wall. Then he opens another pouch, this one filled with a mixture of animal fat and red ochre, a metallic pigment. Rubbing his hand into the mixture, coating it thoroughly, he moves to the cave wall, reaches up, and firmly presses the pigment-covered hand against the wall. He stands back, picks up the stone lamp, and holds the light closer. Yes, it is there: a positive image, a red handprint, a mark of himself. Admiration and awe fill his heart because the handprint says an "I" has been here. An I-self making its mark with a persisting form.

On another occasion Changing Self returns to the cave. This time he uses a mixture called kohl, consisting of charcoal, metal oxide, and fat. Instead of coating his hand and leaving a positive image, he now uses a different method. Placing his left hand on the wall, he dips the index finger of his right hand into the pigment and traces the hand pressed against the wall. Once again the lamp is held high. The stencil outline of his hand, a negative image, reflects back. He has found another way of leaving a mark of self.

Still later, Changing Self returns to the cave with the red-ochre pigment in solution. Using a reed tube, he sucks up the pigment and once more places his left hand on the wall. His breath pulses through the tube as he slowly guides it around the contours of the hand, spraying pigment on the wall. The lamp held high reveals another image of his hand. It is also a negative, with the pigment surrounding the hand, yet the sprayed effect is much different than a simple tracing. He likes this mark of self. It produces a new effect, something he thinks of as beautiful.

The story of Changing Self is based on handprints recently discovered in Chauvet Cave in what is now France. Of course, he is a personification of many people, and we know little about him beyond what can be inferred from the images on the cave wall. Indeed, some of those handprints may have been from a female; we do not know. The approximately thirty-thousand-year-old handprints differ from footprints or other artifacts of that time or earlier because they are clearly the result of intentional acts engaged in to leave a trace or mark of self. Also in that same cave are striking works of representational art, huge animals coming out of the shadows in leaps of artistic imagination as opposed to crude drawings. The purpose of these images is unknown; they may have had spiritual significance.

Because we humans have a fascination for origin, birth, beginning, it is natural to ask: When did the idea of the self begin? For want of a better marker, I propose an origin dating not to the first anatomically modern humans of one hundred thousand years ago but to a self-awareness characterized by deliberately leaving images of one's passing, as with the images of Changing Self's hand of thirty thousand years ago. Significant changes and interconnections in neural anatomy may have taken place well after the formation of the modern skeleton, and those changes likely provided the capacity of self-reference and art found in Chauvet Cave and similar locations.

Whatever their origin, those handprints speak to us today. They tell a story of self. They tell us that Changing Self was right handed because the negative images were probably traced by the dominant hand around the other hand. They are not just physical traces but also marks characterizing stages of planning, foresight, and intention, all directed to leave vestiges that are different from the body, a kind of extension or expansion of self onto rock and into history.

The awareness and deliberation behind these acts is revealing. Lamps must be created, oil collected and processed, a wick made and inserted, and flint provided for lighting the wick. Oxide pigments must be found, ground into fine particles, mixed with binders such as egg or fat, and packed into a pouch for storage and conveyance. A place of meaning must be sought out—the depths of a cave where working conditions are difficult—and then every part of the planning and preparation converges in that cave to freeze a hand image on a rock wall.

In moments such as this, individuality is caught in a snapshot of a hand on stone that is carried forward in time. Such images mark the beginnings of self as a permanent feature of human consciousness. A self characterized by awareness, deliberation, and coordination is born and projected beyond the physical body. This mark of a human hand shouts forth, saying an I-self has been here and will persist.[1]

Images such as those found in Chauvet Cave are part of a long development. Anatomically modern humans began to appear about one hundred thousand years ago in Africa and the Middle East. However, the archaeological record of their tools and artifacts does not distinguish them from the artifacts of the more archaic Neanderthals. As the cognitive archaeologist Steven Mithen argues, in the period from sixty thousand to thirty thousand years ago, something dramatic began to happen, a cultural Big Bang.[2] Specialized tools appeared that were the result of skilled craftsmanship, graves that were deliberate burials made themselves known by the artifacts included within them, and toward the end of that period what we call art began to appear with increasing frequency, culminating in intentional handprints and great paintings as exemplified by those of Chauvet Cave.

William James's View of the Self

We now turn to the intellectual lenses chosen for viewing the present work, the thought of the nineteenth-century psychologist and philosopher William James and the theorizing of contemporary evolutionary psychologists.

James delved deeply into the nature of the self.[3] His method was primarily introspective and informal observation, but his insights were keen. He divided the self into three principal parts—material, social, and spiritual—which he sometimes called the Me. The material self consisted of the body and its radiations: clothing, jewelry, immediate possessions, a house, and the like. The social self consisted of how we relate to others, including relatives, friends, and strangers, in ever wider radiation. Finally, the spiritual self was less well-defined in his original essays, but it was concerned with belief, faith, religious experiences, and the ways we consider and relate to unseen forces in the universe.[4] James then added to this classification an important aspect of the self, an "I" that is characterized by awareness, consciousness, and sentience. This sentient I takes as its objects of awareness the Me of the body, the social self, and the spiritual self.

As we explore the nature of the self, the focus will sometimes follow and sometimes vary from that of James. In particular, the aspect of the material self we will be concerned with is the *body*. Instead of examining the relationships of a social self, we will consider a *persona* that defines an identity and addresses how one thinks of self and presents it to others. Finally, we will consider the *spirit* as a bundle of processes like belief, purpose, and the perception of the sacred, all concerned with how one relates to unseen but deeply felt forces. And the I-self—the part concerned with consciousness, awareness, and the like—will run through the discussion of all of our chosen topics.

To place these aspects of self in perspective, return briefly to the opening story of Changing Self. The affixing of handprints to the cave wall manifests both an aware I-self and a Me-self that is part of the body. He is consciously, intentionally engaged in leaving a trace of his physical body. He may also be doing this for social or spiritual reasons. Perhaps his handprints identify him as a leader of his band, or he thinks of himself in that way. By leaving a mark of his hand, he may place himself in touch with the spirits of the animals painted on the cave wall. So in the handprints and animal drawings on the cave, all the major categories of self may be evident.

Evolutionary Psychology's View

To understand Changing Self's behavior and the current state of the self, the lens of evolutionary psychology is also needed. The evolutionary psychologist believes there is a human nature; we are not merely the products of the shifting forces of culture as the standard social science model and postmodernism would have it.[5] Said in another way, the mind is not a blank slate on which experience is writ but rather a tablet prepared by evolution to receive certain kinds of impressions. There is also a closely coupled action system that is ready for particular deeds in the social and natural world.

While these underlying systems may be influenced by experience and culture, a substratum there comes from our biology. Evolutionary psychology is about the nature of organisms that managed to survive and perpetuate themselves. Sometimes, as a shorthand, I will speak of behaviors that contribute to this process as being *adaptive*: They promote getting one's genes into the next generation, evolution's method of keeping score.

In this account, our distinctive mental nature began formation in our evolutionary past, perhaps beginning six million years ago when our evolutionary line split off from the common ancestors that we share with present-day chimps and other apes. The environment of evolutionary adaptation for humans and their proto-human ancestors required a hunting-gathering lifestyle, and a variety of mental capabilities were formed over that time to mesh with the demands of the environment. Just as the body contains distinct organ systems such as heart, liver, lungs, and circulatory system, so, too, is the brain made up of a variety of different organs or modules with distinguishable functions. In fact, the brain has been compared to a Swiss Army Knife, with the different blades corresponding to different mental modules.[6]

According to the cognitive archaeologist Steven Mithen, the mental capabilities, formed in our ancient past, included:

- general intelligence for dealing with problems that cannot be anticipated, no doubt an important advance over only specific forms of intelligence;
- social intelligence for communicating with others of the same species about social matters;
- natural-history intelligence for knowing about food sources, climate, and shelter;
- linguistic intelligence originally applied to social relationships; and
- technological intelligence first revealed in specialized tool making and tool use.

In turn, these classes were composed of even more specific forms of intelligence.

Mithen believes the order listed above approximates the emergence of the varied forms of intelligence.[7] Many behaviors that seem specific to a particular intelligence are first the province of general intelligence and only later have a specialized mental module associated with them. Thus, stone tools first made their appearance a little more than two million years ago, but they remained unchanged for a very long period of time. Therefore, they are likely to have been the product of a general intelligence rather than a specialized technological intelligence, which really begins to show itself about sixty thousand years ago in an amazing florescence of tool and technological variety that has been likened in cosmological metaphor to culture's Big Bang. No doubt that florescence is the result of many intelligences coming together, perhaps through subtle connecting tracts within the brain.

Not everyone would agree with Mithen and make general intelligence an early development. The evolutionary psychologists Leda Cosmides and John Tooby argue for highly specialized mental modules, ones designed for particular activities such as seeking and selecting food, mates, and the like.[8] If there is general intelligence, in this view, it is likely the result of adding together successive specific modules. Mithen would likely counter that general intelligence can also result from the connection of specific mental modules. Whatever side one takes in this debate, it's likely that our evolutionary past has selected a large number of specific abilities and then through mutational processes has specialized them and managed to hook some of them together.

For each of these conceptions, the driving force behind the development of the mind is the Darwinian notion of natural selection. Those variations in body and mind that pay off in survival and reproductive success are *adaptive*, and they become the ones that endure. Of particular importance are the different reproductive strategies of females and males in this evolution. The female has a high investment strategy and so seeks to have a dependable mate who will supply resources at least through the period of a child's helplessness. This will make it more likely for her to get her genes into the next generation, the name of the evolutionary game. The male, in contrast, has a low investment strategy and is most likely to get his genes into the next generation by having contact with many females. In this scheme of things the biggest threat to the female is that the male will form enduring and resource-requiring bonds with other females. The male's biggest threat is that he will devote resources to a child that is not his, thereby promoting not his own genes but someone else's.

In the process, evolution works in a variety of macro ways. Here are some of its strategies for inventing bodies and minds, if we may speak of a blind force as having strategies:

Make things bigger. Examples include brains and sex organs. We modern humans have the largest penises and breasts of any primate. We do not, however, have the largest brain in primate history. The Neanderthals had brains as at least as large as ours, but they were probably not connected as efficiently. Excess brain tissue is costly, requiring more than twenty times as much energy as an equivalent mass of muscle at rest.[9] The fact that the early artifacts of the Cro-Magnons (people like us) were much more complex than those of the Neanderthals suggests that the architecture of the brain—the specialization of parts and how they are connected—is at least as important as its volume.

Make things smaller. Examples include jaws, muscles, and teeth, all of which tend to be smaller in us than in our protohuman ancestors.

Change shapes. The brow ridge and the head configuration changed greatly over our evolutionary history. Even though our brains are about the same size as those of the Neanderthals, our more prominent forehead conceals larger frontal lobes, an important locus of foresight and planning.

Make the average desirable. The most beautiful faces tend to be the average of other faces.[10] For example, a nose that is neither too large nor too small is most attractive.

Increase or decrease the difference between the sexes. Some of the sexual characteristics that distinguish men and women may not have survival reasons other than for being sexually selected. The analogy is the male peacock's tail or the male Irish elk's massive antlers. Neither of these displays is functional in the sense of navigating an environment or surviving predators, but they tend to exaggerate differences between the sexes, and such extravagant development and display may signify to the female that the male is healthy and desirable.[11]

Add modules. Examples include the language module of the brain and possibly a technological intelligence module.

Connect things already there. Examples include previously independent brain modules that begin to communicate with one another and come to form a system. The Big Bang of human culture, the early glimmer of civilization about sixty thousand years ago, may signify that all the components of self as we know it finally linked together with one another. Said in another way, the self is a lashing together of an ability to conceptualize an I, Me, You, and Other that produces the emergent capability that we call civilization. If that is remotely true, then no study can be of greater importance than understanding the nature and workings of the self.

While these forms of evolutionary change begin at the genetic level, whether they will become widely distributed depends on their macro effects: Do they work in the natural and social environment of the time? Do they enable survival and successful reproduction? Do they provide resistance to disease and parasites?[12] Some of these strategies seem designed for coping skills in the environment (bigger muscles, bigger teeth); others are more likely due to sexual selection. Somewhere in the distant past the hooking together and specialization of previously separate modules of the brain generated linguistic behavior. Still other evolutionary strategies involve trade-offs. A big brain is useful for solving problems, but it is a real energy consumer. So more efficient wiring saves energy and adds brainpower at the same time.

While evolution's strategies served to construct our present bodies and minds, they did so in an ancient hunter-gatherer world. What was once a useful strategy and outcome may be no longer.

Anger in a Stone-Age environment primed the body for defense so that attacks could be warded off or the other party could be bluffed. Now anger has the technology of a three-thousand-pound car to use as a weapon during road rage or an automatic firearm to shoot people who look at us in the wrong way.

More generally, the designs forged from Darwinian selection processes served for one environment and now exist in another. To see this, consider:

A To-do List for Darwinians:
- Get up.
- Survive.
- Reproduce.
- Die.

That may be a good description of life for almost everyone in the not-too-distant past and still for some people in the contemporary world. But for those individuals in the vanguard of voluntary transformation, their days involve only a limited amount of time spent on Darwinian activities. Instead, they are likely to have substantial leisure, financial resources, freedom from traditional ties, access to the diverse information flows sweeping the world, diminishing influences from religious authority, and new technologies to work with.

We do not need to have all of these factors operating as a context for fashioning the self, but in substantial combination they provide the social foundation for self-change. Even the old capacities and behavioral forms of our evolutionary past take on new purposes and functions. Our basic hardware may have been designed for the To-do List of Darwinian evolution, but those particular imperatives no longer hold much of our attention. In apparent freedom from Darwin's dictates, our sexual activity rarely results in reproduction, and we may take special precautions to see that it does not.

Even the most basic of acts now take on signs of self-transformation. When eating, we consume gourmet blends, the elements of which are new combinations. In our free time we may collect stamps, play the guitar, engage in tennis, sky dive, or write poetry— none of which has any direct link to evolutionary selection. To be sure, many people do not have the opportunities such a regimen allows, but it is the fertile ground in which much of contemporary self-creation is taking place. The hand and brain from our past are now turned to serve the emergent elaborations of art, religion, and science. One other factor exerts a profound influence: the realization that we have the freedom to create ourselves, that we can deliberately sculpt the body, persona, and spirit.

Still, evolutionary psychology provides a useful framework, a kind of baseline against which we mark the distance of self-change. But it comes in no one brand. Such evolutionary psychologists as Leda Cosmides and Steven Pinker center on biology and the functions of the brain. A key idea is that we were designed in an evolutionary environment of hunter-gatherers, foraging in small bands, and now we are forced to cope with alien urban environments with millions of people. In contrast, the psychologist Mihaly Csikszentmihalyi writes of an evolving self, one that is steadily becoming more complex, biologically and socially, by virtue of successive differentiations and integrations of brain and behavior.[13]

In a contemporary variation, the evolutionary biologist E. O. Wilson advocates a conscious evolution that begins with a greater integration and unity between the arts and humanities on the one hand and science, such as that of biology and evolutionary theory, on the other.[14] The implication is that a more scientific self will be more capable of dealing with a changing world. Bringing all of human behavior into the evolutionary and scientific perspective will foster more rapid integration and progress. Specifically, Wilson advocates *consilience,* an old word that means a jumping together. Thus the varied disciplines ought to practice consilience, with most of the jumping to be performed by the arts and humanities toward the rapidly evolving sciences.

Surprisingly, such an argument ignores our evolutionary history because the arts, crafts, and storytelling are our oldest forms of understanding. In my view, we should aim for a greater consilience among all forms of knowing, but the jumping together should be more than unidirectional. Science needs to come to terms with our other, older ways of knowing and understanding the world and the self. We need a reverse consilience, one in which the tremendous powers of science come to value and seek understanding of the real roots of our evolutionary past: art, craft, storytelling, plus the perception and valuing afforded by the sacred. As I will show, it is all of these ingredients in combination that are fueling the modern creation of self.

Unity and Harmony

To construct a meaningful self out of the sea of possible variations, we need focus and guidelines. William James had an important idea here, one to which we will repeatedly turn. He was concerned with the idea of unity or harmony, how the various aspects of experience and self fit with one another. An individual thought is an apparent unity, although on reflection we can take it apart and divide it into varied components and attributes. By so doing, we establish it as visual or verbal in mode, short or long in duration, and so on. Here unity is the natural state, something that comes before analysis, and as such it is the proof of a Thinker, a Knower, an I at work that integrates behind the scenes.[15]

James does not describe in detail his conception of unity. I want to use his concern with its importance as a point of departure and propose the existence of a *unity system* as an essential subsystem of the self. It is most probably a relatively recent characteristic of our lineage, perhaps dating to the first appearance of anatomically modern humans about one hundred thousand years ago. Its trace is found in the structure of story, one of the oldest forms we have of knowing self, universe, and the relations between the two. Underneath the surface of story is an architectural system that binds character and plot together. Let us examine the likely sub-components of the unity system and their function:

Consistency. Life's separate parts should be consistent with one another. We don't want to think of someone as a friend and an enemy at the same time, holding out one hand in generosity and the other in threat. Such mental divisions distract, produce unease, and divert energy in different directions. Note that the content of consistency here may be thoughts, feelings, and actions; that is true of the following factors, as well.

Compatibility. More than consistency as a simple absence of contradiction, the separate parts of ongoing life should fit togeth-er at the same time, like the parts of a puzzle, each one contribut-ing to an overall compatibility.

Coherence or Continuity. While compatibility deals with the fit of current activities with one another, coherence is concerned with the fit of activities across time. One wants a life to have continuity and connection with the past. What is done today should grow out of what was done yesterday and the day before that, and those experiences should then blend with the future.

Completeness. One wants to be a complete person, someone who values fully the somewhat separate realms of thought, feeling, and action—or the separate realms of body, persona, and spirit. One needs a work life and a personal life, a time for both rela-tionship and solitude, a time to grow, a time to contemplate fitting into the larger universe—all of these things in balance go into making a complete person.

Compactness. The self should be parsimonious and simple rather than complex and convoluted in organizing our beliefs and actions. Like a ball of string, the more compact the core self, the less chance of raveled and knotted ends.

Community. Life alone is a heavy burden. A person needs to have connections to others. Instead of being an island unto one's self, we want the nurturing of others, of community, and the ability to reach out to others.

These examples of the unity system in action suggest a conscious, volitional system, yet its origin is likely that of a largely unconscious system in development, one that only recently in evolutionary time connected with a linguistic system and became, in part, open to awareness and long-term intention.

We mostly know that the unity system is at work when we depart from it. Then we are punished by anxiety, guilt, shame, ambivalence, and all the tearing forces that body and mind can inflict on one another. These negative states act as warning signals that something is wrong. When we are in balance, in harmony, in unity, we have an ongoing sense of ease. But those moments of contentment are not as sharply demarcated as the times of disruption and the ensuing forms of unease.

In combination, these C-standards—consistency, compatibility, coherence, completeness, compactness, and connection to community—form a system for building a thoughtful, integrated self, one with unity, harmony, and identity across time and place.

To be sure, the components of the unity system are not strong influences like hunger, and their linkage does not bind like sinew. Yet together they form a system that offers great advantage for focusing thought, feeling, and action in the world. While the components may not all function at a given point in time, most of us are guided by them, even if implicitly. Because evolution works over long periods, all that is required of an adaptive system is a slight edge over its absence or its alternatives.

Most important of all is the idea that the separate unity factors should function together as a system, where sometimes one component or principle is ascendant; other times, a different one. The systemlike nature of unity is easily revealed in typical trade-offs. Thus one can have too much consistency and not enough reach for novelty in life. And some components, like completeness and compactness, are forever in tension with each other. The more we seek new experiences in a search for completeness, the more complex and extended we find the self, and the greater the departure from being a simple, compact self. Having a compact set of beliefs that is simultaneously large enough to encompass new experiences is not an easy matter. Clearly, some happy balance of the separate unity factors is worth aiming for, or else the disharmony of mental unease will make itself known through anxiety, guilt, and other forms of distress.

Another basis for a unity system is in formation. Evolution is driven in part by the efficient use of energy. The best brain is small and integrated rather than large with walled-off components—a point made by comparing our brain size and probable integration with the Neanderthal brain. While at least as large as ours, their brains must have lacked a similar connecting architecture and specialization, as judged by the gulf that separated their material cultural and technological achievement from those of our modern human forebears.[16]

The unity system described here provides a way of conserving physical energy while meeting new demands. We try to accomplish several objectives on the same journey—say, both buying milk and dropping off a library book. We devise tools to increase our efficiency—a hammer instead of a hand or a rock. The mental mechanisms behind such economizing acts are not clear. One can argue whether energy saving is a result of carefully wrought general intelligence or a series of separate capabilities linked together. Such energy-conserving strategies are likely to occur early on in evolution, although the conscious awareness of them and their systematic implementation may be another matter, probably much later in development. Certainly we all depart from the unity system and fail to make the appropriate trade-offs from time to time. But an evolutionary capability does not require perfect functioning, only a workable fix for the problems confronted in an environment. One of those problems is surely energy conservation and the associated economy of effort.

Yet there is more to unity than energy conservation. As described, the unity system and its separate components seem to lie at the base of effective storytelling and all those fictions that are believable and moving. Often the most dramatic and troubled characters of fiction are those who significantly violate some aspect of unity. Such characters heighten our interest because we can learn from them. The more global structure of story itself also adheres to unity principles where character and motivation must fit intention and action. Said in another way, when applied to the architecture of story, the unity system slips subtly into a unity standard or norm for telling good stories, quite possibly mirroring the way the mind understands events.[17] To the degree that that is true, the forces of unity will aid us in understanding the construction of the self.

We are now ready for the overall view of the self taken in this book. In graphic form, it consists of three parts body, persona, and spirit as shown in the accompanying Figure I.1.

Symbolically, the circles indicate that the self is a system of interlocking parts, each part with ties to the others. In the middle of the figure is a center, or core, that is the most integrated portion of the self, where everything comes together and interacts, the part we try most to preserve during tension and adversity.

At different times in our lives we emphasize different parts of the self. I am not advocating a stage theory, but when we are young we may place a greater emphasis on the body and appearance, and when we are old we may emphasize more the spiritual aspects of self. Some activities may also emphasize one component more than another: Athletics, the body; social relations, the persona; and solitude, the spiritual. Still other activities may engage more than one component of the self at a time. While hiking over a mountain range we may find the body in a state of fatigue, the persona feeling free and unattached and the spirit grasping something sacred and inspired in the sunset and the shadows.

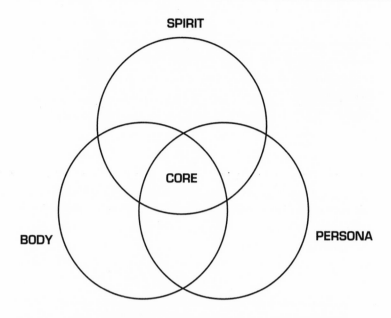

FIGURE I.1. *The three-part division of self: body, persona, and spirit. Each part overlaps with the others, and the center portion—where everything comes together—constitutes the core self.*

The interdependent parts of the self working together form an overall ecology of body, persona, and spirit. We shall probe the complexity of this system as we explore in more detail the components of the changing self.

Creating a Body

[E]ach human mind's appearance on this earth is conditioned upon the integrity of the body with which it belongs, upon the treatment which that body gets from others and upon the . . . dispositions which use it as their tool, and lead it either towards longevity or to destruction. Its own body, then, first of all, its friends next, and finally its spiritual dispositions, MUST be the supremely interesting objects for each human mind.

—WILLIAM JAMES, *Psychology: Briefer Course*

What am I? What should I look like? How should I shape my appearance? Here are examples of the body in transition away from what is biologically given, with methods ranging from a cosmetic makeover to the ever more extensive and deeper penetrations afforded by body painting, tattooing, piercing, surgical augmentation, and the remarkable yearning to create another bodily self through extraordinary reproductive means. Underlying these transformations of body are quests for restoration, preservation, perfection, and extension beyond the physical self.

Chapter 1

TRYING ON FACES

The love of the body of man or woman balks account,
the body itself balks account,
That of the male is perfect, and that of the female is perfect. . . .
I breathe the fragrance myself and know it and like it,
The distillation would intoxicate me also, but I shall not let it.

—WALT WHITMAN, *Leaves of Grass*

The cave wall reflecting an image of Changing Self's hand is a crude sort of mirror. Using a modern mirror, the anthropologist Edmund Carpenter studied the Biami, an isolated tribe of Papua New Guinea. When first exposed to their own images, they were bewildered and frightened.[1] In a few days, however, they came to groom themselves before the mirror. The group, at Carpenter's urging, also used a Polaroid camera to capture their own likenesses. The different forms of technology for capturing their images produced a new kind of self-awareness among the Biami. This is a complex understanding of the self, one distinguishable from the *projected* awareness of leaving handprints on a cave wall. The mirror and photographic forms of image constitute a *receptive,* or reflected, form of self-awareness, seeing an apparent other and realizing that it is one's self.

When chimpanzees and orangutans are exposed for the first time to mirrors, their reaction also reveals fascination.[2] They will examine their teeth or position the mirror to see their own genitals. Especially curious about their genitals are the females, who normally have less visual access to them than males.

Chimps also make faces while studying their shifting expressions in the mirror; they are exploring the varied faces of self. Yet monkeys do none of this. A monkey responds aggressively, as though seeing another monkey, and does not recognize the mirror image as self. Other creatures, like cats or dogs, typically pay no heed to mirror images. For them there is nothing alive in the reflection.

One investigator placed a dot of paint on the face of chimps and orangutans while they were anesthetized; the animals were previously familiar with mirrors and their reflections.[3] When conscious and exposed to a mirror, they would reach up and touch the spot on themselves. The spot evidently constituted a zit on their body image. Again, monkeys displayed no such self-consciousness and did not touch a painted spot. Quite young children act as the monkeys do, with no recognition of the spot; older children act as the chimps do, touching it. Self-awareness in the sense of self-recognition and detection of a distorted image requires intellectual capacity.

The work on recognition of self with other primates shows the elemental nature of the many aspects of self. Yet the recognition of self by chimps is but a foretaste of what we humans can do. William James thought early on this problem of the self and human nature. His view of how we differ from other creatures is not exclusively one of culture but of instincts: We are different from other animals because we have *more* instincts than they do. These instincts are essentially wired-in neural circuits involving a huge array of reactions and response tendencies, ranging from eye movements, suckling, attending, and emotion common to our species and its evolutionary past. As James phrased it:

> Instinct is usually defined as the faculty of acting in such a way as to produce certain ends, without foresights of the ends, and without previous education in the performance.[4]

Why, then, do we little note the instinctual aspects of our behavior? For several reasons. Instincts are numerous and compete with one another, allowing slightly different situations to lead to quite different reactions, therefore having none of the stereotypy we so often associate with definitions of instinct. In addition, when memory and habit are combined, we become capable of predicting how we will behave and therefore come to think of our instinctual reactions as foresight. Once we react with fear to thunder or darkness, we anticipate that those conditions will frighten us. We may then use reason to seek out an amusement park with exhibits that will produce controlled fear. So experience comes to overlay the conditions of the instinct.

The contemporary theorists of evolutionary psychology Leda Cosmides and John Tooby draw deeply on James's insights:

> In our view, William James was right about evolutionary psychology. . . . [O]ur natural competences—our abilities to see, to speak, to find something beautiful, to reciprocate a favor, to fear disease, to fall in love, to initiate an attack, to experience moral outrage, to navigate a landscape, and myriad others—are possible only because there is a vast and heterogeneous array of complex computational machinery supporting and regulating these activities. This machinery works so well that we don't even realize that it exists. We all suffer from instinct blindness. As a result, psychologists have neglected to study some of the most interesting machinery in the human mind.[5]

To this I would add that the self and its workings form our most familiar structure, our most natural competence. This is brought into sharp relief by our concern with appearance, an interest in what James called the *Me*. That interest is already apparent among the early Egyptians, who employed a wide array of cosmetic aids and implements—including unguents, dyes, razors, and mirrors of polished bronze—in their pursuit of preservation and restoration.

Ancient Cosmetics

The time is 3,300 years ago; the place, ancient Egypt. Let us imagine how a queen such as Nefertiti uses the actual cosmetic tools of her time. She is in her bath, holding a polished-bronze mirror beside her.[6] It is a work of art with a lotus-flower handle; instruments of self-awareness are a precious technology and warrant aesthetic embellishment. Two handmaidens are cleansing her by applying natron, an ancient soaplike compound that is a mixture of ashes and sodium carbonate, to her body. Now she stands as the maids pour fresh water over her to rinse. She is a striking woman, known throughout the kingdom for her beauty.

She lies faceup on a pad, and the two maids each take a thin duck-shaped piece of bronze in hand. The curved neck of the duck acts as a handle; its breast is razor sharp. The maid at her feet shaves her legs. The maid at her head shaves underneath her arms. Nefertiti monitors each step of the process in the bronze mirror. Her motives are not transparent to us, but removing unnecessary body hair would help control lice and other body vermin; and perhaps the absence of body hair would be seen as attractive and make her appear younger. From an evolutionary view, all of these motives are adaptive.

Nefertiti has even considered having her head shaved and wearing a wig, a common custom of royal women. For reasons she is not sure of, she has decided to keep her own hair, even though it shows signs of aging, with some early gray streaks.

The handmaidens now wipe her body clean in preparation for anointing. They open vessels of rare oils mixed with aromatics and slowly rub her body. She relaxes, feeling the tension dissolve from her muscles. She rolls over, and fingers work into the muscles of her back. The oil sinks into her skin, the warmth of the afternoon helping its slow, deep penetration.

Now the maids wipe away the oil from her feet and hands in preparation for the next step. One maid applies a dye called henna to Nefertiti's feet while the other applies it to her hands, producing a reddish cast to her skin for this evening's banquet.

The maids help her to a sitting position, and Nefertiti examines her hair, face, and body in the mirror. She shifts the mirror to her hair again and shakes her head. In her thirties, and already she is turning gray. She worries about the signs of aging. Death may not be far away. Perhaps it can be held back by hiding the gray.

She turns to the principal maid. "Yes, it is time to start." The maid pours a rich dye from an urn. It will restore the gray to a youthful black. The dye of her time is a special sacred mixture of blood from a black bull mixed with the fat of a black snake, together with other oils, unguents, and aromatics. The maids rub the dye into her hair and scalp. In her mirror, Nefertiti can see it work as the gray turns to lustrous black.

The maids wipe away the excess with soft linen toweling. Now they begin to work on her eyes. A dark metallic pigment blended with charcoal and crocodile fat is applied above the lid and its line extended outward to exaggerate each remarkable eye. Malachite, a green mineral, is blended with fat, and the compound is applied under each eye. Together the dark and the green pigment mixtures will protect her eyes from insects, reduce the sun's glare, and heighten her beauty. Again, practicality has drifted into beauty—or perhaps it is the other way around.

Nefertiti now stands and is fitted with a gauzy linen dress. One more step remains for the banquet. With several long pins, the maids fasten a scent cone to her hair. The cone is about three inches high and about two inches wide at its base. Its ingredients consist of hippo fat, unguents, and perfumes. As Nefertiti sits at the banquet, her body heat will slowly melt the cone, and its exquisite fragrance will come to her nostrils as it drips down her face and shoulders.

She places the lotus-handled mirror disk into a bag and hangs the strap from her shoulder. She would not be without her mirror—her "see-face," as people called it. Not only does it comfort her to know how she looks at any moment, it also keeps her in touch with her god: When the sun god Aton casts its bright rays onto the polished yellow brass, the mirror becomes a symbol of sun and deity.[7]

Not all in the royal court agree with her choice of gods, some preferring the old system of many gods instead of the single dominant god Aton, the source of warmth and life, the sacred sun disk symbolized by the mirror. She touches the mirror, brushing her hand across it as she puts it into its carrying case. With her precious mirror under her arm, she is ready for the banquet.

In the context of Nefertiti's imagined makeover, it is useful to contrast what is old and what is new relative to her times. Her actions have ancient roots in evolutionary psychology. She is trying to protect herself from loss by preserving or restoring her appearance, continuing themes in the creation of the body. By staying young and attractive, she is more likely to communicate her genes to another generation. Her cosmetics provide a sense of youth, health, and increased fertility. It will help to bond her husband and his resources to her and her children. That is the story that evolutionary psychology tells here.

But there are also new elements. The technology and use of the mirror provides a quantum leap over seeing one's self in water pools and the like. Under the best circumstances, shifting water allows for only poor resolution and flitting images—and that is where the water is quite clear. Any turbidity makes water an even poorer imaging device. The advent of the mirror, the earliest significant technology of appearance, is something new under the sun. The Egyptian polished-bronze mirrors tell a fine story. They are valued, as is shown by the decoration and design lavished upon them. Some also have carrying cases with a strap, making instant self-appraisal possible wherever one goes. The invention of the mirror takes appearance and self-awareness far beyond anything that evolution crafted for us. We know this because the mirror is relatively recent in civilization, no more than four or five thousand years old—far too recent to have had evolutionary significance.

The Egyptian cosmetic materials elaborate on the same theme. The ingredients tell us of hidden presumptions of thought. A linkage exists between the color of a bull's hair and its blood. Evidently hair color is a surface manifestation of blood essence in this implicit theory. Furthermore, that underlying essence is assumed to house a black pigment that can then transfer to human hair. The fat, unguent, and oil act as binders that integrate the essence of different chemicals, although the requirement of fat from a black snake indicates a supposition of pigment once more.

The chemistry of the makeover is once again too recent to have had evolutionary significance. It is the result of emergent capabilities of the mind building upon the desire to look young, healthy, and suitable for reproduction. The effort required to produce the ingredients—complex blends of organic and inorganic substances such as hippo and snake fat combined with metallic oxides—reveals the importance of appearance to the Egyptians. The cosmetics also have varied functions. One is restoration by making gray hair dark and youthful again. Another—most important for the present discussion—is to extend the self beyond the body given by biology; painting the eye with pigment exaggerates the real eye, producing a work of art and idealization outside the realm of evolution's work on the natural body.

Together, the portable mirror and the existence of complex cosmetic materials produce an entirely new level of self-awareness. One sees a concern with aging and vanity. Efforts are made to preserve the body as it is—or perhaps to restore it to an earlier ideal of youth. Carrying a mirror to check one's appearance, tracking one's image and comparing it with an ideal that is part of some mirror image in the mind—these mark essential capabilities of a self, one that seeks preservation and restoration. (That blend of self-awareness and the technology of the mirror continues to our time; the mirror is still our most important accessory in the technology of self-as-body.)

Nefertiti's makeover also takes her beyond the physical body, toward some conception of an idealized or perfect self far from the body that nature has bestowed. Were she to wear a wig, hair not her own, that would be another manifestation of creating a self transcending nature. Whenever there is a concern for perfection, we see signs of going beyond the body that evolution has given us.

Let us jump forward in time, to our own culture. No surer sign of seeking perfection can be found than in annual expenditures on cosmetics and toiletries, which recently in the U.S. equaled more than $29 billion.[8] By far, the greatest proportion of this amount is for female-specific products. Even with shaving and oral hygiene products included for men, women's products account for more than 80 percent of the total. To render in perceptual terms this imbalance between the sexes, visit a large urban drugstore and pace off the shelf space devoted to female and male appearance products. The difference is striking.

Is this a phenomenon specific to our culture, or is it a present behavior rooted in our evolutionary past? The cultural view says that marketing efforts have managed to convince women to buy these things, but why similar efforts have not been able to convince men to do so is not clear. The evolutionary explanation says that the differences between men and women in the use of cosmetics are rooted in the differences in our reproductive strategies. Women have a much narrower window of time than men in which they may reproduce and get their genes into the next generation. Therefore women employ cosmetics to emphasize that window, stretch it, and attract the resources of males as long as possible.

Such an idea seems sexist in today's discourse. But is it really? We are what we are in large part due to our reproductive strategies. Consider the alternative—that women buy cosmetics disproportionate to men because of advertising pressures. That means that women are greater pawns of marketing practice than men when it comes to cosmetics and appearance.[9] Of course, men may be more subject to sales pitches for hunting and sports gear, which themselves may have ancient claims to male reproductive resources. If so, both cases of marketing susceptibility suggest an underlying root difference in evolutionary history that is played to by the marketers.

The cultural position argues in turn that cosmetics are not used in all cultures, that they are now specific to Western industrial society in which cosmetic use is heavily biased toward females. In fact, one of the profit centers of the cosmetics industry resides in getting products to emerging markets where the people are just beginning to have excess economic capacity and be exposed to Western ideas. Women's products, not men's, are the big sellers. For example, in Brazil the demand for women's cosmetic products has been growing by 40 percent a year. The distribution system involves door-to-door selling, with up to two million women estimated to be in the sales force.[10] A basic transformation in emphasis on self is taking place. One may argue whether this is due to cultural influences from affluent countries, or if it is a new chance to play out natural biological tendencies.

A related argument focuses on men in other cultures and their use of body decoration. Does male adornment equally conceal age, or is it more likely a method of revealing wealth, status, and other important notions? In the eighteenth century, well-dressed males of European culture certainly used aids to modify appearance, but there was a sharp difference between the sexes.[11] Women's costume emphasized the bust and hips while showing a slim corseted waist—just the characteristics of a young, fertile female. Male costume of the period did little to emphasize masculine sexual characteristics, instead displaying elegance and status as symbols of power. These are the very characteristics predicted by evolutionary psychology: female fertility juxtaposed with male resources. There may be other explanations for disproportionate cosmetic use apart from biology and marketing, but any such account will have to interpret this huge difference in emphasis.

Let us take one more excursion into change of appearance,

and then we will return with another argument about cosmetic uses that differentiate the sexes—one that reverses the conclusion above and takes us in a different direction than evolutionary psychology.

The Modern Makeover

The American psychologist Mary Harris has written about the fascinating phenomenon of age concealment, noting the "industries designed to impart the appearance of youth or at least to stave off the appearance of aging": cosmetics, plastic surgery, exercise, and dieting.[12] Among her findings for people over fifty, women are more likely than men to color their hair (67 percent versus 32 percent), to use antiwrinkle cream (75 percent versus 13 percent), to use plastic surgery (38 percent versus 17 percent), and to lie about their age (52 percent versus 34 percent). Only in the concealment of hair loss do men exceed women. These figures are not a national sample but a local one, so interpretive caution is needed; nonetheless, they are highly suggestive.

A particularly intriguing result is that people are more accepting of age concealment techniques used by themselves than by others. It is almost as if "I do it to feel good about myself, but you do it to misrepresent yourself to me." That would be very consistent with an evolutionary psychology explanation that emphasizes an arms race between deceivers and deceived. Age concealment is both camouflage and emphasis. The camouflage hides age, and the resulting more youthful appearance displays and says, "Look at me."

Let us examine these tendencies in a modern-day makeover, one that also provides a useful comparison with that of the ancient Egyptians. While few contemporary women have the royal Egyptians' numerous live-in handmaidens, a trip to a spa may not be that different. The mirror—that age-old technology of the self—is once again evident as Ran, a red-haired woman in her forties, visits a modern, technologically sophisticated spa.[13]

Ran likes the spa because everyone concentrates on her. She can see herself in the full-length mirror and in other people's eyes. The treatment is like being a queen in the process of creation. Time stops, space shrinks. Her awareness is of being the center of everything. After bathing in a whirlpool, her body is massaged and oiled. On another occasion she gets a body wrap, something like being rolled in colored Saran with a mixture of herbs and, depending on the season, being heated or cooled.

Later in the day she goes to the Virtual Self Salon, and a video camera captures the image of her face.[14] A computer digitizes the image and displays it on a screen. The technician points out key wrinkles and blemishes, suggesting ways to conceal them or make them less prominent. Portions of the screen image are selected and covered with simulated forms of makeup. Ran likes some of the effects and colors but not others, and she and the technician work back and forth on the screen image until she is satisfied. Then the technician applies varied forms of makeup that match the image on the screen.

The preview of the computer makeover is a new technology of self that may in time come to rival the importance of the mirror. Large cosmetic companies utilize department-store demonstrations of computer-aided makeovers. The customer saves time and can try several alternative appearances with less chance of an unsatisfactory result. The entire process moves rapidly, so the client has a greater possibility of finding a good fit between her physical face and her self-image or ideal. The benefits for the cosmetic company include less trial and error, better customer satisfaction, and increased sales.[15]

Now Ran has her hair tinted to get rid of the gray because, "after all, to the young and attractive go the spoils." Here she has a choice: a tint that merely accentuates the natural color of her hair—it would heighten the red—or completely change the color to another that is also natural, like brunet or blond.

One purpose is restorative—to go back to an earlier time, to recover the image of her youth when her hair didn't show gray. Another purpose is to preserve what she already has. Still another idea that crosses her mind is to pursue perfection. Get just the right tint; accentuate a bit, but don't stray too far from nature. A final choice that she considers, then immediately dismisses is to be audacious and come out with punk-style chartreuse or purple hair. That would be a big step indeed and create a new self by seeking some extension totally *outside of nature*.

She runs through these options and decides her purpose is preservation and restoration. Perfection is for the young; she's satisfied with a lot less. That last notion—green or purple hair—is only for the young and adventuresome. But if one's purpose is attention, green or purple would get it. Instead of shooting the president to get attention, you're shooting your hair—the old idea that it's better to be wanted for murder than not wanted at all.

As she is having her hair done, she thinks about why a woman goes to a hairdresser and decides that basically it's for a couple of reasons: to look good, to get therapy. She had the same hairdresser for many years. She could talk to him about things she wouldn't tell anyone else. A good hairdresser-therapist is someone who can keep confidences. You find that out soon enough. Advice isn't as important as having someone you can dump all your troubles on, someone who listens. As therapy goes, it's inexpensive. By listening, the hairdresser is acting as a kind of mirror for her own innermost thoughts and concerns. She says things, and his silences and nods reflect them back so that she can hear them for the first time as they pass through air where she can better examine them.

It occurs to her that many different kinds of mirrors are at work in a makeover. The physical mirror, the computer mirror, and the silent, sympathetic nodding of the hairdresser that mirrors back her thoughts. As the hairdresser holds up a mirror, she sees herself deeply, all the blemishes and imperfections. Then in another mirror inside her head she tries to see herself as she might be. If the makeover is successful, she moves a little away from the blemish image toward her might-be image. The makeover takes her toward a more perfect self. Then she remembers thinking earlier that she wasn't aiming for perfection. Perhaps she is inconsistent—but it doesn't bother her. Consistency is a virtue up to a point, but it's not the only standard to follow. As Emerson said, "A foolish consistency is the hobgoblin of little minds."

Her makeover complete, she wonders almost aloud why she did it. In addition to preserving, restoring, and perhaps an underlying aesthetic of perfection, there is a satisfaction from the makeover, much the same as from craftwork—building something out of raw materials—a sense of creating. We all want to do that, and what does it matter if we paint on canvas or on ourselves?

Ran also likes looking nice for her husband, which would be consistent with the evolutionary psychology view of attracting male attention and resources. But most of all, she says, the makeover is for herself. She's building something, creating herself a little. It has to do with her body image. She likes the image she presents. She likes the way she feels, and she feels good about herself. It's taking care of herself. Anything she can do to make herself happy is OK as long as it's not obsessive. It's liking what she has, a kind of gentle vanity that most of us have in one form or another. Taking care of one's self is a lifelong project. Every day she is inventing herself as she goes.

Psychological Logic

Ran's account of her makeovers tells an important story, perhaps not too different from that of our imagined Nefertiti. People have a makeover because of restoration and preservation, reasons that are consistent with the evolutionary psychology explanation of pointing attention to one's self and garnering the resources of others. But in addition there are motives for the pursuit of artistic perfection and for feeling good about one's self. Like Nefertiti's makeover, modern makeovers also go beyond our given bodies, resulting in a kind of created self. Hair tints require no explanation; they merely accent what is there or once was there and involve restoration, preservation. Highlighting of eyes and the like is enhancing, perhaps perfecting an already noteworthy feature. But going from, say, brunet to blond or vice versa is a different act of creation. Some women report personality changes along with a major change in hair color. It is like becoming another person, and it gives one the license to act differently.

Still more radical is the person who shifts away from a natural color to employ brilliant purples or greens. These colors outside the human rainbow underscore how imagination trumps the cards dealt by biology and evolution. Imagination extends the self beyond nature—for good or ill.

An evolutionary explanation is that these bodily changes make one stand out in some way and therefore are more likely to command the favorable attention and resources of others, with the end result of enhancing one's reproductive potential. But then again, perhaps not. Evolution does not care a whit about gray hair because it often comes after the reproductive years, particularly for women. Past the window of reproductive time, vanity's client is the self. And the changes totally outside of nature—green or purple hair—may attract attention, but no case holds for their attraction of any other resource. Of course, evolution has no way of knowing just how long one will live and have opportunities for reproduction, so its only reasonable strategy is to overdesign—make a person's concern with appearance last a long time.

But this hardly explains the differences of the sexes in the use of modern cosmetics. If we take at face value Ran's indication of her motivation, she does the makeover for herself rather than for her husband and other males. One might object, saying that the true evolutionary grounding is a largely unconscious process, and people are not aware of their own motivations. The bare-bones counterargument centers on reproductive rates. Do women who spend a lot of money on their appearance have more children than those who do not?

Probably not. The woman who expends the most resources on her appearance likely works in the world of business, government, or education, where such things are valued. In cultivating her appearance, she is not trying to increase her reproductive rate; she is trying to advance her career. She is likely to have fewer children than average if she is really serious about her career, and she is likely to spend disproportionately more on her appearance. The path now is appearance, competence, and power.

If true, such results are at variance with an evolutionary psychology explanation, and they indicate that whatever the original evolutionary basis for appearance monitoring and modification, the rules now are different.[16] The mirror and modern cosmetics provide for changes in appearance never anticipated in our hunter-gatherer evolution. What, then, links the varied reactions to the mirror—from the cave-wall image of prehistoric handprints to the hand mirror placed for the first time before contemporary primal people and chimps to Egyptian queens to a contemporary woman altering her virtual face on a computer screen?

To answer this question, a brief digression is in order. The diverse reactions experienced fit most clearly into a folk psychology framework, what philosophers of mind such as Daniel Dennett call a belief-desire psychology.[17] In this view, one's own mind is filled with such entities as beliefs, desires, intentions, hopes, and fears, and we tend to think other minds have the same furniture. An important part of the belief-desire system of folk psychology is the notion of empathy, the ability to read the thoughts and feelings of others (receptive empathy) and to project our own beliefs and desires into others, as when we urge on a toddler learning to walk or an athlete coming from behind (projective empathy).

These receptive and projective capabilities of empathy are what people use everyday to interpret and understand their own and others' thoughts. Children must mature to understand or apply the ability to read other minds; yet withdrawn, autistic children may never be able to do so and continue to fail the tests of self- and other-awareness that chimpanzees can pass. Thus by a requisite age a normal child knows what a person in another position will see, but an autistic child does not.[18]

American psychologists refer to such capabilities as having a "theory of mind," and British psychologists call it "mind reading."[19] Such descriptions sound ominous in technical portent or even charlatanlike. Hence we will use terms like empathy, in a slightly expanded sense, to mean that we understand ourselves and others by interpreting their beliefs and desires and by projecting the capabilities of our own minds—the presence of motives, intentions, hopes, fears, and other mental states—into their minds. The process may work both ways at once: a receptive capability that allows us to understand others and a projective capability through which we convey our hopes and wishes to another. (These notions will be treated more fully later.) All of this is built in as part of a brain module of self and, in degree, sharply distinguishes humans from other creatures.

While every socially functioning person is expert in empathic understanding of the beliefs and desires of others, the most skilled practitioners are probably novelists, therapists, political leaders, and con artists. They know what we are thinking almost as soon as we do—in many cases, they anticipate us. The evolutionary significance of empathic capabilities is substantial. Insofar as we are social creatures who plan together for hunting-gathering and then share in the results, we must understand others. And much of our time is spent in broadly considered gossip: What are other people doing, how are they doing it, and why? The psychologist Robin Dunbar thinks that gossip is the most important reason for the evolution of the human brain. Nothing is more important than our social environment, and gossip is what keeps us informed of who we can rely on and who we cannot.[20]

Notice that empathic capability, as used here, is a large step beyond the chimp's recognition of self in the mirror. It says, I recognize and communicate with others because I project on to them the same kind of mind that I have, and I read from their expression and behavior the same emotional and intentional structures that I have.

Applied to a makeover, the empathic system works in a reflexive way, something like this: Because I see a blemish on my face, a wrinkle here, a zit there, a roll of fat where it should not be, others will see these blemishes, too, and react much the way I feel, a kind of disappointment if not disgust. Or if I think I am beautiful, with lovely features and an attractive body, others will look at me and think I am beautiful, too. In each case, others do this because the workings of their minds are like my own. At least, that is the operating principle behind belief-desire psychology.

This also means that a central, or core, part of us is operating out of something like a unity system. We crave perfection and its near relatives, preservation and restoration. Perfection is some inner image or standard to strive for to be complete. The self then moves toward perfection by various actions on the body: concealing blemishes, highlighting fine features—anything that reduces the difference between the present situation and the inner ideal. Outside observers never directly see the ideal, only the attempts to reach it. Nor is the ideal always apparent to the self and makeover recipient. It is partly individual creation, partly image that culture interjects, and more than one part may be below full awareness.

Surprisingly, the perfection a person seeks in her appearance is close to being average. The beautiful is often a blend, a kind of averaging, of other faces. To understand this, consider noses. The extremes are a convex hooked nose and concave pug nose. The most attractive nose, then, would be an average of these, one closer to straight, perhaps with a slight inward curve. The same idea holds for other features like the distance between eyes, the width of mouth, and so on. A *Time* magazine cover of a few years ago showed a computer-constructed average face formed from many young women of diverse racial and ethnic backgrounds.[21] The image was truly striking. In later issues readers wrote in saying they were in love with the composite woman. This strategy of making the average beautiful is one of evolution's common paths. The average in this sense, of course, is not to be equated with saying someone is average—that is, not particularly attractive or unattractive. Rather, it is the result of averaging or morphing together a variety of faces.

Later work by the psychologist Victor Johnston has revealed, however, that there is an even more attractive face than the morphed average. In his work, the ideal female face, as judged by males, has a higher than usual forehead, fuller lips, and a smaller nose and chin.[22] These features are a step away from the average mature face and toward juvenilization. In evolutionary terms, men are selecting a youthful woman for the widest possible window of reproductive time.

Whatever its origin, the perfection one strives for is of a changing nature. Most of us as we age come to realize that our standards of perfection must change, or our reality will become hopelessly out of harmony with our ideal. The wrinkle that we now easily accept would have bothered us twenty years ago. Of course, the young have their own angst. The small zit on a teenager's face becomes the focus of all reality. But the same blemish on a thirty-year-old produces no more than mild annoyance, and it is not noticed at all by a sixty-year-old.

What may be most important is not the particular ideal or standard of perfection but having some standard that directs us. The variations in ideal appearance are particularly interesting when we contrast the crafted and the natural look. The crafted person spends time on herself to achieve a particular image. The natural person does not traffic in makeup, for practical or philosophical reasons. For example, if she is an athlete—say, a swimmer—makeup is a nuisance. She receives her self-esteem from activities not strongly tied to her appearance. But she still has an ideal, one of simplicity and naturalness that is not to be confused with the unkempt person who has no design behind her appearance.

The natural person seeks purity in the sense of not putting gobs of chemicals on herself and having easily manageable hair. She seeks a simpler self rather than a more complex one because she would rather spend her time and resources on her most valued activities than in a beauty parlor. In this respect she resembles nineteenth-century writer Henry David Thoreau, who fled the complexity of civilization to lead a life of simplicity and harmony with nature at Walden Pond, Massachusetts.

So far the focus has been on women because at this time in our culture they are the principal users of cosmetics. But if jobs and commerce and culture impress on women the importance of appearance, the same forces are beginning to influence men. Just as women find that they cannot be judged solely by job performance and character, men in public presentation roles like movies and TV also find that appearance is paramount.

Advertisers are beginning to stress the importance of appearance for men, too, emphasizing products that project a "manly" image. Ads in men's magazines stress hair, skin, slimness, and expensive clothes. For a significant portion of business and advertising, the conclusion has already been drawn: We males are far too drab a lot compared to women. If we want to advance in our jobs or just hold on to them—and we are a largely untapped market— we must get on board.

Something like Ran's computer-simulated makeover may be needed by men to see the possibility of the body as a work of art. Our simulated appearances on a computer screen might draw us into the process. As we try on different faces of self, we may approach the female of the species in becoming many-splendored things. In this era of corporate downsizing and public presentation, appearance is becoming at least as important as performance and character, however much we may lament it and wish for a bygone time—one that may never have been.

L et us now make a transition from cosmetics to cosmology. Cosmologists tell us that the universe is expanding. Inspired by the questions of cosmology, I am sitting on a bench in a large urban shopping mall, people watching and wondering if the world of human appearance is expanding or contracting in variety. The array is splendidly varied: hair in every style from ultra long to ultra short and in every color imaginable from natural to tints to the natural colors of someone else to those purple and green colors outside the human spectrum. Plain faces, elaborately made up faces. Clothing from many colors and nationalities, clothing from informal to work related to fashion plate.

My initial reaction to this wonderful variety is that human differences are part of an expanding universe of appearance, ever more diverse. But now I am not sure; maybe that universe is shrinking instead. For example, a Navajo couple is passing by. She has long hair and a traditional velvet dress with many silver adornments, and she clearly adds to the variety in front of me. But he has short hair, jeans, and a flannel shirt, so he is part of the homogeneous end of the spectrum of dress and appearance on display.

Another example of a shrinking universe walks by. Two Muslim women in the traditional chador enhance this array, but their teenage daughters have regular Western dress, the ubiquitous jeans and white shirt.

In addition to people mostly in the mainstream spectrum and people from another culture and guise, there is a third group. These are the people who are architects of their own form. They have tattoos, body piercings, rainbow-hued hair, clothing of so many blends or so much originality that description is difficult.

The variety of appearance here in this one mall is staggering. My impressions of expansion and contraction of self are all mixed together. One moment I am taken with the variety and the next I see tendencies toward homogeneity and contraction, the impression of the majority culture. But the third group, the architects of self, give me a strong push toward a belief in an ever-expanding diversity of self. This is the conclusion that the postmodern theorist Kenneth Gergen has come to. He believes we are becoming a pastiche of cultures and influences, steadily more diffuse with no core.[23]

Even if it is correct that we are moving toward ever-increasing variety, important questions are raised. How would we ever measure such change? Is it accelerating? It is so multidimensional and offers up no obvious metric. How amazing that we can know about the expansion of the whole universe, yet we cannot really tell how to measure the rate of expansion in the variations of human appearance. Still less do we have any indicator of whether the expansions that do occur have a fundamental fit or harmony with one another. As the psychologist M. Csikszentmihalyi expresses it:

> We can measure IQ quite accurately, and can calculate a person's net worth down to the last dollar, indicators we take very seriously. But when it comes to the much more meaningful issue of whether a person's life increases harmony or chaos, we become very tentative and tongue-tied.[24]

Now let us take a closer look at those people who are decorating their whole bodies.

Chapter 2

PAINTING,   TATTOOING,
AND   PIERCING

The pleasures of heaven are with me and the pains of hell
        are with me,
The first I graft and increase upon myself,
        the latter I translate into new tongue.

—WALT   WHITMAN, *Leaves of Grass*

Painting and tattooing the self go beyond the conventional cosmetic makeover centered on the face and head by creating and presenting a body distinctively different than that given by biology.[1] The goal is no longer restoration or preservation but something new. But does body decoration have evolutionary significance?

Kathryn Coe, a scholar of body decoration, claims that the first art is that of the body.[2] In her view, humans have an innate propensity for reacting to color and form, which in combination attract attention to varied parts of the body. She states, "The proximate or immediate effect of art is to make objects more noticeable." Her examples are Neanderthal head binding designed to shape the head, as early as seventy thousand years ago, and Cro-Magnon teeth filing and ablation patterns dating to nineteen thousand years ago. Distinctive patterns of body decoration also communicate information about descent and group membership—important determinants of mating choice and reproductive behavior. For both its attentional and informational aspects, body decoration has a claim to being adaptive in the Darwinian sense of increasing reproductive potential. Let us now consider some specific forms of embellishment.

The decoration of the skin itself is ancient and elemental. Hints of body painting exist in the early years of our species, with a few grave sites of one hundred thousand years ago showing evidence of the metallic pigment red ochre. We cannot be sure that the bodies were painted with it or if it had some other use. However, by thirty thousand years ago many grave sites reveal red ochre, and there is little doubt that the bodies were painted. Whether body painting also occurred during a living state, we do not know. But contemporary tribal people actively paint themselves with red ochre. Perhaps it has an affinity with blood, ritual, and thereby religion.[3]

However, body painting also has a present-day fascination that does not seem explicable in terms of such elemental forces. A local bookstore is having a kid's book day. Patricia, who in her normal everyday life is a book buyer, has put on a costume and is painting the kids—faces and hands and arms. There is a long line of children, each one eagerly waiting to be painted. One boy, Greg, is dancing and fidgeting while waiting his turn. He is the classic example of a hyperactive boy. How can he possibly be painted while wriggling around? It will be like a Jackson Pollack work, except that the painter will not be moving randomly over the medium; instead, the medium will be moving randomly with respect to the painter.

The little girl in front of him is having the finishing touches put on her face. The result is wild colors in artistic asymmetry. She looks in the mirror and is elated with the result. A broad smile fills her face, and she throws her arms in the air in exultation. Then she twirls and dances away in delight.

Greg takes his place, twitches, wiggles, and all. The moment the brush touches his face the movement stops. He is dead still, rapt in concentration. His eyes focus on the mirror, intently studying the motions of the brush on his face. It is as if he had entered another world, become another person—a serious, attentive, focused child, with all the wiggling and wriggling left behind. What a transformation! Such is the power of body paint. Surely an elixir that needs bottling for all time.

Body painting is also portrayed in the cinema. The French film *Cousin, Cousine* has a hilarious scene about lovers escaping from work and engaging in a lunchtime tryst. As part of their lovemaking, they body paint one another in a very arousing scene. Then as work time approaches, they hop into the bathtub to wash away their art. Unfortunately, they have used a paint that does not want to wash away. One can only imagine the laughter of their co-workers. Not all body painting is serious. The theater of the skin sometimes plays to comedy and fun.

While painting is reversible, tattooing is best considered permanent. The earliest known tattoo is that on the so-called Ice Man, a 5,300-year-old body discovered after a thaw in the Alps in 1993[4]. The Ice Man's tattoos are of an abstract form, mostly vertical lines on his back, calves, and ankles. In addition, there are cruciform tattoos on one knee and one heel. The purpose of these marks is lost in the mystery of the ice, but one hypothesis advanced is that of a healing rite. The vertical lines on his back are clustered over the lumbar spine, and X-ray analysis has revealed underlying degenerative spinal changes. Perhaps the tattoos had a curative intention.

Yet that cannot be a complete account because the marks also occur in other areas that did not reveal joint or bone degeneration. Of course, it is always possible to hypothesize some injury, such as a muscle problem in the calf area, but there is no evidence for it, either, and we know that most contemporary tattooing has little to do with healing rites. Also, the vertical lines on the Ice Man's back and legs occur in clusters, and the significance of the lines versus the cruciform marks is not known. Some of the marks could have been self-applied, but those on the back indicate a social act with social significance. Apart from that, all that we can conclude is that tattooing is a very ancient form of body extension.

A prominent use of body decoration is in tribal initiation rites.[5] The passage from childhood to adulthood is signaled by a public marking of the body. If it is tattooing or scarification, the marks are irreversible, perhaps symbolizing that the passage to adulthood is also irreversible. The decoration shows the child-adult to be a full member of the tribal group and distinct from other groups. To the degree that the decoration establishes membership in the group and yet is different from the decoration of other members, it confers both community belonging and uniqueness. Social structure and stability are strengthened as the individual is assigned a new place and responsibilities in that structure.

The social significance of the tattoo varies greatly over time and place. Forty years ago in the United States, only sailors and criminals had tattoos. Anyone respectable with a tattoo had done it as an act of wayward youthful indiscretion and talked about it— if at all—with reluctance. For example, a former cabinet officer is reported to have a tiger tattooed on his backside.[6] Evidently it was the result of a drinking episode while he was a student at Princeton—hence the tiger. And notice the need to justify the tattoo as the result of a drinking bout in which he was not in control of his usual faculties. Today the decision to get a tattoo is more likely to be a deliberate act rather than a drunken lapse.

Forty years ago women in our culture did not get tattoos. Now all that has changed, and many coeds have them. Middle-class girls have flowers on a shoulder, a butterfly on the ankle. Businesswomen have them, albeit usually discreet ones that are certainly the result of a deliberative, conscious, and sober act. High-school students have tattoos. Tattooing has become almost respectable.

Why? Before answering that question, let us consider some examples I have observed, along with stated motivations.

Alex is a twenty-year-old coed, and she has a butterfly on her ankle. It is small, unobtrusive, and artistically rendered. She had the tattoo to be different. She didn't think she was distinctive enough in life. When she arrived as a college freshman, she felt like she was in a herd of hundreds of other students just like her. Her tattoo became a statement of independence and uniqueness—it made her feel special. Even though many young women have tattoos on their ankles, not a few of which are butterflies, she saw her butterfly as different. She has had no regrets about the process and often finds herself admiring the butterfly. Initially she debated on whether to get it on the inside or outside of the ankle. Now she is glad that she had it done on the inside because it's easier for her to see.

In evolutionary terms, her tattoo called attention to her slim, youthful ankles and legs—her femaleness as an advertisement to males. But that isn't the way she thought of it. Did she feel different about herself before and after the tattoo? Yes, the tattoo made her feel good about herself. Once more, self-awareness has captured and claimed the motivation for something that may have more elemental roots, attracting the attention and resources of others.

Her parents had different reactions to the tattoo. Her father liked it. In his eyes, it was a sign of her growing up. Her mother hated it. She and Alex had a big fight about it. Why was the family spending money to send Alex to college when she spent it on getting mutilated? Alex felt this to be a totally unjustified criticism. She worked twenty hours a week and thought of the money for the tattoo as her own. In fact, she may well have gotten the tattoo in part to assert her independence from her mother.

Alex's motivations include: being different, feeling good about herself, and perhaps asserting her independence. Rarely do we humans do something for just one reason. Still, Alex believes her primary motivation was to be different, to be a distinguishable self. The other motivations were secondary.

For Claude, another student, the motivations for getting a coyote tattooed on his bicep were somewhat different. He got the tattoo because all his friends were getting one, so it just seemed like the natural thing to do. Said in another way, Claude didn't want to be different. He wanted to be the same, just like his friends. Did his friends also have tattoos of coyotes? No, they had other designs. (What did his parents say? They didn't care one way or another.) So Claude was at once the same as his friends but—like Alex—different, as well. A wonderful blend of motivations is operating here: being the same and different at the same time. His tattoo also made him feel good about himself. There is another factor, too, the placement of the tattoo. The muscular development of the biceps calls attention to his maleness. In evolutionary terms, it is an advertisement of his masculine attributes directed to females.

Ted, a young carpenter, has an abstract tattoo on his chest. His story is complicated. The tattoo initially was the name of his girlfriend, Melissa. But then they broke up, and he started going with Mary. She couldn't stand to look at his chest, so he had to have something done. He made inquiries about having it removed and found the cost prohibitive. Removal would involve a laser, and because of the nature of the dye, the technique might not have worked very well. He took the practical way out by incorporating the name Melissa into a pattern that obliterated the name by transforming it into a new overall design. Ted's motivation for his first tattoo was to show his commitment and love for Melissa. His motivation for his second tattoo was to obliterate the memory of Melissa and appease Mary.

Jeff was close to his father, who had a butterfly on his sternum. When his father died, Jeff wanted a way to remember him, to memorialize him. Jeff decided the best way to pay tribute to his father would be to get a similar tattoo. His mother thought this a fine idea and paid for it as a graduation present from high school.

She went with him to the tattoo shop to be sure everything was sanitary and provide her support if he needed it. The whole event brought the two of them closer. The act of sharing in the execution of the tattoo was a family and generational rite as well as a living memorial to his father.

Frank has a Virgin Mary tattoo on his back, which reflects both his deeply religious nature and his gang membership. For Frank, his religion acts as a protective veil from the rough life he leads.

Colleen is an ex-convict with a death's head tattooed on her forearm, which made her a member of a group she identified with. The result is not artistic, but it is powerful. She did it in prison with do-it-yourself materials: paper clips sharpened against a matchbook cover and carbon from burned paper to poke into her skin. The paper came from the pages of a Bible. Was this an intentional act of sacrilege or of homage? Homage, because it was another way of getting Scripture into her body. She did it because it was against the rules, because it filled her time, and because it had spiritual significance for her: blending the pages of the Bible with her skin. When asked why a death's head instead of a Virgin Mary, she replied that the Virgin Mary didn't belong in prison—but the death's head did.

Erika, a professional woman in her midforties, has a New Mexico collared lizard tattooed on her left buttock. It took her ten years of deliberation before finally getting the tattoo. Had she been twenty years younger, in another generation, the decision would have been much easier. She thought carefully about the image, its color, and its placement. She read about the process of tattooing, made inquiries about the best artists, and what to look for in terms of sterile conditions. Her motivations were aesthetic. She liked the image; it made her feel good about herself. Her one regret was having the image tattooed on a buttock, limiting its display. She is proud of it and now wishes that it was on a part of the body that could be more readily shown. This is a result consistent with Kathryn Coe's argument that body art is for display and calling attention to self.[7]

Looking over these stories, it is evident that many motivations underlie decoration of the body. It is a way of:

- Initiating into adulthood and one's group.
- Calling attention to selected parts of the body.
- Advertising one's masculine or feminine nature.
- Belonging and being the same.
- Being different, being unique.
- Feeling good about the self.
- Outraging parents or at least showing independence.
- Showing love and commitment to another person.
- Covering up past tattooing choices.
- Memorializing a loved one.
- Bonding in a family ritual.
- Passing time in prison.
- Identifying with a gang.
- Blending the spiritual with the skin.
- Creating an aesthetic object.[8]

Particularly interesting is the joint emphasis on being different and being the same. These are two powerful forces pulling in opposite directions. Being different, indeed being unique, shows up at the biological level: our various facial and body forms, our fingerprints, our DNA, and our powerful immune systems that sharply differentiate self and other. Being the same has its own pull. We are part of a family, a community, a species. We take our identity from these wider associations, these wider examples of sameness. No wonder we use body decoration to be both different and the same.

Other motivations require comment. Gang symbols that are the result of a spiritual act may seem surprising at first, but it should not because it is a blending of what is important to a person with the cohesive power of religion. For these reasons a Virgin Mary representation is common among gang members who need all the protection that they can get. The final motivation, aesthetic creation, comes from thinking of the body as a canvas on which to display art. Many tattoos are thought of as works of art by their bearers. They are proud of them and want to show them off.

When we look at the span of motivations for tattooing, a conclusion follows: The same act can have numerous motivations, many of which would be contradictory if they were housed in the same person.

The question remains: Is there evolutionary significance to body decoration? On the affirmative side, the practices are very old, dating perhaps to the dawn of our own species, so something primary seems to be involved. They are also very widespread, although by no means universal at either the individual or cultural level. They confer the first human resource: attention. In some societies, tattoos serve as an indicator of status or fertility. The frequent placement by males of a tattoo on the biceps calls attention to strength and masculine prowess and resource; rarely do females use this location. In an analogous way, the placement by females of an image on the shoulder or upper breast calls attention to femininity.

At another level, when body decoration is used for initiation and for establishing group membership in a band or tribe, it is a social-solidarity mechanism. The group is thereby strengthened. Indirectly, the individual is also more likely to survive and be reproductively successful by participating in the group process.

The reason that so many social innovations—in this case tattooing—start with criminal and marginal classes is also explainable as a Darwinian metaphor. Variation comes from isolated populations. Subcultures are by definition isolated, if not geographically, then in status. This is the ideal situation for the production of variation. With the attention of and glamorization by media, the innovations of the subculture may spread rapidly.

Body Piercing

If you have ever entered a piercing shop, your experience may have been something like this: A young man with enough metal to set off the detectors in all the airports of the world approaches you. He has a buzz cut, multiple earrings running up and down each ear, a couple of nose rings, and when he opens his mouth, you see at least one tongue stud. And that's just what is visible.

You may be waiting for a rough, uneducated voice. But when he speaks, you find he sounds like you do. In fact, he is a pleasant person to talk to. So much for your stereotypes.

Perhaps you ask him about his tongue studs—he has two of them. Wouldn't that be uncomfortable and not very functional? No, one soon gets used to it. And it does have its functions. It gives one a very sultry, sexy-sounding voice. If the Greek orator Demosthenes could put pebbles in his mouth to practice his diction, why can't a contemporary lad put studs in his mouth so that he can practice the production of sexy tones?

Piercing moves us deeper into the body, below the level of skin. Like tattoos, piercing is also an ancient art. Surprisingly, it is more reversible than tattooing. Rings and bars can usually be removed, and the remaining openings will eventually close on their own.

The variations in the piercing sites are something to behold: ears, nose, tongue, lips, nipples, navel, and genitals.

The form of attachment for a piercing also varies, from pins to rings to bars to crosses. In contemporary American culture, the social acceptability of a piercing site varies roughly in the order of the list above. Ear piercings in our culture attract little or no attention, whether for females or now males. Not long ago, however, it was regarded as a slightly racy thing for a girl to have her ears pierced. She had to be old enough, and she had to have her mother's permission. After pierced ears became routinely acceptable for females, they were still regarded with wide suspicion for males. At first it meant one was gay. Then a male was not gay if he wore an earring on one side—though now no one remembers which ear. Then the meaning of a pierced ear meant only that he had a pierced ear. Cultural symbols change rapidly, and other cultures have their own patterns of what is acceptable.

We still see this progression of acceptance in process for other piercing sites. A nose or a lip pierce will not be acceptable on Wall Street or Main Street because it is visually apparent. If a businessperson wants a body pierce, it is time to go underground and employ one of the sites readily covered by clothing.

Navel pierces now engender the same social uneasiness produced by earrings fifty years ago, but with the difference that they can be covered up. Also, whatever the unease, they are still more acceptable for women than men. Perhaps the navel pierce for the female calls attention to her midsection and the purported waist-to-hip-size ratio that indicates fertility, according to some scholars.[9]

Nipple pierces are still another matter. A teenage girl will have more trouble with her mother over a nipple pierce than a navel pierce. Teen boys with nipple pierces are likely to have even less acceptance.

Finally, the ultimate outrage, right now, is a genital piercing. For women, this might be a labial or clitoral pierce, usually with a ring as hardware. For men, the extreme step is a Prince Albert, a stainless-steel cross surgically inserted in the penis. This is the one piercing that involves surgery rather than pointile penetration.

Many of the motivations uncovered for other forms of body decoration also hold for piercing. The one significant addition involves genital piercing. The proponents of the practice assert that it produces a constant sexual buzz. Each movement of the body produces a movement in the hardware, which stimulates the genitals, which stimulates the imagination.

It is a dubious claim. The body and the mind are set up by evolution to tune out regular, repetitive sorts of stimulation. Our senses adapt to commonplace events. The habituation process will more than likely do its work with genital stimulation, as well. If so, a genital piercing and appliance is more a statement of individual hope than a way to be aroused all the time. A related claim is that these appliances give heightened sexual satisfaction to one's partners—an assertion best left to evaluation by the practitioners.

As to the evolutionary significance of piercing, several issues arise. Much like tattooing, when a traditional society uses piercing, there is a group-solidarity effect: We have all gone through this ritual. Now that you have also, you are a full member of the tribe. In addition, if the claims of the advocates of genital piercing are correct, and they do get a constant sexual buzz and act on it more frequently than others, then there may be a reproductive advantage. On the negative side is the dubious validity of their claim and the possibility of infection from the process. The latter certainly tilts the reproductive balance toward liability.

The deepest justifications for piercing are similar to those of the other forms of body decoration: to be the same or different, to create the body as a work of art. In these matters, one is guided by the unity system: Is the result consistent with the rest of the self? Does it make one a more complete person? Does it link one to a valued community? Tattoos and piercings are clearly expansions of the self, expressive forms that modify the body and take it away from its natural state. Paradoxically, moving the body beyond its natural state seems to be a natural path of the self. In this respect, painting, tattooing, and piercing are just the beginning.

SURGICALLY EXTENDING THE BODY

Magnifying and applying come I,
Outbidding at the start the old cautious hucksters,
Taking myself the exact dimensions of Jehovah,
Lithographing Kronos, Zeus his son, and Hercules his grandson,
Buying drafts of Osiris, Isis, Belus, Brahma, Buddha. . . .

— W A L T   W H I T M A N ,   *Leaves of Grass*

W e create ourselves through surgical enhancement. Contemporary cosmetic surgery provides a deep and lasting modification of the body—whether through augmentation, reduction, or rearrangement—if it is successful. The historian Elizabeth Haiken traces the development of cosmetic surgery and finds it to be a recent phenomenon in acceptance and efficacy.[1] To be sure, as Haiken points out, there are ancient origins, going back to 600 B.C.E. and the attempted surgical construction of missing noses from cheek tissue. There are also attempts late in the nineteenth century to augment female breasts via injecting paraffin. But endeavors like these reveal desire more than success.

A modern impetus for what is labeled plastic surgery came with the trench warfare of World War I and its associated terrible face wounds. But this was reconstructive surgery rather than starting with a normal face and cosmetizing it. Haiken draws a distinction between reconstructive and cosmetic surgery, with the one being an attempt at restoration; the other, an enhancement of the normal.

Other facilitating developments included improved surgical techniques, again given substantial impetus by the reconstructive surgeries of World War I and the later advent of antibiotics. Still another evolution was the shift from the Victorian idea of developing character by bearing a less than attractive appearance to the very different American idea of self-improvement. For Americans, appearance had become one with all the other things that could be improved: craft, process, character. As Haiken points out:

> In 1923, Americans clamored for an explanation of why Fanny Brice, beloved vaudeville actress, successful comedienne, and star of Florenz Ziegfeld's new Follies, had bobbed her nose. Forty years later, in similar circumstances, Americans asked a very different question. When Barbara Streisand emerged on the national scene—ironically, her first significant role was as Brice in the musical *Funny Girl*—Americans wanted to know why she had not.[2]

How do people think of themselves before and after cosmetic surgery? Why do people resort to cosmetic surgery? Most often cosmetic surgery is done to look better according to some cultural or individual standard of beauty.

Before cosmetic surgery became practical with antibiotics and advanced technology, fashion provided antecedents. Women have emphasized their breasts for a long time with uplifted and partially exposed bodices and padded bras. And in earlier times men wore codpieces to draw attention to their genital size and potency. Tribal members in Papua New Guinea still wear a penis sheath— the neck of a gourd covers the male organ and suggests an unreal size and virility. These displays on the part of both women and men simultaneously project endowment and modesty. The organ is at once called attention to while being partially covered—a blend of advertisement, modesty, and mystery.

We humans are vain creatures. In comparison to our nearest relatives, the other primates, we are extraordinarily well endowed. According to the evolutionary biologist Jared Diamond, the human male has by far the largest penis of any primate, and sexual prowess has little bearing on organ length. The orangutan has an erect penis of an inch to inch and a half in length, and this ape still manages extreme sexual acrobatics while hanging from tree limbs and the like.[3] Female chimps have breasts of very small size compared to those of the human female, yet these flat-chested females are quite capable of attracting the male of the species and adequately nursing their own young. In fact, we are the only mammal whose mammary glands stay permanently enlarged whether or not the glands are dispensing milk.

The conclusion is evident: There is nothing physiologically functional about having a big penis or big breasts. Diamond indicates that no satisfactory explanation is currently known for the huge size of these body structures in humans. But evolution suggests at least some general reasons rooted in our past: Large organs are based on sexual selection or dominance in ways not fully understood. Sexual selection works by attracting the opposite sex; perhaps women who have big breasts are more likely to be attended to by men; and men who have big penises are more likely to be attended to by women. In contrast, dominance works primarily within the same sex. Those with large organs are higher in status than those with smaller organs. High-status individuals have priority in their mating choices. In either case, according to the story, those with large organs are more likely to propagate their genes—and organ sizes—to the next generation. As a result, penises and breasts have taken on a size otherwise unheralded in the primate kingdom, much like peacock tails in the bird kingdom.[4]

At this time we have only a just-so evolutionary story, one manufactured to account for a limited set of facts and with no obvious new predictions of any kind. And it is only a partial account at that. Breast size and allied concern have little salience in other cultures. For example, Japanese women have smaller breasts on average, and traditional Japanese culture does not make a cult of that part of the body. In our own culture, advertisers and media presentations have emphasized whatever natural tendencies may be at work, with appeals to vanity rather than physiology. For men and women, this means feeling good about one's self as well as being confident in the competition for mates.

Another subtle source of large-organ need may come from dolls. The syndicated columnist Anna Quindlen has scaled up Barbie to real-life dimensions and arrives at the figures 40-18-32.[5] A real-life sized woman of these proportions would suffer gravitational stress and tend to fall on her face. The usual explanation for the exaggerated dimensions in the doll is that fabric thickness and stiffness is not to the small scale of a doll and it is therefore necessary to exaggerate Bab's dimensions to have her look right when clothed.

An unlikely story. Even with her clothes on, Barbie is superhuman in dimension just as Superman is superhuman in strength. While Barbie does not leap over tall buildings in a single bound, she does leap into the imaginations of little girls and break their normal body images in two. Quindlen wonders aloud: "Has [Barbie] been single-handedly responsible for the popularity of the silicone implant?"[6]

Men are not immune to this process. A new journal calls our attention: *Penis Power Quarterly*. Its Internet ad shouts forth: "Introducing the world's only journal dedicated to reporting the underground breakthroughs in genital enlargement, virility enhancement, potency restoration, and male sex products."[7] Sample articles cover different methods for increasing girth or length of the male organ, increasing the size of the testicles, and new aphrodisiacs for men. All this concern for size and performance is best illustrated by a particular individual's experience.

Simon, an athletic man in his late twenties, became tired of sitting around the locker room and being the smallest fellow there. It was embarrassing. Simon began to do background reading and found the following information about surgical enhancement.[8] For length enlargement the standard procedure is to release (cut) and reposition the suspensor ligaments just above the base of the penis. This allows the penis to move forward and gives it the appearance of being, on average, 1.5 inches longer. The effect is immediate.

Girth enhancement involves other procedures. The older one is called fat transfer, whereby fat is taken from another part of the body—such as the lower abdomen—and then purified and injected under the skin of the penis. The increase in girth is 30 to 50 percent. Unfortunately the fat tends to be reabsorbed by the body over a period of several months, and the result may be a return to previous size or a condition of uneven distribution and lumpiness. To correct such problems, a better girth enhancement method was developed: dermal graft augmentation. With dermal grafts, strips of skin are taken from other parts of the body—usually from areas with creases such as the buttocks—so there is no visible scarring. The strips are then surgically inserted under the normal skin of the penis and wrapped completely around it to leave no ridges. Again the increase in girth is 30 to 50 percent, and the result tends to be permanent.

After much hesitation and uncertainty, Simon sought out a cosmetic surgeon to perform a penile augmentation. He had both a lengthening and a girth enhancement, using the dermal graft procedure. He was well satisfied with the results. His one annoyance was having half the length of his penis now hirsute. The new base, formally part of the pubic hair area, now extended outward, and the lower half was covered with hair. But that was a small price to pay for the desired result. And there's always electrolysis.

Simon's motivations were not so much for attracting the opposite sex—after all, no one would notice his size until a lovemaking commitment had already been made—but for comparison with other males. He would no longer be the smallest man in the locker room, and he wouldn't be embarrassed anymore. That was his stated motivation and the resulting satisfaction from the surgery. Once more, self-image, status, and possible dominance are involved.

Rita is Simon's female counterpart. Her problem was breasts, or lack of them. Breasts are obviously more public than penises, so the process is a little different. Rita just knew she was the smallest girl at the swimming pool, at the dance, at the supermarket, and anywhere else.

Early on she took to stuffing her bra with tissues. When she became older, she wore padded bras. She remembered standing naked in front of her mirror, vowing that some day she'd get surgical augmentation. She wanted breasts to be proud of.

Was Rita's augmentation for the purpose of attracting men? Yes, she said, but also to provoke envy in other women. While it was a different form of satisfaction, it was also gratifying to see other women stare at her. Most of all, though, the augmentation made her feel good about herself—that deepest subjective reason for self-modification of the body that the I-self appropriates for its own, whatever the underlying evolutionary reasons may be.

Both sexes demonstrate the need for attractive appearance through surgeries involving the head.[9] The number of modifications now available is stunning. Here are some of them as used by William, a TV weatherman in his fifties, whose motivation, he claims, is not related to vanity. To hold his job, he must look young and attractive. To appear otherwise is to become ineligible for employment on television.

He had developed a large, shiny bald spot on top of his head, and it was spreading. He initially tried creams, with no success, then a toupee, but he was fooling no one. Finally he decided on surgery. First a large patch of scalp was surgically cut out and the skin pulled and stitched together. That left a much smaller area to contend with. After that he began a hair transplant with micro-grafts. In each micrograft a few hairs are transplanted from the back of the head to the bald spot, and a number of micrografts are transplanted during each session. During the healing and hair growing process, William wore his toupee while at work. One of the high points of his life consisted of finally being able to appear before camera without his hairpiece.

Next, after needing increasingly more makeup around his eyes because they had started to look puffy and sunken with the dark-circles look, he resorted to blepharoplasty surgery, sometimes called an eyelid tuck. In this procedure fatty tissue is removed from the upper and lower eyelids, and the skin is tightened.

That worked for a while. Then William needed a face-lift. As we age, the shape of the face shifts from oval to round. At the same time the skin becomes lax, the muscles atrophy, and fat deposits build up. Creases like the buccal labial fold, the line from the base of the nose to the corner of the mouth, become more prominent. Face-lift surgery moves muscles, stretches skin, vacuums fat, and removes excess skin. After recovery William looked ten years younger. He is now contemplating surgery on his nose because he has never really liked the way it looked in profile.

Here are some current figures on what it will cost William as he explores the boundaries of cosmetic surgery: hair transplants, $2,150; nose job, $2,849; pectoral implants, $4,000; abdominal liposuction, $1,800; varicose vein surgery for a small area, $200; and calf implants, $3,000.[10]

More and more, men are joining women in facial surgeries. In 1980 men accounted for 10 percent of all plastic surgery; by 1994 they accounted for 26 percent.[11] The increase seems to be associated with corporate downsizing and an emphasis on youth. This is certainly true for William's stated reason: To keep a job, one needs to look young and attractive in our appearance-conscious culture.

But vanity is lurking here, as well. In fact, keeping a job becomes a screen for vanity because more men seem to be getting cosmetic surgery for reasons independent of employment. Why, then, does vanity itself need covering with sometimes pseudoexplanations about keeping a job? Perhaps because the explanation's perpetrator realizes the extent of the concern with self and appearance and remembers that "beauty is only skin deep" or that "character is what really counts."

As a culture we are more than a little schizoid here. It is wrong to be excessively self-centered, but it is very important to look young and attractive. With a division like this, naked vanity needs to keep itself covered. Justifications begin as camouflage of vanity, and then at some point a surgery becomes sufficiently acceptable that the I-self may take over and proclaim: "I did it for myself; no one else. Feeling good about one's self is the bottom line."

World-Class Body Modification

William the weatherman is well on his way toward continual body modification through cosmetic surgery. Yet he is an amateur in comparison to Cindy Jackson, a forty-two-year-old woman who has had, at last count, twenty-seven cosmetic surgeries, at a cost of about $100,000.[12] Jackson started life as a farm girl and by her own description was not very glamorous. She attended art school and developed her own ideas of how to construct beauty in herself.

She was most influenced by three models.[13] First, she chose the beauty standards and proportions specified by Leonardo da Vinci for a classically proportioned face "which divides it into equal thirds: from top of the forehead to mideyebrow, from brow to base of nose, from nose to chin. In profile, the upper lip had to be in line with the chin."

The second model based itself on the appeal and vulnerability of a child: "big eyes, full pouty lips and upturned noses . . . there's something innately programmed into the human psyche to bring out the protective, nurturing instinct." She sought to draw on those instinctive reactions.

The third model is the teenage temptress for "the specific

things that make a man want to mate with you. Skin must be smooth; this means you don't have a disease and are likely to be of good breeding stock. The waist must be defined because it means that you are not pregnant by another man."

In addition, "Blonde hair, though not essential, means youth because hair tends to darken with age. And everything you do to elongate the legs is good because the best breeding age is late teens, when women's torsos haven't quite caught up with their legs."

Jackson is giving a textbook-perfect description from evolutionary psychology—which she is undoubtedly aware of—for the biological adaptability of attractiveness, accurately capturing the reasoning of that discipline. To put these goals into action, here is a listing of her surgeries: Eyes widened and lifted, knee liposuction, abdomen liposuction, jawline liposuction, lower face-lift, nose job, outer-thigh liposuction, silicone breast implants, chemical face peel, upper face-lift, lower eyes redone, second nose job, fat transfer and dermabrasion for nose-to-mouth lines, removal of breast implants, facial dermabrasion, ultrasonic liposuction on inner thighs and hips, upper lip and nose-to-mouth line modification, mask face-lift, cosmetic dentistry, chin reduction, laser forehead resurfacing, hair transplant to conceal scars, cheek implants, fat transfer to lips, and semipermanent make up, probably in the form of tattooed eyebrow, lipliner, and eyeliner.

These cosmetic surgeries spanned a period of approximately ten years and formed what Jackson referred to as "the project," now essentially completed. Without much doubt, Jackson views the body as a material to be formed and sculpted at will. Evidently, to good effect. As her interviewer says, "male heart-beats quicken" in her presence.

But what is the *inner* Cindy Jackson like? "I'll tell you what I am. . . . I'm a Trojan horse, because what you see is not what you get. I may look young and bimboesque, but I am nothing of the sort." In addition to being an artist of her own flesh, she is a professional photographer, a member of Mensa (which requires for membership a very high IQ, if not wisdom), and she currently operates a cosmetic surgery advisery service in London.

She is aware that she has been the target of feminist criticism but rejects it, saying that what she is doing is controlling her life, going beyond the body that genetics gave her, acquiring power over flesh. She is at the leading edge of body modification, and her reasons—whether one agrees with them—are carefully thought out.

Of course, she has been lucky, evidently having no major complications to her numerous surgeries. In fact, many horror stories accompany cosmetic surgery, ranging from pernicious infections to permanently twisted smiles to heart attack and death. So Jackson has been fortunate or foolish or brave, depending on one's viewpoint.

To be deeply involved in surgical changes, like Jackson, with multiple procedures in pursuit of bodily perfection instead of just holding back the clock, is to be one of the true explorers of our time. It is to move into uncharted territory, where the rush of excitement and risk becomes apparent on the eve of the next surgery or exploration.[14] Such an attitude is supported by a willingness to see the best possible outcome, an image of a favorite movie star instead of a botched face-lift, a twisted penis, or distorted, asymmetrical breasts.

If I am such a person and am successful in my surgical explorations of self, I will be pleased and society may pay me tribute, especially if my job depends on my appearance. But if the result is less than satisfactory, then I will be like the unsuccessful explorers of history, the ones not in the books and the movies, and my tragedy will be borne largely alone.

But that is the nature of explorers. If all the risks and benefits were weighed—and they are usually impossible to know—no one would explore. Many significant discoveries have been founded on error, misconception, and folly. After all, Columbus was not looking for America. Of course, the explorer of the body may discover something other than what is intended. May my voyage take place in good weather and the surprises be of delectable spices. But if I sail into an unanticipated storm and my ship is blown apart, others won't want to hear about it. Wish me bon voyage.

A Body Virus in the Mind

Western cultures of the twentieth century are obsessed with weight. The casualties are most often women and most recently girls. Let us begin by setting the cultural context:

- 33-23-33. The average measurements of a contemporary fashion model.
- 36-18-33. The projected measurements of a Barbie doll scaled to human size—a bit different than Anna Quindlen's scaling, reported earlier.
- 5'4", 142 pounds. The average height and weight of an American woman.
- 5'9", 110 pounds. The average height and weight of a model.
- 80 percent. The percentage of women who diet.
- 25 percent. The percentage of men who diet.
- 50 percent. The percentage of nine-year-old girls who have ever dieted.
- $10 billion. The revenues of the diet industry in 1970.
- $33 billion. The recent revenues of the diet industry.[15]

The disconnection between the reality of the body and the ideal of the imagination is daunting. Not all ideals serve us well. There is widespread suffering behind these figures and the failure to have a body that lives up to that of a model—the ideal being a thin woman with large breasts and a small waist. Following the Barbie model, the ideal must also have long legs. The social trend in recent years seems to be ever more in the direction of the swimsuit model's look, a woman with larger breasts than those of the fashion model's.

A recent poll shows that 56 percent of women are dissatisfied with their overall appearance, 66 percent are dissatisfied with their weight, and 71 percent are dissatisfied with their stomachs; the comparable figures for men are 43, 52, and 63 percent.[16]

The idea of the average, which helped explain the basis of facial beauty, does not account for the nature of bodily beauty. If these ideals for thinness are the outcome of an evolutionary process, they are certainly not based on averages; they are extremes. Neither fashion nor swimsuit models are examples of women who are outstanding reproductive successes, nor do they promise such. Consider a thought experiment in which a variety of female images are presented, including models and close-to-average women. Participants are asked to estimate the number of children each woman is likely to have. My wager is that those judged most reproductively successful (to have the most children) will not be the stunning models.

How to account for this seeming aberration from evolutionary psychology, where the most idealized are not the reproductive maximizers? Not all preferences are the result of our evolutionary history. Current cultural forces provided by movies, TV, magazines, and marketers are also influential forces in shaping our ideals. Body ideal is a case where culture seems to win over the forces of our past evolutionary preference.

With the figure of the swimsuit model as the ideal for large numbers of women and men, it is clear why people are resorting to procedures like liposuction. The peculiar fact is that the ideal seems to disrupt the whole sense of self and the unity system that underlies it: Conflict among standards is inevitable when ideals are unreachable. The unity system has been disrupted by a virus of the mind, the ideal of a nearly impossible bodily proportion.

The Smallest Implant

Surgical approaches to cosmetic enhancement present difficulties for many people. They are expensive, involve risk, often painful, and may require considerable recovery time. Sometimes, too, their effects are transitory or involve complications. For these reasons, the vain among us want better ways.

The smallest implant, the gene, may provide part of the answer. Not long from now, genetic engineering will begin to contribute to the eternal quest for a better appearance.[17] A biotechnology firm has announced a gene treatment that enhances blood-vessel growth in the legs. Soon it will be applied to heart problems with blocked vessels, hopefully providing an alternative to bypass surgery. But it will also point to possible cosmetic applications because once a drug or therapy has been authorized by the FDA for one use, a physician is free to employ it in other ways. That means that a gene-based drug employed for fostering blood-vessel growth in the legs also might be used in the face to restore old skin and muscles with new blood vessels. Or it might build better pectoral muscles without the agony of having to lift weights. What a promise for those who would like to have better muscle definition without lifting anything! In a fine paradox, one could be heavily muscled without strength.

Think of other cosmetic conditions with clear genetic linkage—baldness, say. In fact, a baldness-related gene (there may be more than one) has been found on the X chromosome.[18] This makes sense of the sex differences for baldness because women have two X chromosomes and men one. Therefore, any defect is going to strike males directly, while females have a backup copy in case one gene has a problem. A missing protein might serve as somatic treatment, or the defective gene itself that underlies hair loss might be restored.

From a drug manufacturer's viewpoint, the ideal gene manipulation would involve those of fat storage and usage. If one or two genes effectively controlled weight, think of the boon to a weight-conscious humanity—not to mention the profit for the manufacturer. But before the forces of vanity emerge triumphant, a question: What if genes that contribute to fat formation also prevent cancer or some other affliction? It is easy to think of modifying only one thing, but it is difficult in practice. Dog breeders know this linkage well. Those beautiful Dalmatians are likely to have hearing problems, and they are not very trainable, either.

An additional difficulty for weight control via gene manipulation is that most conditions of appearance are served by many genes acting in concert and therefore beyond the realm of practical treatment. But for those conditions that are controlled by at most a few genes—as perhaps hair growth is—cosmetic gene manipulation becomes a distinct possibility, and we will have to come to terms with yet another choice.

That evolution provides no precedent for surgical or gene enhancement is both true and false at the same time. It is true because cosmetic surgery is new, and gene enhancement is just over the horizon. It is false because the motives behind appearance modification are ancient: Staying young and attractive are age-old yearnings and are consistent with the idea of attracting resources such as the attention of others and an ensuing reproductive advantage. Vanity is not new under the sun, even though the techniques available to serve it continue to expand. Attracting the opposite sex and gaining status over others of the same sex have a long history. To identify any one practice as natural would be suspect. We may be confident, however, that the feelings associated with vanity and its practice are close to the biological substrata.

Quite apart from evolution's reproductive game, there is something different. Seeking perfection in one's appearance is an aesthetic motive that goes far beyond evolution in other life forms. We continue to care for our appearance after the reproductive years; we also do so if we have decided not to have children at all. Perhaps that is just overbuilding by evolution, a process that cannot, after all, know when we will be no longer fertile or when we will die from predation, disease, accident, or war. So the concern for appearance just extends indefinitely into our life span. Or perhaps this concern with appearance is an emergent capability that arises from all the other capabilities provided by evolution and culture. As with our other capabilities, staying young and attractive is rooted in the desire to be the same and different, to attract the attention of others. That ancient motives can lurk in modern methods demonstrates the joint dictates of biology and culture.

A final thought: Why is it that thinking of technological fixes to bring us in alignment with our ideal bodies is so much easier than thinking of how to monitor and modify our inner ideals about weight and weight control? Why can't we just get rid of our false ideal, the virus of the mind that tells us we must be thin at any cost?

Well, whether or not we like our bodies and ourselves, there is always the possibility of creating another self in the image of the ideal that occupies our thoughts. Let us examine new approaches to that other self, a child to identify with and to mold in the image of our aspirations—an ultimate extension of the self.

Chapter 4

CREATING ANOTHER BODY

I acknowledge the duplicates of myself. . . .
What I do and say the same waits for them,
Every thought that flounders in me the same flounders in them.

— WALT WHITMAN, *Leaves of Grass*

We come now to the third part of the Darwinian To-do List that says *reproduce.* A reproductive module in the mind is evident, with a few important qualifications. Desire and the associated emotional structure are close to universal, but unlike in lower animals, the means of implementation are transferred to culture. How we exercise that desire is a matter of experience and learning. This is also true to a lesser extent of our primate relatives. An old study by the psychologist Harry Harlow demonstrated that monkeys raised in isolation from birth to a breeding age would try to mate, but they did not really know how to go about it, demonstrating awkward and indirect behaviors.[1] Desire was present but not the technique.

Why would evolution transfer components of something as important as reproduction to culture? Probably because it frees up the hardware of the brain for other functions, and it allows for greater flexibility in behavior. This is a common evolutionary strategy that also occurs in feeding behavior. Lower organisms with wired-in feeding as to both preferred food and the behavioral means of acquiring it will be at a disadvantage if the environment shifts on them. The ultimate flexibility comes from transferring food preferences and behavior to culture. It is no accident that our species is so broadly distributed on the earth. Our adaptations are exquisitely nuanced for environments as extreme as rain forests, deserts, and polar regions. The trade-off is a long period of cultural education in which the knowledge and skills required for survival are learned. This is not just a matter of becoming more mentally complex, either. Few of us in a modern civilization could survive for long in an extreme environment. It takes years of learning an environment to fit with it.

To return to reproductive behavior, with large parts of it left to culture for elaboration, it should come as no surprise that new variations in that behavior are now afforded by science, particularly those from the new reproductive technologies. The blend and clash of what seems to be biologically built in and what is technologically possible are now the substrate of the debate on surrogacy, cloning, and the like. Let us examine some actual cases to see the varied forces in play.

The usual evolutionary account is that sex itself is not engaged in to produce offspring; instead, desire fuels behavior that gives rise to these progeny. Then other built-in tendencies work to insure care and nurturing of these progeny. The missing nexus is the wanting of children themselves, and, insofar as it exists, that is a cultural add-on. If so, it is an easy addition. At a deep level, in the ultimate extension of body, many of us want to create another body, usually through the normal process of sexual reproduction.

But other means are now at hand, involving the new reproductive technologies. A *New York Times* headline reads: WHEN GRANDMOTHER IS THE MOTHER, UNTIL BIRTH.[2] Far from a tabloid freak account, as suggested by the title, the tale is one of courage and love among the participants, while the spectators find it a tale of fascination, mixed feelings, or even Frankensteinian portent. This is a story of self creating another self that would have been impossible and unimaginable until a few years ago.

Here are the facts: Arlette Schweitzer, a forty-two-year-old woman, is carrying twins. The eggs are from her married daughter, Christa, who was born without a uterus, a rare condition occurring in one in five thousand women. The sperm was supplied by Christa's husband. Together, egg and sperm were mixed in a laboratory petri dish—in vitro—and the resulting zygotes were implanted in Arlette's womb. When the twins are born, they will be raised by Christa and her husband.

Notice that this is very different from the controversial cases of a contract surrogate mother supplying her own egg. Arlette Schweitzer is acting in a different capacity, as a *gestational surrogate;* none of the genetic material is directly her own, even though there is some overlap because the egg is from her daughter. Moreover, the contract surrogate mother often receives pay for her role. It is quite the opposite for Arlette, who had very different motives: "You do what you do for your children because you love them. . . . If you can do something to help your children, you do it."[3]

To understand the inventive nature and logic of such new forms of parenthood, I want to take a brief excursion. First we will consider a simpler analog involving bacterial reproduction with structure-function splits, then a second analog from physical invention with its own splits, and finally a third analog involving a division of roles.[4]

In bacterial reproduction, every so often there is a split down the middle, leaving two bacteria where previously there was one. It is impossible to know which is the older, and indeed that is a meaningless question. While individual bacteria can be killed by viruses, antibiotics, sterilizing agents, and the like, barring such bad fortune they are immortal. Many people think that because of their mode of reproduction, bacteria are all genetically the same. Not so—at least for some of them—because in their spare time bacteria connect microtubules between one another and swap DNA back and forth.[5] What makes this so interesting is the contrast with human repro- duction. In bacteria the swapping of genetic material and repro- duction are split off from one another; they are separate activities.

Consider a structure-function split involving invention. Imag- ine a standard kitchen knife, one with a long blade and a handle. The knife may be used for a variety of purposes: reaming potato eyes, cutting carrots, chopping meat. The same structure has many functions, but they are not optimized. It is difficult to ream potato eyes with a long kitchen knife, but cutting carrots may be fine, while chopping meat is also awkward. By splitting apart the structure of the knife for specialized functions, a more optimal shape and resulting function occurs. A potato peeler with a rounded point is ideal for digging the eyes from potatoes; a cleaver is ideal for chop- ping meat. Of course, neither the potato peeler nor the cleaver has the general-purpose capability of the regular kitchen knife.

The splitting of structure and function also occurs with the same logic but different terminology for people and role splits. The manufacturing process illustrates this nicely. In a typical craft operation such as making chairs, one worker has all the roles: cut- ting, shaping, assembling, and finishing. But in an assembly line those roles are split between a number of different people—one person cuts, another shapes, another assembles, and still another finishes. It is easy for a worker to achieve expertise on a simple component task and become very fast; it is much more difficult to acquire expertise on all the elements of making a chair.

Now consider how these different forms of splitting and recombination relate to Arlette Schweitzer's surrogate mother role. Obviously she is not the usual mother. Typical motherhood has its remote origins in attraction between a woman and a man. This attraction leads to passion and then usually marriage or some other kind of commitment. At some time unprotected intercourse takes place and is followed by pregnancy and birth. Then begins the long process of rearing a child. All of these functions occur in the same woman. When we divide or split these functions, we find several customary parental roles, as in this sequence:

Attraction Parent → Passion Parent → Married Parent → Intercourse Parent → Genetic Parent → Womb Parent → Birth Parent → Rearing Parent.

In the usual case, each of these roles is bound to the others; together they constitute a bundle of roles in the *same person,* one that we call the mother. Structure and numerous functions are tied to each other. Of course, many departures occur in practice. Often rearing parents have had no part in the other parental roles, as in adoption or when grandparents raise a child. And sometimes conception does not involve attraction or passion or the commitment of child rearing. But for the most part there is a common sequence to the many important roles of being a mother.

What Arlette and Christa have done is to split the sequence into a set of roles divided much further than before. Grandmother Arlette is not the Attraction Parent, the Passion Parent, the Married Parent, the Intercourse Parent, or the Genetic Parent. She is the Womb Parent and the Birth Parent. After the children's birth she will not be the Rearing Parent.

Daughter Christa is the Attraction Parent, the Passion Parent, and the Married Parent but not the Intercourse Parent since the egg and sperm were combined in a petri dish. However, Christa is the Genetic Parent while neither the Womb Parent nor the Birth Parent. Yet she will be the Rearing Parent. The role of Christa's husband remains similar to that of most fathers; he is a Genetic Parent and a Rearing Parent, although he is not the Intercourse Parent in this case. In a surprising convergence, Christa's role is now very similar to that of her husband's—and any typical male's: She is a Genetic Parent and a Rearing Parent.

The various functions of motherhood have been teased apart, or split, and they no longer take place in the same person; now they occur in separate people. This logic of structure-function splitting has enabled a splitting apart of parenthood. On the surface, what is happening here is like the trading around of DNA independently of reproduction in a way not altogether different than the bacteria, the invention, and the assembly line examples already mentioned. Christa and her husband have given their DNA package to Arlette for the gestation that Christa is not doing herself. At another level of description, the varied roles of motherhood have been split or assigned to different people, just as the assembly of the chair moved from a craft operation with one builder to an assembly line with many builders.

While the parallel with the splits from bacteria, knives, and chair assembly is evident, there is much more to Arlette's case. Ethical concerns apply to birth if not to bacteria, knives, and chair manufacturing. But following the logic of structure-function splitting in these contexts suggests the possibility of some women becoming specialized as donors of eggs or gestational surrogates. For example, to provide convenience, a rich couple might enter into contractual arrangement and provide a zygote to a poor woman, who then serves as a gestational surrogate for a fee. Or the surrogate might contribute both egg and gestational services. Or the poorer woman might contribute her egg to the richer couple in exchange for a fee. Many variations are possible. Here is a recent classified ad from the Harvard alumni magazine:

> Devoted Harvard couple with one lovely child seek exceptionally intelligent and attractive egg donor to help us complete our family. Ideally she should be young, even featured, of slender to medium build, with lighter colored hair and eyes. Musical, artistic or scientific gifts are also appreciated. Very generous compensation is offered and discretion is assured.[6]

It is comforting that what Arlette Schweitzer and her family did was ethical by almost any standard. The procedure they engaged in was done not for experimentation, convenience, profit, or any other detectable negative motive. Indeed, the entire story is an act of maternal love freely engaged in. She wanted to help her daughter have children.

Where, then, should the larger society fit into this picture of the reinvented parental self? Various doctors and medical ethicists are greatly concerned. Dr. Jay Katz, a professor of law, medicine, and psychiatry at Yale, believes that Arlette Schweitzer's actions were "a very, very bad idea. . . . Is the grandmother the grandmother or the mother? . . . It may ultimately create too many tensions for the child and for the family. I appreciate and I would not dispute the loving intentions of the woman's mother. But sometimes love can create problems of its own."[7]

Dr. Albert Jonsen, a University of Washington ethicist, has this to say: "The question is, are there kinds of altruism that may be so troubling to important social and cultural traditions that we'd rather not have that altruism take place?" He believes that this is a case in point.

Other ethicists have a different view. Dr. Arthur Caplan, of the University of Minnesota, said: "I think it is a very kind, generous act. . . . Therefore, I think it is ethically admirable. . . . Although . . . it sounds a little bizarre, a little crazy, when you think about it, this may be the least problematic case for surrogacy. . . . You could argue that this is the ideal form [because money was not involved and love was the motive]."

Interestingly, Arlette Schweitzer has said she has never received an adverse comment on her actions. Perhaps the public is simply watching with fascination and either cheering her on or waiting to see what happens.

In perspective, then, what Arlette and Christa did is both less and more than conventional surrogacy with egg donation and gestation. On the less side, their child is not the direct genetic offspring of the birthing mother, and no money has changed hands. On the more side, novel human relationships are involved. The birth mother and the grandmother reside in the same skin; the birth mother, the daughter (genetic parent), and the child are related in ways for which we have no words. Once the component functions and structure of reproduction are revealed, as by modern birth technology, new combinations and arrangements become possible. Arlette and Christa seized upon these. In doing so, they were reinventing motherhood, the nature of the reproductive self, and the forms of possible kinship relations. Here is a birth process that requires not just two parents but three.

Stepping back from the process, it is easy to see that Arlette's motives are admirable. Her reason for helping is love. Many children are conceived with lesser motives in mind, if any at all. So a cautionary note is in order. Under these circumstances, should medical ethicists remain noncommittal and governmental regulation hold off until wisdom shines through the dust? The whole situation is just too complex to know much about the implications. The total number of surrogacy cases is small, and those of Arlette Schweitzer's type will obviously remain even rarer. Other than reasonable legal provisions to guarantee responsibility for children, the appropriate role of society at this time may be curiosity—it is so interesting! As long as no malevolence is evident, let us give people some room to reinvent the idea of parenthood. After all, when evolution transferred the precise behaviors of human reproduction to cultural instruction, was it not to allow for innovation?

The counterargument is that the potential for abuse is substantial. Imagine thoughtful parents of the next century routinely conceiving identical twins by having a pre-embryo split. With development, one of the resulting embryos will be placed in cold storage, where it will be reserved as spare parts for unfortunate accidents or diseases befalling the other embryo implanted in the womb to become a child. What might we say of such a practice? Would our answer differ depending on whether someone in the news did it or we did it to provide for a bone marrow transplant for our own child?

In all of these surrogacy cases involving new expressions of the reproductive self, two possibilities offer concern. The first is that the previously yoked body and role of what we historically call the mother will become so fractured that we will end with something like embryo farms. The second concern is that the role of being a mother, a role etched deeply in tissue and mind, will thereby be split off and shed from what it means to be a reproducing self. The embryo farm implies just such a division if the reproductive self proceeds solely on the path of efficiency, as in technological invention. Then we as women, men, and humans will be diminished by a separation of body and being from mind and role.

As in previous ways of inventing the self, these cases of varied surrogacy transcend nature by redefining and inventing anew what it means to be a parental self. The technology for recreating biological parenthood, for all of its difficulties, is easy in comparison to recreating the sense of parenthood that has been refined by eons of evolutionary history.

Further variations on the separation of structure and function are provided by the legal case of Junior and Mary Sue Davis. The Davises tried for years to have a child.[8] Mary Sue had repeated tubal pregnancies requiring surgical interruption. First her right fallopian tube was removed. Then after her fifth tubal pregnancy she had her left fallopian tube ligated. She could no longer hope for a conventional pregnancy, and attempts at adoption failed. The couple resorted to in vitro fertilization.

IVF began with hormone treatments to stimulate the production of ova, or eggs; the ova were then extracted from the ovaries, using a long needle, and placed in a petri dish, where sperm was mixed with them. The result was a zygote, a fertilized egg with one complete cell. Forty-eight to seventy-two hours later, the developing pre-embryo (now four to eight undifferentiated cells) was transferred back into the uterus.

The Davises went through this procedure six different times

without success. Mary Sue became fearful of the needles. Then the clinic they were working with acquired the capability for freezing unused pre-embryos consisting of four to eight cells, to be used for later backup and to avoid more hormone treatments and needle aspirations. On her next attempt, multiple ova were extracted and fertilized, then allowed to divide into the pre-embryo stage. The plan was to implant one pre-embryo in the uterus, and the remainder were to be frozen as backups for subsequent use, a process termed *cryogenic preservation*. The first attempt at implantation again resulted in failure. Before another attempt could take place, Junior Davis filed for divorce.

The divorce process seemed to be amicable, except for the disposition of the remaining pre-embryos. The dispute went to trial at the state-court level. Junior Davis told the court that he did not want to be a compulsory father. Mary Sue did not want the pre-embryos he had fertilized to be destroyed. The trial court judge ruled that the pre-embryos are really "children in vitro" and awarded Mary Sue custody.

Junior Davis disagreed and took the case to the state Court of Appeals. That court rejected the trial judge's reasoning and ruling. Ultimately the case went to the Supreme Court of Tennessee. The court made a number of distinctions pertaining to gametes, zygotes, pre-embryos, embryos, and still other stages of development, with the idea that a separate law may apply to each stage.

In its technical deliberations, the court considered just what form of property, if any, pre-embryos are. It also considered a number of models for disposition of pre-embryos, ranging from custody to Mary Sue to use by other infertile couples to medical research to disposal. Ultimately the Supreme Court sided with Junior Davis: A man cannot be compelled to become a father against his will.

What were the motives of Junior and Mary Sue Davis? He did not think he should be required to be a father. His former wife, he maintained, would be in the position of requiring him to participate in fatherhood and all of its legal implications against his will. In contrast, she wanted to be a mother and perhaps believed that she already was.[9]

This is a tangled issue, one that we will surely hear more of as technology makes possible the ever finer splitting of structures, functions, and roles that, from the dawn of our evolutionary past, always came as a unified bundle. Here is one such futuristic scenario that draws on an ancient drama.

In the fifth century B.C.E. the Greek dramatist Sophocles wrote his play *Oedipus Rex*, from which Sigmund Freud arrived at the idea of the Oedipus complex. In the play a son unwittingly slays his father. In Freud's delineation of the complex, a son vies with his father for the love of his mother. Without passing on the merits of Freudian theory, I believe it is safe to say that the reproductive technologies now available—and others soon to come—will create entirely new possibilities for psychoanalytic speculation.

Consider but one example: giving birth to your own brother. Why would you want to do this? Suppose that shortly after you were conceived (in a fertility clinic's lab dish, of course), the other pre-embryos were frozen, as backups. Your parent's reasons for doing this are not altogether clear and cannot be recovered, since they died in a car accident several years ago. At any rate, you and your husband now want to have children. After repeated attempts and numerous medical consultations, the verdict is in: You are infertile.

Alternatives are considered, including using your husband's sperm to fertilize the egg of a donor, an embryo that you would then carry. Before this possibility is taken very far, you find that your husband is the carrier of a potentially lethal gene. Of course, with the wonders of amniocentesis it is possible to discern early in the pregnancy whether the fetus caries the gene. But you are opposed to abortion for any reason.

All of which drives you and your husband to an unusual decision. The frozen pre-embryo of your brother is available. It could be implanted in your womb, it would be genetically similar to yourself, and your husband is agreeable. When the baby is born, you will have given birth to your own brother.

Think of the new complexities of relationship here. Now the normal tensions between parents and children are further complicated by having the mother-son relationship combine with a sister-brother relation. Previously separate structures and roles are now merged in the same person: mother-sister and son-brother. The logic of recombination is now a structure-function integration. It yields sibling rivalry on top of generational angst. The whole thing boggles the thinking mind.

Sophocles would also have found fascination in the cloning of a sheep called Dolly. To clone her, a mature somatic, or body, cell of a sheep was selected; it had all of its chromosomes and genes. The nucleus of that cell, the part with the genetic material, was stripped out. Then an ovum from another sheep was selected (remember, it contains only half the somatic chromosomes, the mother's half of the genetic material) and its genetic material stripped out. The nucleus from the somatic cell with all the chromosomes and genes was now inserted in the ovum; this is the equivalent of a zygote, a joined ovum and sperm with all the chromosomes. The resulting cell was then implanted in a surrogate mother who later gave birth to Dolly. Note that Dolly was genetically identical to the sheep from which the somatic cell came.

Human implications are not hard to find. A woman could give birth to a copy of herself. The nucleus from one of her somatic cells would be stripped out and substituted for the half-complete genetic material in one of her ova. The result would then be implanted in her uterus and, if everything worked, nine months later she would give birth to herself—or more precisely, an exact genetic copy of herself.[10]

But that is not the most incredible implication of the new reproductive technology. Far from it. According to evolutionary psychology, we are built by evolution to get our genes into the next generation. Normal mating means we get 50 percent of our genes into our progeny. Cloning means we get 100 percent of our genes into the next generation. From the perspective of evolutionary theory, *the optimal method of reproduction is cloning.* Following evolution's logic to the limit, we should first choose to clone ourselves before the normal reproduction of mating with another. The result truly is a brave new world.

A man could also duplicate himself, but the procedure would be slightly different. The complete nucleus from one of his somatic cells would be stripped out and joined with an ennucleated ovum as before. The difference is that he would now need to find a surrogate mother to carry his genetic material.

An infertile couple could decide to have a boy and a girl, each a clone of one partner. If the developmental routines in the infertile woman's ova were functional, a somatic nucleus from either herself or her mate would be implanted in the ennucleated ovum. The resulting cell then would be implanted in her womb. Nine months later, a genetic copy of one of them would be born.

Is this unethical? The first rush of opinion on the cloning of the sheep Dolly sounded many warning notes about it being a deviation from nature's way. But opinion has been shifting rapidly, and the normal cycle of horror to no to curiosity to partial acceptance to why not? has taken place in a remarkably short period.[11] Fertility centers that initially said they would never consider cloning are now taking experimental steps in that direction. Monkey research is being funded by the U.S. government to develop clones—and for good reason: When random statistical variation is eliminated, the effects of different experimental drug treatments are much clearer. Though monkey clones are being developed for one purpose, the techniques are likely to be easily translated to human use.

As we have seen, evolutionary theory carried to the limit of its logic tells us that cloning is the very best individual strategy for getting our genes into the next generation, but it cannot be a good general strategy. If everyone clones, the overall population becomes a fixed genetic pool and a more likely target for disease, assuming the endless recombination of sexual reproduction provides a moving target that protects us from the afflictions visited on us by the microbial world.[12] This would be particularly true if large groups of clones arose in one place—a dictator, for example, might decree that all children in the palace must be his clone. Then any disease to which he displayed special susceptibility would be visited with vengeance on his progeny.

Cloning has one further implication to consider, an idea from Robert Wright:

> If cloning becomes an option, what kind of people will use it? Exactly—people who think the world could use more of them; people so chipper that they have no qualms about bestowing their inner life on a dozen members of the next generation; people, in short, with high self-esteem. The rest of us will sit there racked with doubt, worried about inflicting our tortured psyches on the innocent unborn, while all around us shiny, happy people proliferate like rabbits. Or sheep. . . .[13]

To place the material of Part I in perspective, the body that biology and birth give to us enjoys substantial modification in pursuit of restoration, preservation, or perfection. Sometimes, too, there is an element of exploration and experimentation. The methods of change take a variety of forms: cosmetic enhancement through accentuation and camouflage; additions of tattoos and piercing hardware, penile and breast augmentation, and other bodily implants; deletions via nose reductions and liposuctions; and, finally, the rearrangements and recombinations of role and gene splittings from reproductive technology and cloning.

These categories—addition, deletion, rearrangement, and recombination—are the very stuff of physical invention where almost no prior rules of constraint have applicability.[14] Thus part of a tree can be used to carve a facsimile of a duck to produce from that strange mating a decoy that attracts real ducks for the purpose of humans hunting them. In raw nature there is little if any connection between trees and ducks, but this relatively free-form linkage and combination in physical invention means that anything is fair game for an attempted pairing with anything else. Whether it produces a viable invention is another question, but we can't rule it out a priori.

The same free-form pairings do not occur for the extensions of the body, in part because we have immune systems that are choosy about what the body is combined with. But these constraints of compatibility are being overcome gradually as new materials, surgical techniques, and knowledge of the immune system are developed.

Yet any new form of the body must be more than workable invention. We also want beauty and grace as much or more than function. As a result, our bodily extensions must be not only invention but art, where the body itself is becoming a material to be sculpted at will. The nature of the resulting invention and art is not always clear. In some cases it is beautiful; in others, grotesque or damaging. But that is the nature of the creative process. Sometimes it works and other times it does not.

PART II

Creating a Persona

[A] man has as many social selves as there are individuals who recognize him and carry an image of him in their mind. . . . [H]e has as many social selves as there are distinct groups of persons about whose opinion he cares. He generally shows a different side of himself to each of these different groups. A youth is demure before some groups and swears before others.

—WILLIAM JAMES, *Psychology: Briefer Course*

Who am I? In part a persona supplied by culture and in part one crafted by myself. My persona is the image I have of myself and what I want to project to others, how I connect to others, a set of self-concepts. While no sharp line separates my body from my persona, they are frequently linked by self-consciousness and vanity.

Yet persona goes far beyond the body. It is a self of social connection, of autonomy and distinctiveness, and of sameness spanning change. It also has its own internal dynamics, allowing it to contract or expand, to reach out empathically and partake of another's mind, to identify so completely with someone else as to want to be them. Finally, it has the capacity to create imaginary friends and lovers.

Chapter 5

THE CONNECTED SELF

Is this then a touch? quivering me to a new identity,
Flames and ether making a rush for my veins. . . .

— WALT WHITMAN, *Leaves of Grass*

We begin by considering the persona as a web of relationships and connections to others. This is what William James meant when he talked of a social self. It is what marks us as a distinct person, separate from others yet connected to them. We value most that distinctness and pattern of connections when they are taken away from us. There is first a biting sense of loss and then a scramble to regain what has been taken away. Here is a tale of that loss, a breakdown in the usual social links that define one's sense of identity.

On his way to a grant visitation meeting, Earl, a biochemist from Stillwater, Oklahoma, traveled to Las Vegas, New Mexico. During his journey he lost his billfold.[1] He discovered this when he changed planes in Dallas. Perhaps he had left it at the airport newsstand. He retraced his steps. No sign of it. Had it slipped out of his pocket while on the plane from Oklahoma City? He inquired at the gate, and an attendant went back on the plane to check his seat. No, not there. He called Oklahoma City. Nothing there, either. Had someone picked his pocket? The airport police couldn't help him. He had only loose change, and it was Sunday and no one was at Traveler's Aid. Quickly, he became a nonperson: no money, no credit cards, no name, a nobody because he had no verifiable connection to other people or to society's institutions of commerce and credit.

He remembered his telephone calling card number, however, his one fragile link connecting him to his dispersed self of credit and finance. He called his wife, requesting that she cancel his other credit cards. He still had his airline ticket, since it was in his shirt pocket, so he continued on to Albuquerque. His rental car was reserved, but—surprise!—he couldn't have it, not only because of an absence of a credit card but because the car rental required a driver's license, now missing. He called a friend in Albuquerque, who brought him two hundred dollars cash. Another member of the grant visitation committee showed up at the airport, so the car was secured in his name.

At the hotel in Las Vegas he sought to restore his lost self. He called American Express. They could get a replacement card to Albuquerque but not to Las Vegas because it's a small town in a remote area. Hotel accounting then called American Express. To verify that Earl was who he claimed, he had to answer a number of personal questions: recent purchases and orders—what was charged, where, when—the last bill paid, his work phone number. He was given some hints: Where's your last charge? It was in Maryland; give the name of hotel. His memory acted as an internalized connection of events to match external billing records. His credit with the hotel desk was then authorized, and he canceled his old card. (Restoration often requires destruction.)

Exhausted, Earl slept soundly. Waking early, he went for a walk. During his walk, he began to wonder if it was a good idea. Here he was, a black man in a strange town—perhaps the only one—wandering around very early in the morning. What if the police stopped him? He had no identification of any kind, no money. Walking around like this was not a good idea. When you have no ID, you're not only a nobody, you're a suspicious person. He had lost more than his billfold.

His meeting over, he arrived back in the Oklahoma City airport and started his car. He then realized he had no driver's license, and to get back home was a sixty-five-mile drive. He drove very carefully, once again wondering what would happen if he were stopped for any reason.

Once home, he canceled his phone calling card, his last remaining numerical tie to the codes of his old credit life. Now the process of restoration began in earnest. His first task was to get a new driver's license. But he found out at the Motor Vehicle Department that he couldn't get a license because he didn't have any identification. That would require a birth certificate or passport. He went home, found his passport (it had a picture), and went back. The driver's license bureau then called a computer to verify the information on the passport. Did his weight and height information match? Yes. So he finally received a new driver's license. The moral: You need identification to get identification.

Next he went to his university to get a new faculty ID card. Personnel would not accept his driver's license as proof that he was whom he claimed he was. He needed a personnel action form from his department. He obtained it and returned to Personnel so that they could compare it with the other form on file. A ten-dollar charge and twenty-four hours later he had his faculty ID. He was beginning to exist again, regaining a sense of self.

In his adventure, Earl discovered that there are two great symbolic systems for getting around in the world, and he had lost both of them: ID and money. Even money wasn't enough to be able to rent a car or get a new driver's license or faculty ID. If he hadn't memorized his phone card number, it would have been much more difficult. To be sure, Traveler's Aid in the airport—if they had been open—would have eventually come to his rescue, but it would have taken longer.

Another aspect of his experience is the different levels of identification he required. First there's financial ID, as on a credit card; not having that, he wasn't able to rent the car. Lacking the same ID made it difficult to register at the hotel. Then there's state ID—a driver's license. Without it, he couldn't rent the car, and it made him uneasy while driving back home from the Oklahoma City airport. To renew his driver's license, he used a national ID—a passport—although a state ID—a birth certificate—also would have worked.

These different forms of identification connected his name to financial records that certified his ability to pay based on past information and established a kind of abstract container, or file, for future billing and record keeping. They connected his name to state records, where a driver's license certified a minimal competence on the road. That license also connected him to a computer file with his record, indicating any past infractions. The passport meant that he was a citizen of this country, that the picture on it matched with whom he claimed to be, and that he was not a criminal whose right to travel outside the country had been revoked.

Beyond all of these levels of identification and connection to previously abstract social institutions there was the feeling of unease during an early-morning walk in a strange town, a fear of being stopped for vagrancy or loitering, a sense of discontinuity of person. He had something almost taken away from him: his sense of person.

Identity Theft

Earl's experience could have been worse. What happens when your purse is stolen and someone hijacks your identity by charging your accounts for their purchases, by acting as you in numerous capacities? Each new day presents the possibility that some aspect of yourself will be taken from you. The psychological effect is halfway between being raped and reading your own obituary. Here is the experience of Marcia Vickers, who had her purse stolen from a restaurant.[2] She had put it on the floor beside her—and then it was gone.

She became the victim of what law enforcement officers call "true name fraud," or in everyday language, identity theft. Marcia did most things right from the beginning, but her ordeal was still compelling. Immediately after the theft, she canceled most of her credit cards (she wasn't sure which ones were at home). Then she canceled her ATM card and checking account. As soon as she got home, she called a locksmith to change the keying on her door, and then she sorted through her other credit cards and canceled the remaining stolen ones. Once again, the restoration of self required the destruction of prior connections because they might have been taken over. The analogy is to cancer. When a cell has been invaded, it must be destroyed to regain health.

That evening she received a call from a man who claimed to be with her bank, saying he had a report that her ATM card had been stolen, and he needed her to enter her personal identification number in the phone so he could issue her a new one. Surprised, she asked him for a phone number to call him back, telling him the call was being traced. He hung up immediately. The likely scenario is that since her personal identification number was not in her purse, the thief used the phone ruse in an attempt to get it.

Next, Marcia, who is blond and in her thirties, began to get calls from stores to confirm that an applicant for instant credit was in fact her. Usually, just her answering machine message with her name was enough for the store to grant immediate credit of one thousand dollars. On one occasion she answered a call from a store that was in the middle of a transaction with her alter ego impostor. The store detective described the woman as large and with black hair dyed orange. She was attempting to purchase "six extra-large Triple Fat Goose down jackets." Marcia wanted the woman arrested, but the store wouldn't comply because she hadn't yet bought anything. They simply denied her credit, and she walked away. Stores are naturally reluctant to arrest someone on the word of someone else. Think of the liability problems.

Marcia knew she was in for a siege. One of her most effective strategies consisted of leaving a message on her answering machine saying that her purse had been stolen. That helped cut down on the issuance of new credit cards. Nonetheless, she found herself in an ongoing battle with merchants and credit bureaus, trying to keep her good name in the clear. It became a minioccupation, requiring ten hours a week for the first few months to keep up with the identity thief's commercial purchases. The added insult: She kept receiving catalogs for extra-large women, a constant reminder that someone very different from her had taken over her credit identity.

The identity thief is the contemporary equivalent of a stagecoach robber of the nineteenth century or a bank robber of the early part of the twentieth century. But the identity thief earns a living with considerably less risk. Even if caught, she will not get shot, and the sentences are light compared to those incurred by the robbers of old—or for that matter, contemporary stick-up artists. The odds are better, too. Often the thief is successful. Once she gets your identifying credit cards, social security number, and driver's license, she can use those for completely new credit cards. A common gambit is to also send in a change of address for you. Your mail is rerouted to a vacant house, and the new credit cards are picked up by the identity thief. Even as you read this, there may be another you out there making purchases in your name. At the very least, it will cause you great inconvenience and perhaps a denial of that mortgage you have applied for. Good luck—to all of us.

Even more insidious and malicious forms of identity theft are possible. For example, suppose the identity thief was near you in the restaurant, listening to you talk, before making off with your purse. Further assume that she is an excellent mimic and enjoys sadistic pleasures. Now the thief's voice is no longer distinguishable from your own, and she begins to burrow deeply into your own identity. If the thief is truly malicious, she may call your friends or family, imitating your voice, and making strange requests—or maybe insulting them in your name. What would your reaction be? Perhaps as if a cancer had invaded your body, your whole existence. One of the most frightening aspects to contemplate about this form of theft is that the cellular machinery of your identity has been taken over by a malignancy that you do not know how to combat.

Sudden Identity Shifts

We value a certain constancy in self not only in ourselves but in the people we meet, and we want that self to be real or true and not just a facade designed to con us. When another person shifts characteristics quickly, or takes on a false identity, the effect on us is substantial. Here is a famous case of a young man who turned out to be different than he represented. The people affected were disturbed, to say the least, because his identity halo was not real.

The young man called a New York couple, saying he was a friend of their children at college.[3] He said his name was David Poitier, and he was the son of the actor Sidney Poitier (who has no son). Furthermore, he, David, had just been mugged. His money and his thesis on the criminal justice system had been taken. He desperately needed help and a place to stay until his father, Sidney, arrived the next day. Could they aid him? He was invited to the couple's home, ate dinner with them, borrowed money, and slept over.

He had asked to be awakened in the morning. When the wife did, she found him in bed with another young man. He was asked to leave. Soon the couple found that other friends of theirs had had the same con worked on them. David then called to apologize, requesting a meeting in Greenwich Village. Instead, the couple called the police. David Hampton—his real name—was arrested and arraigned on charges of petty larceny, criminal impersonation, and fraudulent accosting. He pleaded guilty to attempted burglary, a lesser charge. The court ordered him to make financial restitution to his several victims, but he violated the court order and served almost two years in state prison.

As one of his victims said: "He defrauded more of the spirit than the flesh."[4] That is precisely the point about this kind of fraud. Hampton took relatively little of financial worth from his wealthy victims. Instead, it was that fragile bond of trust and vulnerability, the connection that makes us human, that he managed to destroy.

There is still more to David Hampton's story. The playwright John Guare went on to write *Six Degrees of Separation*, based on the incident; the play later served as the basis of a fascinating movie of the same name. At this point, Hampton sued Guare seeking "$60,000,000 compensatory and punitive damages against the author, producers, publisher and purchaser of the film right to the award winning play. . . ."[5] Of course, anyone can sue anyone else; collecting is another matter. The court did not recognize Hampton's claim for commercial misappropriation or invasion of common-law right to privacy. Further, he had no property interest in making himself seem other than he was.

Hampton's suit is remarkable under these circumstances. It is almost as if he thought his con was a part of his own persona, an intellectual property, and anyone using it should have his permission or pay him for it.

Here is another variation on the false-identity con game. A man claiming to be Harry Edwards, the well-known sociologist of sports, calls you, a lesser-known professor of sociology, and tells you he has a problem.[6] His nephew Bill is in your town on a job interview and has had his wallet stolen. The caller, posing as Edwards, says he will be in town in a few days himself, but in the meantime, could you please help out his nephew? As soon as he comes to town, he will reimburse you, and for your trouble he'd be glad to give a free seminar for your department.

While you're thinking over this request, "Edwards" may say

how much he has admired your work. If you had any reservations, they now rapidly melt away. A distinguished professor admires your work, you'll be given credit in your department for getting him to give the seminar, you'll be introducing him, and you can imagine talking to him over dinner about your article that he so admired.

In a few hours, Edwards's nephew shows up at your house. He talks knowledgeably about his uncle Harry and the sociology of sports, and then he thanks you for your willingness to tide him over with the money he needs. You don't know it at the time, but this will be the last you see of him, and Harry Edwards never comes to town.

This is a wonderfully slick con. Like all great cons, it appeals simultaneously to your generosity and your vanity. The perpetrator knows about this and has studied your weaknesses. He is doing this to make money but evidently it is much more: a game to put down those like yourself who are accomplished enough to have a doctoral degree and be a university professor, those who are confident of their intellectual abilities and who would normally think of themselves as impervious to being outsmarted.

From the perpetrator's point of view, he is a fine actor engaged in a great performance; each performance stretches and improves him. He prepares for his performance and has studied the real Edwards, either by having heard him speak in public or by calling his office and listening to his answering machine until he has the voice down. He has read an article or two by you. He is a lifelong student of human vanity. He will know the quality of his performance quickly, not by some silly theater critic's review in a newspaper but by how much money he can extract from you.

In the process, your tormentor will have destroyed some of your most ingrained assumptions about trust, belief in your own judgment, and the delicate membrane of human identity that both separates and connects you to others. You will see the true importance of a social self and the value of regaining it when it is lost.

Chapter 6

THE UNITARY SELF

Singing the song of These, my ever-united lands, my body no more inevitably united, part to part, and made out of a thousand diverse contributions one identity, any more than my lands are inevitably united and made ONE IDENTITY . . .

—WALT WHITMAN, *Leaves of Grass*

William James asked a seemingly simple question about identity: How is it possible that when I wake up in the morning, I have the sense of being the same person who went to sleep the night before? Before answering the question, some context is needed. For James, identity marks off an *I-consciousness* and a *me-body* as a unity of self that is distinct from those of other people. This is the distinct "I" that others see as they relate to me; in short, my personality. Said in another way, identity is formed by an invisible surrounding membrane that separates an "I" and a "me" from everyone else.

To return to his question of how identity is preserved overnight, consider how my body has changed. I am eight hours older, my gastric, circulatory, and nervous systems are all in different states, and my dreams have altered my consciousness and my memory. At a different level, my electrons and atoms have undergone significant change from the day before. Yet through all of this I think of myself as a constant self, one persisting across time.

Longer time intervals only aggravate the problem: How am I the same person I was five years ago even though most of the cells of my body have long since been replaced and my neurons are the victims of significant cell death? And if I think of myself as I was ten or twenty years ago, my dimensions are quite different, not to mention what has and hasn't sagged. How can I be both the same and different at once?

Even when I think of myself in less physical terms, I believe I have the same mind I did years ago, although I have learned many new things and forgotten many old ones. Emotionally, too, there is a sense of continuity, even if numerous catastrophes of flesh and triumphs of feeling have taken place between my earlier and present emotional self, then blended together in some indecipherable mix.

The problem of identity is not confined to me. I go to a professional convention and see an old friend for the first time in several years. I'm shocked. He has changed greatly—more weight around the middle, hair now gray—but I see far less change in myself. Of course, if you were to ask my friend, he would no doubt tell you how *I* have aged. We see the changes in others, but somehow *we* are constant—or at least more so than others.

The problem of identity is easier to understand and more powerfully brought home when it is personalized, as James himself realized.[1] I'm reading in the newspaper about some poor wretch whom tragedy has smitten. It's a terrible story, dreadful, but no real emotional involvement on my part. Through no fault of his own, the fellow has lost his life savings in a bad investment. Then he lost his spouse and children in a horrible accident. He tried to commit suicide, but he botched it and is now paralyzed. The tale moves me a bit more but only in an abstract way as I read it in the newspaper.

Then I notice that this poor, sad, pathetic person has my own name. I feel a clutch in my chest. Hurriedly, I read on. The man in the paper lives in the same city I do. I look around to make sure that the world has not shifted on me and the sun turned black. I breathe a sigh, and relief mingles with the release of sympathy; he is older than I. The similarity is just a coincidence. Normally I'm not this superstitious. I take another deep, deep gulp of air.

A modern version of the same story is provided by the philosopher Daniel Dennett and the computer scientist Douglas Hofstadter.[2] Pete is in the checkout line of a department store. Idly, he stares at the overhead TV monitor, watching people in the store come and go. Then something catches his attention. A man is getting his pocket picked. Pete raises his hand to his mouth, and so does the victim on the screen. A shock of self-recognition passes over him. He is the one whose pocket is being picked. He, Pete, is the victim. Notice the change. At first, he is in a state of low interest and motivation, casually watching the monitor. Later, his interest picks up as he detects a crime in process. Then, with self-awareness, complete recognition captures all of his attention.

The conclusion is inescapable: A sense of self underlies the significance of events. When something happens to a stranger, it's too bad, an unfortunate circumstance. When it happens closer to me, as with a friend or relative, my sympathies are more readily stirred. When it happens to me, the lens of interest becomes more focused, the visible light more intense as the "me" is illuminated most sharply in attention's focus. Others more distant from me shade into darker corners of my consciousness and interest.

These examples show that the self is separated from other people in space. Why, then, is the self not separated from its different circumstances in time? What is the glue used by the self to hold together a sense of identity in a field of constant change? For William James it is a core of memory and the feeling of unity across time that together serve as the connective tissue. At different times we look back on life and have a rich set of memories. No matter when we repeat this exercise, the memories of the past are more or less the same: an early birthday party, a first love, a wedding, the birth of a child, the death of a parent. And with each successive look, we also find the tracks of previous looks nested orderly in the present recall. Therefore, the different selves that change from instant to instant are all connected to a common pool of memory and a corresponding feeling of unity, a feeling of oneness across time and from one place to another. These memories and feelings glue the separate-seeming selves together to make a single person.

The processes of identity normally operate effortlessly and naturally. Preservation is the default operation because it happens without effort in an unconscious way. But there is a conscious part, too, when we become more deliberate and intentionally strive for unity in our varied experiences by seeking consistency from one occasion to the next—when we can, and when it is not too inconvenient. But being consistent is difficult work. We must *learn* to tell the truth because it is so natural to impose wishes upon the world and our friends. We must *learn* to think of others' welfare as much as our own because we are inclined to think of ourselves first.

Perhaps this is why lying is so problematic. It lays down tracks of experience that are not orderly—that is, aligned in one direction with time's arrow and a journey's step. Instead the tracks keep shifting their compass bearing and their content, circling without a fixed course. Lying requires a fraudulent relation to the world, a false identity that takes attention to keep discordant memories functioning.

When experiences do rub against one another in discord, a next step is to cut and shape them so that they fit together in a broader pattern, as in a jigsaw puzzle where one is not yet aware of the finished picture's appearance and must continually look for pattern and meaning.

In the extreme, when pattern and meaning are unattainable, identity is incomplete, and the self becomes a receptacle where battles of ambivalence and doubt take place on the field of divided consciousness. When disunity reigns, the self becomes little more than a box filled with contradictory jumping beans that bounce in all directions at once, leaving not a unified self but a division producing inconsistent movement—or even frozen immobility.

We can choose to worry about our contradictions or ignore them, wall them off or try to fit them together in a less friction-prone pattern. Or we can seek for a greater unity and understanding. The worry strategy may be our first reaction, and it is normal enough. How can one reconcile being a tough guy at work, in charge of office downsizing and reorganization, while being a warm, caring husband and father at home? Sometimes the inconsistency of life plants a burning spot in the middle of the chest. Because worry does not seem to help one way or another, we now decide to ignore the contradictions. For a while we wall off our different lives from one another.

But soon the ignoring strategy doesn't work anymore, and we try still another approach to contain contradictions and paradoxes. We try to encapsulate them much like the body builds scar tissue around a splinter. Whenever we are at home and think of problems at work, we give a leg a good hard pinch. Whenever we are at work and think of trouble at home, we pinch ourselves again. Over time, we encapsulate our two different existences. We are no longer sure which is the splinter and which is the flesh, the work self or the home self.

Maybe none of this works, and we seek a different way out. We look for some higher pattern or unity to fit both work and home into. We begin to construct stories about the economy: Certainly it is difficult to fire people, but if the company is going to survive and be profitable, it is necessary. If a sizable number of companies such as ours did not behave this way, we would all end up as victims of foreign competition. If we did not have a vibrant national economy, sooner or later our own kids would suffer—they would not be able to go to a good school or get a good job when they graduate. Therefore, we must fire Mrs. Jones tomorrow, even if she has been with the company for twenty years. And when we get home, we will try not to think about it.

All of these are potentially workable methods for dealing with contradiction in life. Instead of one being better or worse than the others, we use them like a tool kit for shaping ourselves as we encounter life's inconsistencies. With the right tools applied in the right way—and a bit of luck—we manage to preserve some semblance of a unified self, although often less than we would wish and sometimes with adverse consequences for others.

Some of the strategies used to preserve identity warrant closer inspection. The encapsulation process of building separate identities with no connection to one another is particularly intriguing. Encapsulation is appropriate when we have different identities that may clash when they come together. Amanda, a young woman from a strict religious background, goes to college and takes on a series of lovers. Chances are she'll want to keep her family self well separated from her college self. She will encapsulate these different selves, much as a time-sharing arrangement for a condo works only when the different tenants don't show up at the same time. When home she acts one way; when at school, another.

In this case, Amanda is like a series of selves that time-share the same body, different ones for different occasions. Not only are her different behaviors time-sharing one body, she is helped by the different spatial contexts, as well. To the extent that school and home are distant from one another, her task will be easier. If she lives at home and attends school, her separation of selves will be more difficult. Phone calls for the wild self will come to the home of the conventional self, making the time-sharing of selves precarious. In part, that is why many young people prefer to go away for school. It is easier to try out a different self when its territory is separate from that of the usual self. Of course, these different selves are not completely independent of one another, as in a case of radical multiple personality. Rather, they overlap, with the nonintersecting parts specific to given times and settings.

These notions apply not just to the young. We all have different identities that we time-share a body with as we keep our separate identities from rubbing against one another. Yet our encapsulations must repeatedly defend themselves from some hidden force, a unifying self that strives to keep everything together and consistent. The unifier keeps us from splitting into a thousand shards, but it is a demanding overseer, repeatedly jabbing us for telling little social lies like, "I love your hair." (Translation: You're really brave to have done whatever that is.)

In more extreme cases, when our divisions become too outrageous, the unifier administers anxiety and gastric upset. It does not want any selves too far from that center core. Just when the unifier seems to be winning and pulling us toward the center, the explorer part of us that would extend beyond where we are now is unrelentingly pushing toward the edge. The edge and center selves alternately lead in this waltz, this dance of explorer and unifier.

When the unifier gets overly zealous about matters like 100 percent truth, it, too, must be walled off. After all, truth is not the only value in life; it must also compete with survival and compassion, to name but two contenders. And when the explorer becomes too adventuresome, too daredevil and carefree, another time for walling off and encapsulation has arrived.

Omni-Bob

Unity sometimes requires a separation from others. Like a cell membrane, unity keeps some things inside so that they will not go outside and keeps other things outside so that they will not come inside. One's name is an important unifier and separator in this sense, a membrane around the self, and disrupting the function of a name serves to destroy the membrane.

Here is a tale of two boys with the same name. Six-year-old Miguel did not think that his newly born nephew, also named Miguel, could have the same name. Miguel #1 got very upset; someone was taking his name from him. What would he have done if someone had told him that from now on every new baby boy would be named Miguel? No doubt he would have been very perturbed.

The distinction between Miguel #1 and others depended on everyone else having a different name. Evidently, his underlying model of self assumed that everyone was unique, that a name was owned or at least reserved for each individual, maybe even being a part of the self, like an arm, and someone else having his name constituted a personal violation like taking an arm or leg from him—or occupying his very same point in space and time.

I am sympathetic about this matter of other people taking one's name. Once I was on a four-person committee with three other Bobs. Maybe this was due to coincidence, or maybe my department chair was secretly malicious. Almost immediately we, the committee, were in trouble. The membrane, the distinctive name boundary separating selves, had broken down, and the difficulty of communicating was exquisite. "What do you think of this, Bob?" Everyone would answer. "What if we did it the other way, Bob?" No one would answer, everyone deferring to another Bob. Then we tried last initials. I'd be Bob W, and the other Bobs would have their last name initials. Unfortunately, two of us had last names with the same letter. Moreover, the whole thing sounded stilted. So we communicated by gesture and eye contact. Stare straight at the person you're talking to, and nod your head toward him, hoping he would know who was being addressed and others would see the same cues.

The meeting was like an existential drama of the absurd, with its own developing emotional tone. At first we thought it hilarious, then inconvenient, then damned annoying. What if everyone had the same name? What if everyone were Bob?

As an exercise, what would the world be like if every man were Bob, every woman Mary, and all dogs named Rover? Maybe this needs to be a TV sitcom—something funny if it happens to someone else.

Let us carry the idea further. A spoof church in Texas is called the Church of Bob, where the founder is named Bob and the deity is named Bob.[3] Bowing down toward Sacred Bob just does not sound right. Of course, we could really get extreme and also name girls Bob. Mary would become Bob. In that case, the Church of Bob might have as a special deity, the Virgin Bob. That sounds like too much. I spoon the dog food into a dish and call, "Time to eat, Bob." Instead of coming with his tail wagging, my dog sits with eyes glazed.

Communication is impossible in the land of omni-Bob. Miguel #1 was right. When someone takes your name, it is like breaking down the membrane that separates selves, like losing an arm. Your separate identity is lost and along with it your ability to function as a distinct person in the world.

The Unity System

The psychologist Howard Gardner writes of multiple forms of intelligence. One prominent form is intrapersonal intelligence.[4] Possible manifestations include understanding one's own motives, emotions, and thoughts; being able to predict and explain one's actions; and being able to fit into new settings. While Gardner does not discuss it, an important part of intrapersonal intelligence is likely to be the unity system that we touched on earlier, one grand component of the architecture of self.

To more fully preserve identity and self, it is not enough to let built-in tendencies automatically shift for themselves. The unity system must be brought to attentional foreground and actively applied from time to time. To be the same person in a body that is growing older and in a world that is forever changing all around, one must employ at both unconscious and conscious levels the varied elements of the unity system:

Consistency. The separate parts of our lives should be consistent with one another, or encapsulations, time-sharing, or rending of the self takes place. We do not want to be simultaneously engaged in writing a poem of love and a list of curses. We do not want to use a croquet swing with a golf club. And we want our thoughts and actions to be consistent as well, not saying "I love you" while thinking about cheating with someone else.

Compatibility. More than just consistency, the separate parts of ongoing life should be compatible so that they fit together like the parts of a puzzle. If we are equally engaged in playing piano and boxing, raising flowers and skydiving, and blackmailing while helping the poor, we may have too many passions without linkage, a life with parts that do not fit with one another. If compatibility is not possible, then separations along functional lines, such as work and home, may make sense.

Coherence or Continuity. While compatibility deals with the fit of current activities with each other, coherence is concerned with the fit of activities across time. So we also want life to have continuity and connection with the past. What we do today should grow out of what we did yesterday and the day before that. Life should have a trajectory, a line or arc of development. Otherwise our passions move from varied pursuits, such as playing cards to buying clothes to golfing to bird watching to mud wrestling, without any mental connection among them. Of course, care in judgment is needed. Activities that make no sense to others may have their own inner logic for their practitioner.[5]

There is nothing contradictory about these pursuits because they occur at different times in life. For the same reason, they do not present problems of compatibility. Yet they have no trajectory or arc of development. They just drop into life like a series of unrelated visitors. Far better to have one passion in life lead to another, a natural growth instead of hopscotch emotion. Progress not from singing to archery but from singing to composing songs.

Completeness. We want to be a complete person, someone who values fully the somewhat separate realms of thought, feeling, and action. Or the realms of body, persona, and spirit. We want a work life and a personal life, a time for both relationships and solitude. All of these things in balance go into making a complete person. By moving toward a complete self, we will better anticipate situations and problems that have not yet come to pass. Otherwise we may require too many cut-and-paste revisions of self. Where each new experience is an isolated event, we do not know how to handle it, and life becomes an unorganized sea of raw experience.

Compactness. The self should be compact—that is, parsimonious or simple rather than baroque in organizing beliefs and actions. Like a ball of string, the more compact the core self, the less chance of raveled and knotted ends. The self should be integrated like a Swiss Army Knife instead of a junk drawer full of miscellaneous tools.

Community. Life alone is a heavy burden. We want a life to have connections to others. We do not want to be an island unto ourselves. We seek the nurturing of others, of community, and we want to reach out to others.

Most important of all is the idea that the unity components must function together as a system, where sometimes one principle is ascendant and other times, a different one. Such a system then gives rise to capabilities not present in its parts.

The systemlike nature of the self is easily revealed by noting the workings of the different components. Some, such as those of completeness and compactness, are forever in tension with one another. The more we seek new experience in a search for completeness, the more complex and extended we find the inner core of self, and the greater the departure from a simple compact self. Having a compact set of beliefs that is simultaneously large enough to encompass all new experiences is not an easy matter.

In practice, often one or the other principle must yield. If compactness is hallowed, we must withdraw from experiences that make life messy as they enlarge it. If we emphasize completeness and seek experience, we will no doubt have to sacrifice compactness to the rich and disorderly nature of life. Always there is tension between the richness of fragmentation and the attractiveness of a unified self.

In a related way, consistency and completeness are also difficult to simultaneously hold. Indeed, the same may be said of almost any pair of principles that make up the unity system. No one principle is more important than the others; all must be honored, and that means we are in a perpetual flux of balancing the varied principles against one another because none of them is absolute.

Clearly, some happy balance of the unity principles is worth aiming for because disharmony produces mental unease. For example, when coherence is not present and the dilettantism of hopping from unrelated interest to interest is ascendant, no strength flows between the separate parts of life because connection between the parts is absent. One's boxing and pianistic endeavors do not fuel each other in the same way as singing and playing the piano.

When consistency is absent, when one says "Yes, I love you" and means "No, I want to be with someone else," the mental gears grind with contradiction. Lack of consistency may mean that the mind is not very orderly—or it may mean something more formidable, such as being a liar.

When an effort toward completeness is absent, we cut ourselves off from the richness of life. Or when we encounter a new experience, which even the most encapsulated life may become heir to, we have no tools for working it into a meaningful context with the rest of life. It is like going into a toy store and rejecting the merits of play.

Finally, when there is no inner core or center, no compactness of ordered self, we are buffeted by the chaos of experience. Every experience becomes as good as any other; one might as well rob a store as write a song.

The self is always in tension with what it is and what it might be, a present self and a want-to-be self. That tension produces change and, ideally, growth. So, too, can a certain healthy amount of contradiction. "Do I contradict myself? Very well then . . . I contradict myself; I am large . . . I contain multitudes,"[6] said Walt Whitman, poet of the self. Whitman's insight is that consistency cannot be the sole standard for ordering life; it must trade off or negotiate with other principles. Whitman certainly had a core self, coherent in the dedication to his art, the alleviation of human suffering, and the description of the aspiring heart. Sometimes that core required a toleration for contradiction so that other standards might enliven the whole.

What all this means is that humans are more than consistency machines, more than contradiction makers. We seek experience, but we want to integrate with a core self, to wear that self without too many sleeves that do not quite fit. We are standard creators, too, even if those standards must all be worn at the same time, their mutual seams bulging and twisting and sometimes tearing as they pull against one another.

When we successfully fit all these standards into the same system, when we do all this in a reasonable, balanced manner with reasonable trade-offs, we have a personal identity functioning as it should. The unity system then takes on an evaluative nature. New forms of self are appropriate when they satisfy the dictates of the unity system. With unity, there is an overall sense of harmony.

THE INTERPRETING SELF

I know I am solid and sound,
To me the converging objects of the universe perpetually flow,
All are written to me, and I must get what the writing means. . . .
Singing the true song of the soul fitful at random, any man trans-
lates, and any man translates himself also. . . .

— WALT WHITMAN, *Leaves of Grass*

G eneralizing on Darwin's idea of selection for reproductive fitness, William James pointed out the importance of selection in mental life. Each sense modality is tuned to particular energies or molecules: vision, hearing, touch, smell, taste. For events or objects that simultaneously excite several modalities, consciousness may focus on one more than another. And across time, consciousness prefers some events and emotions over others. The possibility of selection from complex experience affords grist for the interpreting mind. The same event may be seen in multiple ways, the same memory recast in diverse frames of interpretation.

We see that memory itself is an important selector, definer, and preserver that goes far beyond sheer storage as it exercises its preferences and aversions. What memory selects to encode and value serves to define the self. In the process, memory provides a basic constancy that helps preserve a sense of identity across time and place.

Thus we remember some things and not others. Some of us

remember mostly the good things; others, the bad things. If we are extreme about this, and our memories determine our present mood and future action, we are typed as a grouch or as a happy person—another way of saying that we are defined by the memories we keep.

Here is a story of two contrasting rememberers and how selective memory contributes to constancy in identity. Fifteen years ago, Jack and Frank, two friends, were on their way back from a fishing trip. They each caught many fish, were bitten by numerous mosquitoes, drank a lot of beer, and discussed a business opportunity that later showered profit on them both. As they drove back, they had a blowout, swerved off the road, and the car's front end was damaged. They had to stay over in a small town for two days while the car was being repaired.

Now fifteen years later Jack remembers the trip as a disaster. "Got bitten to hell by mosquitoes, had a bad car wreck, and had to stay over in this dingy little town and eat in a café where the food tasted like rat poison."

Frank has a different memory of the trip. "Wonderful fishing. Caught the biggest trout of my life. Jack caught an even bigger one. Beautiful fish. The mountains were just spectacular." Anything else happen? "We had some kind of car problem—can't even remember what. Stayed over in a lovely little town at the base of the mountain. Those people have a hard life up there, but they're really honest and hardworking. The fellow in the garage saved our skin. He must have worked half the night on my car. We ate in a little café near the garage. Really warm, friendly people there. Oh, yes, we got a terrific idea for a business venture together. We've pursued it with profit for both of us."

Two different memories recall the same events, and the recollections couldn't be more different. Jack's memory system is tuned in to record what goes wrong, Frank's to record what's right. One is an old curmudgeon—admittedly with a fine acerbic sense of humor, but a little of him goes a long way. The other is a generous, open man, who is good company. Whatever the basis for their friendship, it has lasted a long time.

The experience of Jack and Frank illustrates how we may create ourselves via the *interpretation* we impose on experience.[1] First of all, interpretation will determine how our *present experiences* are encoded, evaluated, and filed in memory. The assumption here is that the selection of interpretation can be a conscious process, even though it often is not. Knowing that there is an interpretive system helps free us from seizing on the first frozen view of events. As an overall assessment of their trip, Jack and Frank provided dramatically different views.

Second, we create ourselves by virtue of which memories we keep or get rid of. Once something is in memory, we can dwell on it or shed it, after a fashion. I don't know if we can voluntarily rid memory of something in the sense that it will never show up on a recognition test. But we can functionally remove a memory by the interpretation of it as having little significance. This process bears some resemblance to the Freudian notion of repression. While psychoanalysts regard repression as a bad thing, it clearly has its uses in ordering our memories and consciousness. With some such process, Jack kept his bad memories and Frank kept his good ones.

Third, we create ourselves by choosing the interpretation we impose on already *existing memories*. Suppose looking back over the years, Frank relayed to Jack that the fishing trip was the beginning of their friendship. It showed what they had in common, and it provided the basis for their going into business together. Now, after a joint discussion of the experience, for the first time Jack sees the set of events in that more pleasant light. By so doing, he is *reinterpreting* the original experience, turning it on its head from what was once negative into something now positive. Psychotherapy is extensively involved in the reinterpretation of memory, but interpretation is also a common act of the untroubled mind.

That memories can be reinterpreted, even if they were formed many years previously, warrants another example. Mary had been happily married for thirty years. Then her husband went through a middle-aged crisis and left her for his high-school sweetheart. Mary's initial response: All those years were just a sham; he didn't really love me. How could he be so deceitful?

Then Mary started reevaluating. Deceit was one way of looking at it, but another way was that they had had twenty-nine good years together, and then they changed in different ways. Few things are forever. So now it was time to pick up her life and build on her success in knowing how to succeed in a relationship for multiple decades. She knitted her brow, shook her head sideways, then up and down. In a short time she had gone from thinking she had a happy marriage to thinking she had been betrayed to thinking she had enjoyed many good years of marriage after all. This last insight helped her because she began to look at her marriage history, her former husband, and herself differently—not as a case of deceit but as two people having a different arc in their lives. Once again, interpretation has the power to turn experience on its head.

Einstein's Memory

The powers of memory to effect one's view on life do not limit themselves to the ordinary among us. They apply with equal or greater force to the significant and the famous. At age sixty-seven the physicist Albert Einstein was persuaded to write his biography.[2] He looked back on his life and noted tongue-in-cheek that his autobiography was like an obituary; it is significant both for what it says and what it leaves out. On the left-out side of the ledger, he includes no reference to wives, children, close friends, or the normal human pains and sorrows—which is where most of us would begin our account. If this were to protect his privacy or that of his loved ones, we would applaud. But perhaps his motivation for exclusion was altogether more complex.

An early significant event, at age twelve, was Einstein's

conviction that much in the stories of the Bible could not be true. The consequence was a positively fanatic (orgy of) freethinking coupled with the impression that youth is intentionally being deceived by the state through lies. . . . Suspicion against every kind of authority grew out of this experience. . . .

And here is the significant point; this experience was a

> first attempt *to free myself from the chains of the "merely-personal," from an existence which is dominated by wishes, hopes and primitive feelings.* Out yonder there was this huge world, which exists independently of us human beings and which stands before us like a great, eternal riddle, at least partially accessible to our introspection and thinking. . . . The mental grasp of *this extra-personal world . . . swam as highest aim* half consciously and half unconsciously before my mind's eye. [Italics added.]

What is evident in these statements is a lack of interest in the personal, perhaps even a flight from it, and at the same time a fascination with what is external to the body and mind. His early memories reflect this emphasis still further. His first formative scientific experience seemed to be receiving a compass from his father at age four or five. The behavior of the compass represented "Something deeply hidden . . . behind things." Then at age twelve a similar epiphany seized him when he learned of the certainty and purity of thought behind Euclid's geometry.

What Einstein is remembering, then, is the source and inspiration of ideas for the exploration, through science, of the world out yonder, the physical world. What he is ignoring—at least in his autobiographical account—is the whole internal world of "wishes, hopes and primitive feelings" as well as the pain and suffering of human relationship and the body. The selectivity and stamping of relative importance on these two worlds may have something to do with his troubled personal life, one lacking closeness to his own spouse and children.

But there is still more. He talks of memory trade-offs between the contrasting cases:

> If an individual enjoys well-ordered thoughts [of the physical world], it is quite possible that this side of his nature may grow more pronounced *at the cost of other sides [the personal]* and thus may determine his mentality in increasing degree. . . . [S]uch an individual *in retrospect* sees a uniformly systematic development, whereas the actual experience takes place in kaleidoscopic particular situations. . . . In a man of my type the turning-point of the development lies in the fact that gradually *the major interest [physics] disengages itself to a far-reaching degree from the momentary and the merely personal* and turns toward the striving for a mental grasp of things. [Italics added.]

Einstein goes on to talk of two very different approaches to physics. The first is the quantum-theory view requiring probabilistic treatment of the discrete, discontinuous, and temporally indeterminate characteristics of a system. The second—and the one he prefers—is a theory that describes the world with continuous functions because he believes the underlying nature of reality is continuous and deterministic rather than chance governed.

Einstein's view of memory comes to be modeled after his view of the physical world. If the world underlying perception is continuous and not the subject of chance, experience and the way memory interprets it must also be more than kaleidoscopic. And therefore memory must exclude the personal, the hopes, wishes, and wants, the sufferings and sorrows that are so human defining, so discontinuous, probabilistic, and chaotic in their nature.

His account once more reveals that the memories we store, keep, and interpret help define us as a person and preserve a constancy of identity across time. Or maybe the causation goes the other way: The kind of person we are determines the nature of our memories. I prefer to think of it the first way because then I have much more control over myself. I can decide within limits what to remember and what to forget, at least in terms of emphasis and valuation.

Journals of Self

Insofar as memories influence our sense of self, we shape ourselves by how we remember. To aid personal discovery, we seek a glimpse of the memorial and interpretive self in motion. No better way exists for keeping track of memories and their interpretation than regular journal entries. Looking over journal writings spanning a year or two quickly reveals the kinds of memories we hold on to and the interpretations placed on them; the constancy of self is revealed in the repetitions and the patterns. The entries may also reveal a certain incoherence and thereby offer the opportunity for reordering and reinterpretation. Do they fit a larger pattern? How are they coalescing? Are they acting to determine a direction of movement?[3]

An important variation on the memory journal is the family album. Every family needs a keeper of memories, someone who tracks significant events. Sometimes the keeping track is just in biological memory and thought; other times it is an external memory, a series of mementos of family: locks of hair, first teeth, old shoes, pictures, audio- or now videotapes. These keep us in touch with personal history by providing a bridge between a previous self and a present self. They are like William James's examples of memory that are available to the self at different times, and they reveal and preserve our identity across all those occasions of self-awareness and pondering of the essential question: Who am I?

I may have forgotten who was at my wedding, but looking at the pictures again returns me to old friendships, to a startling realization of what I looked like years ago, how my spouse has also changed, how my friends have transformed themselves—like me—in some ways for better and other ways for the worse. My youthful arrogance has been replaced by a calmer countenance, and the once athletic body is now less so.

While the pictures are visual, they evoke other senses in memory: the sound of voices and music, laughter that comes back to renew the present self. But the pictures leave out other senses. Too bad touch and smell cannot be recorded so as to better remember the caress of a first kiss and the perfumes of youthful passion. These are memories that also need the support of record keeping, but in their absence the imagination tries to fill them in.

Turning back to what is remembered, I concentrate on images of beginnings. In fact, a beginning—a new thing with sharp demarcation from what went before—is one of memory's best landmarks. A beginning sticks out like a mountain on a prairie. Here are some beginnings: My walking to kindergarten on the first day of school, a first dog in the family, a first car, a first date, the birth of a child—all these become landmarks for remembering. Other events then coalesce around and build on top of these landmarks, making them even more prominent. That is why initial interpretations are so important. They establish the architectural siting for building a memory.

Sometimes endings provide landmarks. A senior prom, a graduation, the image of a mother in her deathbed—all are different landmarks in memory. Still other events coalesce around such endings. A memorial is an ending surrounding a death. It organizes scattered memories, fills in blanks, and puts to rest a whole landscape of thought, making it a constant marker for drawing bearings in the years ahead.

The way I keep memories, the temporal landmarks I see, and how I interpret them—all these factors contribute toward the construction of a self across time.

Dream and Interpretation

The role of interpretation in furthering the preservation of identity and the creation of self is brought out in dreams. In February 1906, William James recorded a sequence of dream experiences that had taken place over the previous two nights. The dreams were disturbing to him. He was able to overcome the disturbance, however, through a supreme act of interpretation, involving multiple levels of analysis that brought him back to his own life and values and therefore left him undisturbed. This is an account of the interpretive mind at work, striving for identity preservation:

The night before last, in my bed at Stanford University, I woke at about 7:30 A.M., from a quiet dream of some sort, [which] seemed suddenly to get mixed up with reminiscences of a dream of an entirely different sort, which seemed to telescope, as it were, into the first one, a dream very elaborate, of lions, and tragic. I concluded this to have been a previous dream of the same sleep; but the apparent mingling of two dreams was something very queer, which I had never before experienced.

On the following night (Feb.12–13) I awoke suddenly from my first sleep, which appeared to have been very heavy, in the middle of a dream, in thinking of which it became suddenly confused by the contents of two other dreams that shuffled themselves abruptly in between the parts of the first dream, and of which I couldn't grasp the origin. Whence come *these dreams?* I asked. They were close to *me,* and fresh, as if I had just dreamed them: and yet they were far away *from the first dream.* The contents of the three had absolutely no connection. One had a cockney atmosphere, it had happened to someone in London. The other two were American. One involved the trying on of a coat (was this the dream I seemed to wake from?), the other was a sort of nightmare and had to do with soldiers. Each had a wholly distinct emotional atmosphere that made its individuality discontinuous with that of the others. And yet, in a moment, as these three dreams alternately telescoped into and out of each other, and I seemed to myself to have been their common dreamer, they seemed quite as distinctly not to have been dreamed in succession, in that one sleep. *When,* then? Not on a previous night either. *When,* then, and *which* was the one out of which I had just awakened? I *could no longer tell:* one was as close to me as the others, and yet they entirely repelled each other, and I seemed thus to belong to three different dream-systems at once, no one of which would connect itself either with the others or with my waking life. I began to feel curiously confused and *scared,* and tried to wake myself up wider, but I seemed already wide-awake. Presently cold shivers of dread ran over me: *am I getting into other people's dreams?* Is this a "telepathic" experience? Or an invasion of double (or treble) personality? Or is it a thrombus in a cortical artery? and the beginning of a general mental "confusion" and disorientation which is going on to develop who knows how far?

Decidedly I was losing hold of my "self," and making acquaintance with a quality of mental distress that I had never known before, its nearest analogue being the sinking, giddying anxiety that one may have when, in the woods, one discovers that one is really "lost." Most human troubles look towards terminus. Most fears point in a direction and concentrate towards a climax. Most assaults of the evil one may be met by bracing oneself against something, one's principles, one's courage, one's wit, one's pride. But in this experience was diffusion from a centre, and foothold swept away, the brace itself disintegrating all the faster as one needed its support more direly. Meanwhile vivid perception (or remembrance) of the various dreams kept coming over me in alternation. Whose? whose? WHOSE? Unless I can attach them, I am swept out to sea with no horizon and no bond, getting lost. The idea aroused the "creeps" again, and with it the fear of again falling asleep and renewing the process. It had begun the previous night, but then the confusion had only gone one step, and had seemed simply curious. This was the second step—where might I be after a third step had been taken? . . .

At the same time I found myself filled with a new pity toward persons passing into dementia . . . or into invasions of secondary personality. *We* regard them as simply *curious;* but what *they* want in the awful drift of their being out of its customary self, is any principle of steadiness to hold on to. We ought to assure them and reassure them that we will stand by them, and recognize the true self in them, to the end. We ought to let them know that we are with them and not (as too often we must seem to them) a part of the world that but confirms and publishes their deliquescence.

Evidently I was in full possession of my reflective wits; and whenever I thus objectively thought of the situation in which I was, my anxieties ceased. But there was a tendency to relapse into the dreams and reminiscences, and to relapse vividly; and then the confusion recommenced, along with the emotion of dread lest it should develop farther [*sic*].

Then I looked at my watch. Half-past twelve! Midnight, therefore. And this gave me another reflective idea. Habitually, on going to bed, I fall into a very deep slumber from which I never naturally awaken until after two. I never awaken, therefore, from a midnight dream, as I did tonight, so of midnight dreams my ordinary consciousness retains no recollection. My sleep seemed terribly heavy as I woke tonight. Dream states carry dream memories—why may not the two succedaneous dreams (whichever two of the three were succedaneous) be memories of *twelve o'clock dreams of previous nights,* swept in, along with the just fading dream, into the just-waking system of memory? Why, in short, may I not be tapping in a way precluded by my ordinary habit of life, *the midnight stratum* of my past?

This idea gave great relief—I felt now as if I were in full possession of my *anima rationalis. . . .* [I]t seems, therefore, merely as if the threshold between the rational and the morbid state had, in my case, been temporarily lowered, and as if similar confusions might be very near the line of possibility in all of us.

The dreams of William James are marked by multiple layers of experience, introspection, description, and interpretation. All of these layers function to fit the dreams into his ongoing life, to provide a sense of minimal disruption. Therefore, the interpretive process is employed to preserve unity and self-control: Instead of his disturbing sequence of dream events being indicative of pathology, it has a rational explanation that is consistent with his overall life. But let us examine the steps to this conclusion.

In the beginning there is the raw experience of one dream

and then its recall on waking—followed by a written description, as with the rest of the episodes. There is also the raw experience of another dream and its subsequent recall and description. In addition, the two dreams somehow telescope, becoming integrated with one another, although they seemed to have nothing in common.

During James's recollection, the later experience of in and out telescoping is identified as something new and disturbing "which I had never before experienced." Here he is comparing his present dreams with all his past dream experiences. It is not the content of the dreams that is of particular interest but their intermingling.

Compounding it all is another dream on the next night that seems to further intermingle with the first two. Again, the content is of no particular interest; it is their telescoping together that bothers James. He is now consciously reflecting on the dream experiences and trying to understand them, noting that the present happenings are unlike his other dreams—a matter of recollection, as before, and now a classification of novelty, as well.

His mood takes on confusion, fear, and dread as his mind lifts to a higher level of interpretive possibility: "[A]m I getting into other people's dreams?" Is he experiencing the first indications of double or treble personality? Perhaps he is losing his sense of a unified self, a frightening thought to one who so values unity. Or maybe he is having a stroke, a thought that would occur to someone with his medical training. All of these interpretive possibilities come to the fore as the waking mind tries to make sense of his dream experiences.

He wonders if he is having a telepathic experience or an incipient episode of multiple personality. Here he is linking his dream with his other interests, including a fascination with the paranormal. The dream experience has sent ripples to the furthest reaches of his life. This is a kind of distress he has not previously known (memory comparison), so he draws on metaphor: It's like being "in the woods, one discovers that one is really 'lost.' " In this way he is connecting a novel feeling to an approximation of a more familiar one. It is possible to be lost not only in a forest but also in a dream.

Once more he turns to a rational process, extrapolating on his experiences. Strange dreams have happened twice now, on successive nights. If he falls asleep again, will an even more foreboding dream experience occur? How can he escape this line of thought? He becomes an objective scientist and humanitarian at the same time. He is "filled with a new pity towards persons passing into dementia . . . [or having] invasions of secondary personality. . . . We ought to assure them . . . we will stand by them. . . ." By implication he hopes that someone will stand by him, too, if he is in the grasp of dementia.

Yet his capacity for objectivity reassures him. "I was in full possession of my reflective wits . . . my anxieties ceased." As a scientist he theorizes that such dreams occur normally; he just isn't aware of them since he sleeps past them. "This idea gave great relief. . . . [S]imilar confusions might be very near the line of possibility in all of us."

The entire sequence now makes sense to him. It is simply an unusual concordance of events. Most likely it occurs for others, too. The interpreting mind has encircled apparent irrationality and squared it with full rationality.

Others might have interpreted the same events differently. History contains many examples of dreams that are thought to come from God, Satan, or a departed ancestor. In these cases the content may be less important than the interpretation. That was also true of James. What seemed to disturb him most was not the content but the thought that the dreams indicated the onset of a dissociative pathology.

As William James's experience reveals, dreams provide endless material and fascination for an interpreting mind, one trying to fit the experience of the dream state to ongoing life.

This is yet another variation and way of remaining the same person over an extended period of time, one that uses a common interpretive lens in the face of changing experience. The interpretations of our dreams may say less about the nature of the content than about the nature of the lens that interprets.

Historically, the interpretation of dreams has taken many forms. Here are some of them, with their corresponding origin and lens:

A dream is:

- A message from God that one must pass on to others. Possible origin: Ancient Hebrews. Lens: the wishes of a monotheistic, personal god.
- A prophecy or omen of ill tidings about to happen to one's self or to others. Origin: Ancient Greeks. Lens: Greek mythology, a story of family relations writ large.
- A symptom of a disturbed or guilty mind. Origin: Freud. Lens: Freudian theory, in which the dream is a way of preserving sleep by covering up deep disturbing motives.
- A racial archetype or experience common to all humans in all times; the materials of myth that bind us together. Origin: Jung. Lens: Archetypes of the past.

Each origin and interpretative lens acts to preserve a system of belief. The Hebrew God provides a stern constancy when everything else is changing. The Greek myths tell us how to interpret chaos and turmoil in terms of familiar family relationships. Freud tells us that dreams are the fruits of enduring unconscious motivations. Jung appeals to inherited mythic states, a cross between the Greeks and Freud.

In the absence of a definitive perspective to present on dream interpretation, I want to embrace a Jamesian-like view and treat the dream as a rich human experience that needs cultivation and consideration. Here is a way of providing the due diligence we owe to our dreams.

Just as memory is illuminated by a journal, so, too, are dreams. A journal provides the raw material for narratives, for making dream entries to construct stories that fit one's life. Those of us with an active imagination will weave dream material into a story and produce something meaningful out of the whole. We need not know what our dreams mean—or if they mean anything in raw form—but after we put them into a story, they acquire meaning. Like James, we may try to make these stories link the dream content with the way we see our overall life. In so doing, they contribute a constancy of purpose, a kind of continuity that is as much as anything crafted to make a meaningful tale. The psychologist Jerome Bruner has written extensively on this point. Experience takes on meaning when it is incorporated into story.[4] Our overall lives come to form an ongoing narrative with its own logic and direction.

When thinking about dreams, different lenses yield various meanings. As with any interpretive art, often no one right story is lurking behind a dream. Many interpretations well serve the same dream content. But that does not mean that anything goes. Clearly there are wrong stories where the flow does not fit the materials, the images, or the mood. Last night, I dreamed about the play *Hamlet*. What did it mean? Well, it can be interpreted as dealing with uncertainty, doubt, awakening responsibility, or revenge—any of these are fair game. But *Hamlet* is not easily interpretable as constructing pyramids or going swimming with a polar bear. While no one view definitively captures the play, other views are clearly wrong or forced. That is the nature of all interpretive art.

Memories, dreams, and interpretations all flow together to create a part of the self. Of these, the most subject to conscious influence is interpretation.[5] Let us look closely at what it entails and how it works.

The interpretive system:
• Acts as a filter for the contents and workings of mind and new expe-

riences.

- Preserves or restores existing attitudes, beliefs, values, and states of being.
- Places interest or importance of a positive or negative nature on memory and dreams.
- Amplifies or makes experience more or less salient.
- Determines the value of what is remembered or dreamed.
- Defines us through our way of viewing memories and dreams.
- Reconceptualizes events and thereby makes the old new as well as the new old.[6]

These many workings of the interpretive system add variety to human experience beyond the perception of events. The functions of interpretation are important because our experiences come to us when and as they will, for we have only limited control over the flux of actual events. Interpretation provides a controlling power over that flux, but its influence is not unrestricted. For example, it is difficult to interpret as pleasant the experience of having one's neck on an executioner's block while he lifts an ax. Similarly, it is difficult to interpret as unpleasant a dinner party with good friends, fine conversation, elegant food, and the laughter of fellowship.

But in between the scenes of the executioner and the dinner party—where most of life's experiences reside—the possibilities of interpretation are wonderfully flexible. That flexibility acts as an interface, or bridge, between experience and the self concept, providing a fuzzy translation capability that preserves our sense of identity as shown by James in his interpretation of his dream. In this way interpretation is a buffer between the chaos of the world and the deep ordering systems of the mind.

In the normal course of events, we have much to say on how the memories of our experiences are encoded, assessed, and stored—or cast away, as Jack and Frank's auto accident reveals. Our dreams are even more flexible and open to interpretation and remembering. They afford fine raw material for a story, for weaving into our ongoing life and consciousness, for creating an inner life with the constancy or variety we want. Perhaps that is why these experiences are called dreams.

A final comment. The goal of interpretive art—whether in dreams, story, or life—is not to be right, not to find the one true meaning, which is unlikely to exist. Instead of abstract truth, most of us want an interpretation of life that makes it possible to fit everything together so that all the parts flow into one another in a powerful way. The resulting narrative is the meaning behind memories and dreams. The more it covers every part of experience— allowing thoughts, feelings, and actions to cohere—the less important is its truth in any final, abstract sense.[7]

That would be consistent with James's notion of pragmatic truth: The practical and useful consequences of a belief are really what count. Just as a tool must be evaluated by how well it performs a particular task, so, too, must beliefs and truths be evaluated by how they contribute to the evolving story of one's life. Interpretation is the Swiss Army Knife of experience, a tool for every occasion and every want, one that helps greatly in the task of creating a self that is somewhat unified across the chaos of experience to which the senses and the flesh are heir.

Chapter 8

THE CONTRACTING AND EXPANDING SELF

Why what have you thought of yourself?
Is it you then that thought yourself less? . . .
From this hour I ordain myself loos'd of limits and imaginary lines,
Going where I list, my own master total and absolute. . . .

— WALT WHITMAN, *Leaves of Grass*

Having considered constancy of identity as a foundation of self—and interpretive conditions that may contribute to stability—it is time to go forth and examine the changing self. In this light, William James talks of many possible selves to choose from, all with their own appeal and allure, each pulling for our attention. Yet once a choice is made, the unchosen selves recede into the shadows. Just as when a figure is picked by the eye from a background and the background then drops out of attention, so it is with the focal attention of the self chosen and the disappearance of selves unchosen.

A consequence of choosing one self over another—say, being an actor over a pianist—is that we are no longer responsible or subject to shame for not doing well what we have not chosen. What does it matter that I am not an accomplished pianist? It is no longer my chosen expertise because I really want to be an actor. As James put it so well: "With no attempt there can be no failure; with no failure no humiliation. So our self-feeling in this world depends entirely on what we back ourselves to be and do."[1]

James then goes on to conceptualize these ideas in an equation:[2]

$$Self\text{-}esteem = Success/Aspiration$$

We can increase self-esteem either by increasing our success or decreasing our aspiration. But what do we make of this equation? As a mathematical expression it is problematic because there is no obvious and principled way of measuring any of the variables used in the equation. Nor is it clear whether it is only a definition where an entity called Self-esteem is *defined* as a ratio between two other observable quantities or if there is a *real quality* or feeling we call Self-esteem that is a mathematical function of the variables Success and Aspiration.

Of these alternatives, James seems to have in mind much more than a definition. Instead, he is claiming a feeling state corresponding to Self-esteem, and the magnitude of that state is directly related to the degree of Success and indirectly related to the degree of Aspiration in a causal relationship.

Yet the equation is profound because it says we can have more self-esteem. If our self-esteem is not satisfactory, the solution is at hand. Expand the reach of the self by increasing effort and the consequent probability of success. A big reach, after all, stretches us to the edge of our ability and makes possible a joyful life by successfully playing on that edge. One grows by stretching.[3] That is the nature of the *expansive self.*

But a caveat is in order. A greedy reach is what all the motivational speakers at business luncheons would have us cultivate—flail the flesh and scale the heights—and if we do not succeed, it is because we have not tried hard enough. Still, the downside of overreach is hugely important: Being too expansive inevitably leads to failure. Why, then, is success so often accompanied by stories of superhuman effort and failure by stories of not trying hard enough?

Expansion of reach is a strategy that is often validated by the curious logic of survivor bias—we hear only of the successful practitioners and never the casualties. It is a strategy heavily dependent on the opinion of others and little dependent on our own inner values or pain. The risk here is overreach that is so extreme as to guarantee the inaccessibility of one's goal.

The opposite solution to maintaining self-esteem, one that the business luncheons never mention, is to cultivate by nature a *contractive self.* When overwhelmed by demands on us, when our capacity is stretched to the breaking point and nothing positive happens, we drop back or contract the reach of aspiration. The result is a restoration of self-esteem—at least according to James's equation—because it is now possible to achieve and match the reduced aspiration.

For James, the Stoic philosophers provide an example of contractive reach. Indeed, the Stoic's prescription for contentment is to shed in advance all that is out of one's power to influence. Then "fortune's shocks might rain down unfelt."[4] This is self-protection by exclusion and contraction, a drawing back into the turtle shell of self. While it is a strategy almost guaranteed to succeed in cutting back on disappointment, the result may not be worth having. With a contractive strategy, the risk is in being timid, prematurely subtractive. By having too short a reach, we never come to the high water of where we might rise.

Here is a more analytic look at the two strategies of contraction and expansion, each with a potential difference according to the concern addressed, as in Table 8.1.

For each concern or focus of attention there is a contractive and an expansive strategy. The list of concerns is just the barest sampling and far from complete. Furthermore, we may be expansive for one concern and contractive for another. Each person has a particular profile of contraction and expansion, perhaps eschew-

Concern/ Focus of Attention	Contractive Strategy	Expansive Strategy
TABLE 8.1. TWO STRATEGIES OF SELF-CHANGE		
Ambition	Cut back on aspirations	Desire the large, want more
Power, influence	Eschew, devalue	Seek out (can be for self/others/ideals; not good/bad in itself)
Possessions	Get rid of	Acquire
Skills, ability, ego	Deny value of special skills like art, math, music, and associated ego	Become artist, mathematician, musician; there is nothing wrong with ego when it is attached to accomplishment
Loved ones	Hold down commitments, eschew, leave	Find, embrace, hold on to
Community	Be individual, exclusive; attachment only leads to sorrow	Be inclusive, part of others; attachment enriches, enlarges

ing power while being inclusive of community or seeking power while caring little for community. That said, there is not complete independence across the areas of focus. Those individuals who are ambitious may well be inclined to seek power, as well.

Of the two strategies which is better, expansive reach or contractive withdrawal? In practice, most of us are neither completely contractive or completely expansive. Instead, we mix and match situation, ability, and inclination. Rather than a single strategy, what is needed is access to both modes so that depending on the situation we can use either one. There is also a large learning component here. We must become expert at appraising environments and situations with regard to knowing how our own capabilities fit with them. Sometimes we will find that the fit is best realized with a contractive strategy; other times, with an expansive one.

Now consider more closely these broad operations of the self, contraction and expansion. The treatment of contraction will be brief because the primary strategy for creating a self centers on expansiveness.

The Contractive Self

The contractive self is manifested most clearly under two principal conditions, affliction and simplification. In affliction, we suffer illness, pain, stress, or adversity that tends to cut back our normal voluntary responses for engaging the world. In each case the question is, How do we make inner contractions to deal with the outer impositions? In simplification, we feel the need to cut through the complexity of an unsatisfying and stressful way of life, and we do so voluntarily and intentionally. Sometimes, too, simplification is an aesthetic matter.

An example of contraction mediated by affliction is starkly evident in concentration camp narratives.[5] Viktor Frankl, a psychoanalyst, was a captive during World War II, along with the rest of his family. While his account is well-known, we will try to place it in a somewhat different context than usual.

Frankl describes three stages of realization and coping that take place with internment: the initial shock of admission to the camp, learning its ways, and liberation and freedom from confinement. As prisoners are admitted to Auschwitz, an overseer gestures some of them to the right and others to the left. While being processed, Frankl is stripped of all belongings, including his clothes and his most valuable possession, the manuscript of a book he has been working on.

Soon he learns that few, if any, will emerge from this ordeal alive. He finds later that day that a friend chosen for the opposite line, by a gesture of the overseer's thumb, is ascending in smoke from the stack of a crematorium. Frankl sets about coping with his situation, trying to find meaning in his abject circumstances. He thinks about the sources of meaning in life: creative deeds, love of another, and discerning some purpose in one's suffering. He tries to find opportunity for each source of meaning, but at the same time he is constricting himself in his overt acts. Anything that draws the guards' attention to a prisoner is inviting disaster.

Some men handle their confinement by running into the electric fence, committing suicide. Early on, Frankl makes a pact with himself not to do that. He begins helping others as best he can—small acts where there is little other creative possibility. A camp ethic holds that no one is to stop another from suicide once the act is underway. Thus anyone seeking to run into the fence would not be restrained, nor would a man hanging himself and dancing on the end of a noose be cut down. But the ethic does not proscribe helping the dangerously suicidal *before* an overt action on their part and trying to give them a reason for life. Frankl makes this one of his small tasks.

Because the present and the future are so bleak, he spends many hours reflecting on the past: imaginary conversations with his wife who, if she is alive, may be in another part of the camp. He is reconstructing from memory and imagination the pleasant aspects of his past, pushing out of consciousness present realities. But he also seeks to avoid living entirely in the past. The people who do that soon give up. There are actions to take in the present, helping others and trying to reconstruct on scraps of paper the manuscript of the book taken from him. And sometimes he escapes into the future. He imagines, after his book is published, giving a university lecture on the workings of the concentration camp. He is connecting his present with his hoped-for future.

Finally, when things are so unbearable that he cannot concentrate on the pleasantness of past memories or the promise of imagination projected into the future, he makes the ultimate constriction in mental life. He will push everything else out of his mind and decide how to bear his suffering, the attitude he will have toward it—sniveling or brave or with dignity. He decides to bear it as bravely as he can. That is his ultimate choice: how to bear inescapable suffering, what it will mean for him. That is his core self, stripped of everything else, in ultimate contraction.

In the midst of terrible adversity, all that is left is hope and the freedom to choose one's attitude toward suffering. And it is a choice because a human is

> ultimately self-determining. What he becomes—within the limit of endowment and environment—he has made out of himself. In the concentration camps, for example, in this living laboratory and on this testing ground, we watched and witnessed some of our comrades behave like swine while others behaved like saints. Man has both potentialities within himself; which one is actualized depends on decisions but not on conditions.
>
> Our generation is realistic, for we have come to know man as he really is. After all, man is that being who has invented the gas chambers of Auschwitz; however, he is also that being who has entered those gas chambers upright with the Lord's Prayer or the Shema Yisrael on his lips.[6]

With liberation from the camp (only one in twenty-eight survived), there was a long learning period for Frankl to accept freedom. Its appreciation came slowly. Many events had to be reconciled with his own survival. He learned that his parents, brother, and wife had perished, although because of their separation he did not realize their fate until liberation. Earlier he had feared as much, but the hope of their survival offered comfort to him.

Frankl's experience underscores one of the great paradoxes of evolutionary explanation: The deterministic and chance processes of evolution have designed a creature that believes strongly that it has freedom to choose under the most constricting of conditions.

William James had a similar view. After finishing his medical degree, he went into a deep depression that lasted several years. What brought him out of it was a decision, not unlike Frankl's, that he had free will.[7] Such a belief is contrary to that of many scientists who espouse determinism and perhaps a dollop of chance in their chosen subject. But watching the scientist-determinist and the ardent believer in free will as they shop in the supermarket is not likely to reveal behavioral differences. Philosophy and practice are not the same. The seeming practice of freedom of choice in daily life is probably universal and is a likely part of our mental furniture. To believe one has free will is to believe that one is an agent, actively engaged in the struggle with the world. Probably this is an adaptive belief, paradoxical for the scientist, natural for the layperson, but helpful in evolution for the species and the changing self.

Simplification is the second reason for constricting the self. Previously, we alluded to the idea of simplifying life in Part I. The young woman who was a swimmer and chose to avoid makeup of any kind served as an example of simplification of appearance.

At the level of the persona, one may simplify by choosing to leave a complex life and find a lower-paying job in a small town. John, now thirty-five, was a hard-charging computer software executive who had resolved to become a multimillionaire by the time he was thirty. He had come close but found that the stress of deadlines and managing other people had taken the joy from life. He had no time for his family and no time to spend all the money he was making. So before his thirtieth birthday he stopped caring about money and moved from San Francisco to a small town, where he now writes computer games in an unhurried way. He has time for his wife and children, teaches about computers in a public education class offered by the library, and takes classes on painting.

Finding pure cases of simplification is difficult. John's life is at once a simplification and an expansion in an intricate mix of the two. He has simplified his professional life, but he has also enriched his personal life. The relief from deadlines and management has given him more time for his family and to explore other interests. At the same time, the push of ego, competition, and advantage have narrowed and become smaller influences in his life. When he looks back, he wonders why these were once such powerful forces.

Sometimes he wonders if he could simplify life even more. What if he had no wife or children? What if he became a monk in a monastery where no one spoke at all, where the daily routine rarely varied—an ultimate simplification, the greatest contraction of all? But there is such a thing as too much simplification. He needs some involvement with the world, and what he now has seems right for him at this time, in this place. However, his verbal qualifications and hedges suggest that he is still in unstable equilibrium.

The Architecture of the Contractive and Expansive Self

Is the expansive-contractive capability a mental system of self? Likely so because it is the internalization and broad elaboration of natural tendencies to approach and avoid. At that level it is seen throughout the animal world, where much of it is prewired and of clear evolutionary significance. Yet the human use of it is more abstract, and its application involves extensive learning and practice. Learning the intricacies of contraction and expansion that are needed to fit with a moving environment is a lifelong task, one that requires knowledge of context, self, and the fit between them all in good measure.

Clearly, fit is an active process, and here is a possible model of how it works. I have illustrated it with a diagram, but it is not necessary to understand the diagram to realize the most important points. Figure 8.1 shows what engineers call a *control system* and what physiologists call a *homeostatic system*.[8] It is exemplified by the way thermostats work or, more directly, the way we manually control our body-surface temperature. When we are cold (our interpretation), there is a discrepancy between the world state and our ideal state. Accordingly, we take actions: put on a sweater, stand in

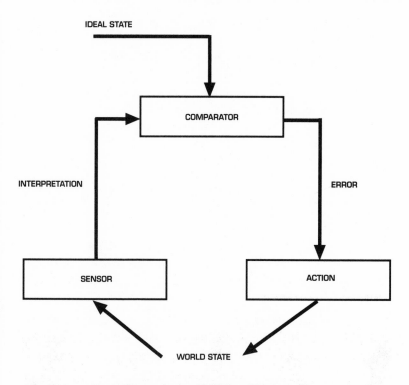

FIGURE 8.1. *A control system for the self. With modifications, the system also allows for contraction and expansion of each of its components.*

the sun, or turn up the furnace thermostat. When we are too warm, we execute different actions: take off the sweater, move into the shade, or turn down the thermostat. In the case of the furnace thermostat, there is a consequent change in the ambient environment of the world state, bringing it closer to our ideal. This process keeps cycling to maintain the body-surface temperature as close to our ideal as we can make it.

The same logic applies to goals more abstract than a desired temperature, perhaps to goals like maintaining self-esteem or happiness. Here are the specific ingredients of this control system for the self and how they may work:

- My ideal state or goal may be thought of as my standard or indicator of success.
- My world state is perhaps the work environment that I try to make consistent with my ideal of success.
- My sensor is any way I take in information from the world that has bearing on my approval or disapproval by others.
- My interpreter evaluates the incoming information; my boss is pleased or displeased with my work.
- My comparator determines whether there is a discrepancy between my interpretation and my ideal of success.
- The error signal from my comparator indicates whether there is a discrepancy between the ideal of success and the interpreter's evaluation of the information from the world of work.
- My action component is anything I do to operate on the work world to change it so that my ideal state is realized; I had better work harder to reach my ideal because my performance is lagging.

There is an important caveat here for complex examples like that just given. The control system of Figure 8.1 applied to the world of work and success is metaphorical because personal success is not a one-dimensional variable like the temperature controlled by thermostats. Nonetheless, metaphors can be powerful. Let us continue its development. So far we have examined the nature of a control system that is seeking to reach its ideal state. To understand how contraction or expansion of self takes place requires more steps, with several possibilities suggested, each emphasizing a different component of the self as system.

The self may change by altering the ideal state. For contraction, that means choosing an ideal easier to reach. In the real world of self, as opposed to the one-dimensional model, that may require relaxing some of the goals one wants in life (getting away from that high-paying but stressful job) or lowering some standards or values (being less committed to helping others in a concentration camp). For expansion, one increases the difficulty of goals, taking on more, reaching further. Wanting to earn more, accomplish more, help others more in that concentration camp.

The self may also change through action. Instead of employing the same actions to realize our ideals, we try other actions. Some of those actions may be easier, or they may be more difficult. Rather than trying to change the state of the world alone, we join with others in concerted action or become part of a community effort, an important expansion in the realm of action.

The self may change by altering the domain of the sensor. We may choose to seek out or ignore certain information. The more we ignore, the more we are likely to constrict; the more we take countenance of, the more we expand.

The self may change through altering the interpretive component. The criteria of acceptability is changed. When we are working and going to school at the same time, the nature of what is an orderly, clean house changes. Some people may say this is a change in the standard or ideal, but just as certainly it is a difference in how we interpret or monitor our surroundings. Here we are engaged in a trade-off: We constrict our notion of neatness and expand our minds by learning new things at school.

The self may change because of the comparison operation. Perhaps it becomes less sensitive and not capable of picking up fine discrepancies between the ideal and the world. The violinist in his seventies may not be able to detect the subtle imperfections of pitch that he once would have. Or the comparison operation may become more sensitive, and with increasing expertise the young violinist hears imperfections in pitch that once were unnoticed

These same ideas generalize beyond the self to incorporate relationships between separate selves, each with its own control system. No doubt many marriages founder on the reef of identity change. One partner stays the same, and the other changes. Sometimes sameness is valued; other times, change. It depends on which state the viewpoint character is in. If I change and she stays the same, then she's just not growing. But if I stay the same and she changes, then I don't know her anymore, she's so unpredictable.

For a marriage to remain happy over many years, the same two people will each be married to many different partners, each other's shifting personas. That means that they must be sensitive to one another's constancies and changes. Each must be able to track the other's changes through contraction and expansion of self and then mesh them with their own shifting trajectory of constancy and change. Not an easy thing to do—maintain the right balance between these two forces, constancy and change—through the joint operations of contraction and expansion. And of course each partner must be willing to slip into many roles and identities.

While the self enjoys preservation and sometimes undergoes contraction, its expansive forms are what astonish. The remaining chapters in Part II pursue the expanding self, in a few of its many forms.

Chapter 9

THE EMPATHIZING SELF

Agonies are one of my changes of garments,
I do not ask the wounded person how he feels, I myself become the
wounded person,
My hurts turn livid upon me as I lean on a cane and observe. . . .
I AM he that aches with amorous love. . . .

—WALT WHITMAN, *Leaves of Grass*

We now introduce the empathy system, one of the primary structures that underlies the expansive nature of the self. Through its workings we participate in the minds of others, draw out their ways of feeling and thinking, and sometimes incorporate them into our own self. Many of the workings of the empathy system lie below consciousness. Yet with only a little inward analysis, large parts of the system can be brought into awareness and used to expand the self through conscious design.

Earlier we mentioned the psychologist Howard Gardner's notion of *intra*personal intelligence and assigned the unity system a likely role in its architecture. Now we turn to what Gardner calls *inter*personal intelligence, how we understand and relate to other people.[1] A likely cornerstone of interpersonal intelligence is the empathy system, but as we shall see, empathy has other uses, as well, where we attribute humanlike characteristics to animals and inanimate nature as a first explanation of their functioning.

No operation of self is more suffused with expansive capability than empathy, a way of reaching out to others. Pooling across dictionary definitions, we find that empathy is:

1. *Identification with* and *understanding* of another's *situation, feelings,* and *motives.*
2. *The attribution of one's own feelings to an object.*
3. *A very close relationship between persons*, especially one resulting in *mutual understanding* or *affection* and *sympathy*.

Notice that several forms of empathy are defined here, and together they constitute an interlinked system. Let us consider them in more detail.

The first form we will call *receptive empathy,* the ability to *understand* the situation, emotions, motives, or more generally the mental processes of another. It includes the ability to read facial expressions, hear voice inflections, and interpret body language as a basis for knowing what is happening in another person's mind.

To be sure, these readings are imperfect. They begin at an early age, based on a rudimentary built-in nonconscious process, maturing with age and practice and ending with additional conscious strategies and a finely tuned interpretive ability. In contrast, autistic children, socially withdrawn even though some are possessed of normal intelligence, have an impaired empathy system and experience extreme difficulty in interpreting the motives and thoughts of others.[2] Psychologists refer to being able to understand these inner states of others as having a "theory of mind," or being able to "mind read," and their absence as being "mind blind," but my own preference is to stay with the more familiar notion of empathy.[3]

Receptive empathy enables us not only to understand the interior lives of others but also to copy or infer those aspects that are noteworthy for use by one's self. We see a person ahead of us on a hiking trail stumble on loose rock, fall down, and grab his knee in agony. We understand the situation that caused the accident, understand the victim's pain and suffering, so we decide to be more careful ourselves.

The second form, *projective empathy,* is also a tool for reaching out to others, but it is a giving relationship more than a receiving one. It is the ability to propel our own thoughts, feelings, and motives into another. Silent advice is proffered to the object of our empathy, and our own thoughts are projected into the body and the point of view of the other, perhaps to check the fit and generality of our own thoughts by seeing how they might be experienced through her eyes. In giving advice to a soap opera heroine, we silently tell her, "No, no, don't fall for that guy's line. He's more trouble for you." In simulating a situation, we may think of an idea and imagine how the president or a favorite actor might express it.

Projective empathy also begins early in childhood and is involved in doll and stuffed-animal play. It occurs in adults when we encourage and urge on a child who is just learning to walk. It surges to the fore when we read fiction, identify with a character, and implicitly start telling that character what to do. And when we watch a favorite sports team, we send them, via empathic imagination, our hopes and admonishments and advice.

A final component of the empathy system is the closely linked concept of *sympathy,* a special form of emotional contact.[4] Sympathy involves an emotional identification, most often for distress or misfortune: "I feel your pain," as politicians tell us. Sometimes sympathy is distinguished from empathy, the one giving rise to *feeling* and the other to *understanding.* I believe there are enough overlapping aspects among receptive, projective, and sympathetic forms of empathy to indicate the functioning of a common system. Hence, when speaking of empathy, I usually mean the entire system, its receptive and projective forms as well as the capacity for sympathy.

The adaptive value of an empathy system is apparent. We come to understand other minds, and we try out our own thoughts and actions in the different context of another's skin and point of view. By doing so, we test and validate our thoughts and values. From these receptive and projective journeys of mind, we add to our own persona, delete from it, rearrange its parts, and recombine new ingredients with already existing states and structures. When all the forms of empathy occur together and intensely, the result is an ability to *identify* deeply with another person and to create a sense of community. In extreme cases we become that other person in imagination.

All of these components of empathy contribute to being part of a larger community, as we come to explain and predict the thoughts, feelings, and actions of others. Mature adult empathy, built on innate tendencies, is an act of invention, an important process in the creation of one's own self and in the building of connection and community.

Charles Darwin anticipated many of the principles behind the empathy system in his book *The Expression of the Emotions in Man and Animals*.[5] In the terminology here, the empathy system is based on the match between behavior and internal states. That makes it possible for perceiving organisms to accurately interpret what is going on internally in another creature's mind. So there are really three coevolving subsystems here: the internal expression system, the behavioral expression system, and the match between the two. Of course, the match between internal and external expression is not perfect because our interpretations may err.

The adaptive value of such a system starts within a species. For example, in Darwin's view, a dog's snarl is the reduced symbolic correlate of a full-fledged attack. Other dogs read such a signal and may back away or prepare themselves for attack—also adaptive reactions. To the extent that the snarl produces intimidation while not requiring aggressive action, it has achieved its ends without the hazards of combat. Other species, such as we humans, also know how to interpret a dog's snarl, and we similarly back away or prepare ourselves when the matter contested is worth fighting over.

The snarl has function for its producer, for observers within the same species, and for observers of other species.

In humans, the empathy system spreads beyond its original motor and perceptual components as it links up with symbolic systems of storytelling, dramatization, and other fictional what-ifs. All of these are potentially adaptive, insofar as they help us anticipate possible worlds in which the cost of not knowing how to react can be severe. Experiencing them first as fiction involves negligible cost. Let us now turn to the application of these notions.

Princess Diana and Mother Teresa died within a week of one another. The media coverage and the public's apparent grief for Diana far outweighed that for Mother Teresa and provides an indicator of each one's ability to evoke empathic reactions in the public.[6]

Diana's death resulted in a great outpouring of public sympathy, especially among women. Many of those aroused to sympathy were surprised by that feeling. Around the country in the days following Diana's death therapy sessions for female clients were often devoted to the mythical connection of the average woman to Diana.[7] Apparently there were no therapy sessions devoted to a mythical connection to Mother Teresa. In addition, a number of arguments between men and women took place because men did not experience the loss for Diana that women felt. In further contrast, news accounts did not reveal any such arguments between men and women regarding their differential loss for Mother Teresa.

On the surface, all of this is surprising. There is little doubt that Mother Teresa's accomplishments significantly outweighed those of Diana's. There are similarities, to be sure. But while Diana demonstrated a public concern for AIDS victims and was an advocate of banning land mines, Mother Teresa addressed human suffering at a deeper level and in a more sustained way. Why is it that Diana's death provoked so much more interest? Why the disproportionate news coverage for her?

First we will examine preliminary explanations and indicate why they are inadequate. Then we will consider what may be the real reason for the greater coverage of Diana.

Princess Diana died first, and she exhausted a finite supply of public grief, so there was not much more left for Mother Teresa. But this is unlikely because Princess Diana not only died first, she was in the news longer, overlapping the coverage for Mother Teresa. Journalistic speculation maintains that the news coverage for Mother Teresa was greater than expected because of professional ethics: "Mother Teresa's legacy also got a cosmic boost from the shame felt at hyping an adulterous princess over a living saint."[8]

Mother Teresa is a more difficult model to relate to because of her remoteness from our own experiences. How can one identify with an apparent saint? She was unreachable because she was so different from the rest of us in her devotion to duty and in her willingness to associate herself with that most unpleasant of human problems, dying and death. While this may be a partial explanation, Diana's social life of formal balls and weekend escapes to the estates of the superrich was as remote from most of us as Mother Teresa's activities. And, in fact, Diana's charities were also concerned with dying and death—AIDS and land mines specifically.

Princess Diana was attractive, Mother Teresa, old and worn. The public prefers to read about the one more than the other, the glamorous rather than the dutiful. Also true but only in part.

Princess Diana died of an accident at a young age, and Mother Teresa died a natural death at an old age. The first is the greater tragedy because the second is the result of a natural progression, the one unexpected and the other all too expected. But this is also unlikely to be the whole story. Many people, including celebrities, die early and attract none of the public caring shown for Diana. Truly, there is something distinctive about Diana still awaiting explanation.

What, then, may be the real reason for the greater coverage for Diana if it is not social importance or one of the aforementioned factors? The answer is that Diana was easier to *identify with* than

Mother Teresa. But what does that mean? To begin with, people—women especially—felt that they knew Diana almost as a friend. But who of us could say that she felt she knew Mother Teresa?

How is it that people felt they knew Diana but not Mother Teresa? Well, Diana had a full set of entangling human relationships: a husband who was unfaithful, children being educated in ways she evidently did not care for, and in-laws who were cold and unsympathetic to her. These are all conditions that we readily understand and relate to, either directly or indirectly through close friends and family. In contrast, Mother Teresa had no family as such, no similar entangling relationships, and as a result she had less connection to the rest of us—at least those in this country.

People also knew Diana much better because she told them more about her personal life than did Mother Teresa. Indeed, Mother Teresa seemed to have had no personal life. Diana was an expert at using the media to deal with the turmoil she suffered at the hands of the royal family; she revealed her vulnerability to the world. Since we are all vulnerable in many ways, that sense of frailty provided another anchor point for identification. Mother Teresa had no such sense of vulnerability. While she was definitely a compassionate person, she was also an in-charge person, one who could create and organize an entire worldwide order of nuns, the Missionaries of Charity, devoted to her idea of human and religious service. And evidently she did so in a demanding and authoritarian way. She was not frail and defenseless.

If people believed they knew and understood Diana better than Mother Teresa, then the basis for that belief requires closer scrutiny, for it is yet another way of extending the self, a way of sharing in the life of someone else through the remarkable processes of the empathy system. That system allows us to regard a distant celebrity as a friend, even though we have never met her. Or we may even imagine that we are the other person. In fact, identification was the likely mental state for millions of Princess Diana's mourners. They empathized with her struggles, her marital difficulties, her savaging by the media (receptive empathy). In imagination they sent her their best wishes, their cautions about love, and their hopes for a more normal life (projective empathy). They also shared with her the pain produced by the betrayal of her husband (sympathy) and the coldness of the other royals (a lack of sympathy). With her tragic early death, people felt that they had lost a friend, and indeed she was a friend constructed of the imagination. Perhaps they had even lost an alter ego of the self.

The difference in news coverage between Mother Teresa and Diana becomes explainable as the difference between coverage of a remote person versus the coverage for a friend or an alternative self. Why shouldn't we hear more about a friend or an aspect of one's self? Journalists understand this well. They tend to cover people who are easy to identify with or—the reverse—people who are easy to hate.

Personification and Vivification

Along with empathy, two closely related processes share a key importance for the way we understand the world: personifying and vivifying. *Personification* attributes human characteristics to nonpersons. In the process the nonperson is invested with human qualities such as personality, motives, intentions, emotions, and hopes. We regularly do this with animals, "Your tail is wagging so fast; you really *love* this food." It is probably a reasonable attribution of *like* but perhaps not *love*. We empathize with pets whenever we talk to a dog or a cat, investing them with a kind of human intelligence while feeling their pain and anticipating their wants. My mother used to talk to her chickens as if they were people, urging them to lay more eggs and do the right thing by one another: "You can do it. Stop pecking that other chicken. What if he did the same to you?" Unfortunately, chickens are inept students of empathy, and they will peck to death an injured fellow stuck in a fence.

Sometimes we even personify plants. A friend who is a skilled, no-nonsense gardener tells her plants: "I'll give you one more chance to grow. *Shape up* and start growing, or I'm going to cut your *heart* out." Shaping up and having a heart are person characteristics, not really shared by a plant. And a *threat* is an action to take against another person, not a plant.

At other times the nonperson we direct our thought to can be a force of nature: "The sky is *angry* tonight." Or "That was a *biting* wind, a *vicious* tornado." These are all examples of personification, attributing human characteristics to nonhumans.

Finally, personification can be extended to nonliving objects. I have heard an elderly man talk to his tools as if they were a person. When cutting wood, he might say, "Now, don't do that again [tool as agent]. Be more *careful* next time [tool as careless]. Or I'll trade you in on a new saw."

The meaning of a personification while not literal is instantly clear because it employs terms we use to describe ourselves and our own thinking, something with which we are on intimate terms. It is nothing short of applying our mental model of persons to nonpersons.

In this regard, *vivification*[9] is even more general than personification, attributing not just human characteristics but a more diffuse life force to the nonliving: "I see the clouds changing into *animals*. All of nature—the rocks, the sky, the water—seems to be infused with *spirit;* the earth seems to be *alive* tonight. I can feel nature's *breath* on my face, its *pulse* in the seasons." To be sure, the dividing line between personification and vivification is not always clear. Nature's breath could be a human characteristic or a more general reference to life. For the most part I will speak of personification, but I wanted to make clear that it is an instance of something even more general: using life to explain the nonliving.

When I was a graduate student in psychology, the name for applying human mental states to nonhumans was *anthropomorphizing,* and it was a cardinal sin. The argument against it was twofold: excessive sentimentality and a lack of parsimony.

The first of these was directed against pet lovers who talk to their poodles, and the second was based on the notion that simpler processes than humanlike thinking can explain the behavior of animals—perhaps processes like classical or instrumental conditioning, two relatively simple forms of learning. Now we recognize that conditioning is anything but simple, and it is far from a complete explanation of animal behavior. In addition, studies of primates reveal remarkable abilities closely linked to what is here called empathy. As the primatologist Franz de Waal remarks, the most parsimonious explanation for animal behavior may be a human one such as empathy because it applies to multiple species, ourselves included.[10] Perhaps the poodle owner knows something that psychologists do not know. Parsimony is itself an unclear notion.

The modern scientific view of the world does not much care for these processes of personification and vivification. Yet they are the underlying mental models that most people through most of human time have used to explain life, the world, and the cosmos— a kind of universal folk psychology in which consciousness and feeling are extended or projected outward to other creatures and the larger universe itself.[11] The reason for folk psychology is not hard to see. A model of intentions, emotions, motives, and hopes works well for understanding other humans, so why not extend it to animals, plants, and the universe? That is the essence of folk psychology.

Science and reflective sense tell us that characteristics personified in nonhumans do not always work well. No matter what a *good friend* my pet wolf is, he may at some time take off one of my ears. And the pet boa constrictor wrapped around my neck might seem to be a *trusting* pet until it gets large enough to choke me. Plants respond even less well to personification, and depending on one's cosmology, the forces of nature are little mollified by rituals, offerings, and feasts.

Nonetheless, we persist in personifying because we may not

have a better way of understanding. This often happens in arenas ruled in large part by chance. The stock market is regularly personified and vivified: "The market is *seeking* a correction." or "The market *wants* a period of *tranquillity* after all this movement." It is as if the market were a living thing, with goals and emotional needs.

Why this attribution of life to nonlife? Once I heard the eminent sociologist Semour Lipsett talk about conspiracy theory. His point: Far more conspiracies are imagined than really take place. The reason: It is better that our enemies control the world than no one. This is so because if no one controls the world, then that stock-market dip or that tornado or hurricane that wiped me out last year could come again. Also, if the market or a tornado is personified, I know how to deal with it. Such events are just like big, angry, unpredictable people—say, a *capricious* king or boss to whom I give *compliments,* bestow *favors* upon, and *prostrate* myself before when I cannot escape his wrath.

If it works for my boss, why not for the personified tornado? Even when personification is not a good model of a system, I may derive comfort from its application because it works so well for me in human contexts—and similarly for vivification. To think otherwise is to admit the frightening prospect that much of life is affected by the forces of chance, against which I have no influence. Personification overcomes this feeling by providing the comfort of an explanation and a strategy that at least works in other contexts.

To summarize, personification works well for understanding our fellow humans, not too badly for our dogs, and less well for plants and for the material universe, where science has made important contributions to our understanding. Clearly, personification builds on the empathy system. Even though empathy has antecedents in other species, it reaches its zenith in our own. It is adaptive because we get along better in the world by using it to understand and reach out to people. In a Darwinian sense, adaptiveness means being reproductively successful relative to others.

Being able to explain, predict, and feel the reactions of others are important abilities for competing, meeting, and mating. It's only natural to extend such abilities to nonhumans.

Reproductive success originally forged the development of human empathy. But as we have seen, empathy is a powerful system that goes beyond its original uses, allowing us to identify with the likes of animals, plants, and other forms of nature—to apply the model of *person* to their diverse forms. In all of this, we see processes that further the extension of the self beyond the body. We now turn to how the empathy system allows us to understand historical figures from the distant past, to learn from fiction, and to grasp the reasons for identifying with an athletic team.

Historical Empathy

The English historian R. G. Collingwood thought long and hard about how to understand people who lived in another time.[12] He advocated an empathic approach, putting one's self in the shoes of a person long since gone, and seeking to understand that person's experiences, decisions, and actions. A guiding principle is charity: Choose the interpretation that makes the other person most rational. Instead of explaining away his actions as, say, crazy, unbalanced, or due to luck, figure out reasons why in the same situation we would have behaved as he did. Perhaps stress produced the irrational behavior; if so, what kind of stress? Or love for his family may have led him to a seemingly evil betrayal of others. When we can see reasons why we would behave as the historical protagonist, we have touched him empathically and bridged the temporal gap that separates us.

In addition to rationality, historical interpretation is facilitated by thinking of shared traditions with the person from the past. Do we share a legal system, a common literature, a set of customs, a religion? Even if we are of a different culture, that is not an insurmountable barrier because no present-day cultures have found it impossible to communicate on a broad range of fronts. Moreover, by having a mind of the same biological kind as the historical figure, we will have the same emotions of anxiety, fear, and exhilaration, even though our situational triggers may differ.

For example, the military historian John Keegan tries to imagine the Battle of Waterloo of 1815 where the English general Wellington defeated the French general Napoleon. Keegan gains a contemporary understanding by drawing on his own knowledge of fatigue:

> We ought to take account . . . [of] several common factors that helped to determine [the] human context. The first of these was fatigue. . . . [B]oth armies on the morning of Waterloo . . . had been on the march the whole of the previous day, carrying fifty to sixty pounds per man, had fought the day before that, and had been living on rations issued the day before that again. . . . [I]t prompts speculation whether the men . . . were not helped to endure the horrors of "their" battle by the semi-anesthesia of extreme physical tiredness.[13]

In this process, the interpreter of history is trying to get to its psychological bedrock through an empathic reach across time and place that may go back centuries or millennia and stretch to never-seen parts of the world. That means knowing as much as possible about the historical context of the person and understanding the reactions of one's own body in context with shared conditions (certainly everyone is familiar with fatigue, for example). By so doing, the length of empathic reach is increased to span history.

Storytelling and Theater

Another important consequence of empathic capacity is the art of storytelling—be it as theater, cinema, or, more generally, make-believe. Without the capacity for empathy it is difficult to imagine the possibility of such art forms. For the characters on a page to take on the reality of warm flesh and pulsing blood, we must understand their mental life, feel their emotions, and tell them what they ought to do to escape the current plot crisis. We want heroes to succeed. While empathy provides heroes with a positive identification, something like a negative empathy exists, as well. It leads to the mirror-image fictional creation: the jerk, the cad, the villain. We want the villain to fail.

Both of these empathic variants—positive and negative, hero and villain—are first apparent in children's play: cops and robbers, earthmen and aliens, fair maidens and evil stepmothers. A more adult example is that of Shakespeare's *Hamlet*.[14] In brief, Hamlet's uncle has killed his father and married his mother. Hamlet is unsure of his course of action.

> To be, or not to be: that is the question:
> Whether 'tis nobler in the mind to suffer
> The slings and arrows of outrageous fortune,
> Or to take arms against a sea of troubles,
> And by opposing end them. To die, to sleep—
> No more—and by a sleep to say we end
> The heartache and the thousand natural shocks
> That flesh is heir to! . . .

How can we appreciate such a play? We are living four hundred years after it was written, and few of us have had an uncle kill our father. To start, we will need to relate historically to the event, as with Collingwood. Here Shakespeare has helped us mightily by providing context, atmosphere, and metaphor. A more difficult problem is that most of us have no direct awareness of Hamlet's situation. Therefore, a deep emotional understanding of the play will have to come about as an empathic construction.

While my father has not been killed by my uncle, perhaps I have had tragedy heaped upon me. Possibly someone in my family was killed in an auto accident. Maybe my mother was killed in a car driven recklessly by my cousin. How did that make me feel about my cousin? Well, I felt intense anger and wanted to direct that anger to the person who caused this, my cousin. But at the same time, the loss of my mother sent me into a deep depression. I wanted to say or do something to my cousin, but the anger was not enough to overcome the depression. I became listless and unsure about what to do.

Such a reconstruction is very similar to the method actor's preparation in mastering a role, a way to develop an empathic resonance to Hamlet's situation and indecisiveness. However, method acting requires a deliberate conscious effort, while understanding story can be immediate and direct, a natural enlivening. The difference is that of creation versus recognition. Whether understanding comes from natural connection or from deliberate artifice, empathy's reach is clear: It makes fiction come alive. We have spent our lives understanding uncertainty, pain, and sorrow in the lives of others as well as ourselves. Because of such experiences we quickly grasp the truth of a fictional character's experience. Without the empathy system there would be no interest in novels, theater, or cinema.

The ability of a skilled actor to assume the persona of another character, to try on for a brief period a character role that serves as another kind of mask, is so miraculous that it warrants closer examination. The Broadway actress and teacher Uta Hagen presents two different ways of going about the creation of a role. The first one I call *imitative,* and it is associated with the famous late-nineteenth-century actress Sarah Bernhardt; the other I call *interior,* and it is associated with an equally famous actress of that time, Eleonora Duse.[15] In the first acting style, the actor seeks to imitate the character's behavior. It is associated with grand stage gestures, like appearing to tear out one's hair at the death of a lover. In contrast, the interior style seeks to produce an inner set of feelings and actions compatible with the character, letting the outward manifestations of the character flow naturally. This is a more subtle and psychologically deeper portrayal, requiring an understanding of the character's internal states. Instead of tearing out her hair at the death of the lover, the actress will stare into space, and a tear will run down her cheek. Hagen very much argues for the interior style of acting, preferring Duse over Bernhardt.

The interior style requires an unusual form of training that makes it a model for the construction of other selves, ones we can try on by assuming their thoughts and feelings as well as their actions. Here is Hagen's account of how it works, contrasting the performances of Bernhardt and Duse in an act of denial:

> Each, in her native tongue, had played the same popular melo-drama of the time, the high point of which was the moment when the wife, accused of infidelity by her husband, swore her virtue. "Je jure, je jure, JE JUUUURE!" Bernhardt proclaimed in a ris-ing vibrato of passion. Her audience stood to scream and shout its admiration. Duse swore her virtue softly and only twice. She never spoke the third oath, but placed her hand on her young son's head as she looked directly at her husband. Duse's audience wept.[16]

I can see myself as the accusing husband confronted by these two entirely different reactions—and I have no doubt that I would be more deeply moved by the more subtle voice and gesture. It is one that plays not to rage but to hurt and the fracturing of trust.

Hagen goes on to describe how she herself constructed the character of Blanche DuBois in *A Streetcar Named Desire.* In this play by Tennessee Williams, Blanche is a southern belle who visits her sister and brother-in-law, Stella and Stanley. Soon afterward, trou-ble starts.

To construct her portrayal, Hagen begins by listing needs of her character, Blanche: perfection, beauty, gentleness, tenderness, delicacy, elegance, decorum; being loved, protected, and possess-ing delusions to cloak unpleasant realities. Hagen's own image of herself is quite different; she describes herself as a "frank, gutsy child of nature."[17] How, then, can Hagen create a character so dif-ferent from herself?

She does this by drawing on her own experiences and substituting them for Blanche's. She recalls getting ready for the opera, "bathing and oiling and perfuming my body, soothing my skin, brushing my hair until it shines."[18] That takes her into some of Blanche's characteristics—the need for perfection, beauty, and delicacy. Now Hagen recalls reading a poem by Rainer Maria Rilke and how she wept; that helps her understand and create the sentimentality of Blanche. Then she remembers the tenderness experienced at twilight, the manners of a gentleman; and other related life events. Through these past experiences and memories, she begins to find an internal reality to match Blanche's. By the assembly and synthesis of the right memories and emotions, she is becoming Blanche, becoming another person by seeing that person's needs and then constructing their match out of her own experiences.

Since reading Hagen's account, I have tried to do this myself. It is easy with people I readily identify with, more difficult with strangers in news accounts, and most difficult of all with people I despise. Yet it can be done, getting inside that person, understanding why he does what he does, and making his behavior seem natural and inevitable.[19]

With this process, I can create a character who has never lived and make him believable, alive, and interesting. If I like that person, I become a little bit of him, too. If that part of him persists in me, I am creating my own persona as I try on these different masks, different roles. The experience is unnerving and powerful. The technique for persona creation is so useful, it should find currency beyond the stage.

For the most part the empathic response is good—it helps make us caring and considerate humans. But sometimes its wiring becomes crossed, and a master at empathy becomes a con artist or a game-playing seducer. Even more extreme, the empathy master may become a demagogue who inflames a whole country with hatred because he has the remarkable capacity to see the incipient fears and antagonisms of a people and the ability to play to them for his own purposes. At the same time, he is altogether lacking the vital component of sympathy. I call this *predator empathy*, the ability to read the thoughts and minds of others with the intention of exploiting them or doing them harm.

Examples are not hard to find. In my youth I knew an older Danish woman who had witnessed the rise of Hitler. As she told me, many people thought at first that he was a clown to amuse the lower classes, and then he was an efficient way to get the riffraff off the streets. Only later did his power of oratory and his deep insights into human irrationality fully reveal themselves. He knew and understood people's weaknesses and anxieties, and he was a master at projecting his own evil aspirations into the minds of his followers. Only when it was too late did the full truth and tragedy of his talents become known.

Team Personification

Personification combined with intense empathic reach is the basis of team identification in spectator sports. Once we identify with a sports team, we own a little bit of it and root for it—a form of projective empathy. The resulting identification is no longer with an individual but with a collective of individuals called a team. The team as collective, through an alchemy of personification, becomes a superperson.

Tom, a man in his early sixties, is a devoted baseball fan. He thinks that what makes identification with a team easy or difficult is a matter of place. When he lived in Detroit, he was a Tigers fan; when he lived in Chicago, he became a Cubs fan; and now that he lives in Albuquerque, he's a Dukes fan. As he explains it, because the Dukes are a principal farm club for the Los Angeles Dodgers, by association he has also become a Dodgers fan. Being a fan means that a linkage of places, loyalties, and hopes have all come together in unity, focusing on a favorite team.

Tom's identification continues even after he leaves a city—he hasn't lived in Detroit for thirty years and not in Chicago for fifteen, but he still cheers for the Tigers and the Cubs. Is the identification with the team or with the individual players? What happens when a player he really likes is traded to an opposing team? Tom experiences conflict for a little while, but the loyalty seems to be primarily with the team and not the person. If a star acts as a free agent and goes to another team, Tom may even boo him the next time he comes to town. When the two teams he roots for—the Cubs and the Dodgers—play one another, he is neutral and just enjoys the game; it doesn't matter who wins. Does he identify with managers, who also come and go? No, it's hard to identify with administrators.

The identification process is also helped along by winning. When a team is hot, attendance is high. When it's consistently losing, attendance drops way off. But even then some fans remain staunchly loyal. Oh, yes, distinctive T-shirts and the like also help.

What if a team leaves a city, as when the Dodgers left Brooklyn and went to Los Angeles? Tom felt real anger there. Even though that move took place years ago, fans still regard it as a betrayal. Someone even said the move marked the beginning of the decline of Western civilization. Team identification is a serious matter.

What is happening in this identification with team? Evidently the team has become an extension of one's self, perhaps a part of the self. Like a favorite shirt, the team is invested with something of us. In empathic projection, fans talk to the team and yell at it, offering advice. In an act of receptive empathy, they feel pain when the team loses. If a favored team loses the World Series, the loss is a little bit like the cutting off or mutilation of a body part—something of the self is lost in the process. In this respect the team is an imaginal extension of the self to be looked after, cared for, and invested with emotional energy.

Feelings for a team are mediated most easily by a sense of place and community within that place. It's no accident that when we meet a stranger at a party, a natural question concerns where the person is from. Place is a powerful holder and receptacle of commonality and community. When a team is near us in a physical place or in emotional association, we personify it, we treat it as though it is a friend. It takes on the drives and hopes of individuals. It has life. It is a personification on which we project our hopes.

E mpathy and personification provide us with the ability to identify with others across an immense expanse of forms and objects, times and places. Within reason, it does not matter whether the other is a celebrity like Princess Diana, a hero like Jackie Robinson, or a baseball team like the Cubs. We project our aspirations onto them, understand their situation, and feel their pain. Almost by definition, the celebrity or a hero we identify with is one whose mind we share or even attempt to take over, by anticipation of the person's moves or by implicit advice on what should be done. Or we may wait for the voice of the hero to advise us in a nocturnal dream or a daydream. And the baseball team, even if an ensemble of individuals, is easiest to think of as a single organic entity from which we receive emotion and to which we project our advice.

This is the same empathy-personification system that allows us to understand and relate to story and novel. Without it, we could not identify with fictional characters, enter their lives, feel their feelings, and offer mental directives to them. Without it, we could not identify with teams. Without it, we would be like an autistic person. The empathy-personification system is a mighty contributor to what makes us human, extending us beyond our own time, our own place, our own skins.

Chapter 10

WANTING TO BE ANOTHER SELF

*If I worship one thing more than another it shall be the spread of
my own body, or any part of it,*
Translucent mould of me it shall be you!
Shaded ledges and rests it shall be you!

— WALT WHITMAN, *Leaves of Grass*

The expansive self draws on the empathy system for its understanding of others when we drift into fantasy to take on the life of another, to be someone else, wholly or in part. Wanting to be someone else is a desire of most of us at one time or another. A possible insight into the process is offered by the work of the cognitive scientist D. N. Perkins, who writes of distributed thinking and learning. When we remember something or try to solve a problem, we do not exclusively draw on material within the skull. We look at books, notes, and maps. We seek out others who may have useful information. In all of these ways, knowledge is a "sum and swarm of participations" *distributed* across places and minds.[1]

Perkins's notion of distributed cognition may also be applied to the creation of a persona. From an early age we have heroes and celebrities to whom we feel a special resonance. The identification with those individuals makes us a part of a distributed self from which we draw knowledge of how to act, how to feel, how to love. They are our satellites—or perhaps we are theirs—and we connect regularly with them as we create our own personas. In this way the self is much more than simply the workings within one's own skull. Let us now look to specific instances of this process at work.

Extraordinary accomplishment acts as a beacon for identification. The home-run feats of Mark McGuire and Sammy Sosa created an interest in baseball as a game for countless people who wouldn't ordinarily think of themselves as baseball fans. More than one of us has found it an easy feat of imagination to be in the shoes of one of these superb athletes, swinging a bat, feeling the impact of a hit, and watching the ball lift and head for the stands. Years from now children who were inspired by McGuire and Sosa will become baseball players because of their influence.

Incorporating others into the self and projecting the self into others are powerful aspects of the empathic system. To understand them better, I started asking people to tell me about their experiences in wanting to take on the persona of someone else, their experience in forming an expansive identity in a complex society. In the process, I found that the nature of incorporation and identification are intricately nuanced. Here are some other examples.

The someone else we want to be does not even have to be a real person. As a child, Ralph, now a college teacher, wanted to be Tarzan because his hero's courage impressed him and helped him to overcome his own shyness; Tarzan's idealism became part of him, and persistence in the face of failure illuminated his own path. To be sure, Tarzan would now be seen as a cultural stereotype, a superman white guy among a bunch of slow-witted savages, but that was not the message Ralph received from him. Instead, his identification with Tarzan gave him a little bit more courage, idealism, and persistence.

In wanting to be Tarzan, Ralph extended himself by incorporating new aspects of someone else into his own persona. That is exactly what heroes should do: allow us to idealize them, reach out to them, and then copy some of their properties into our selves as we incorporate what is positive and admirable in them. No matter if they have flaws; we can overlook and filter out any number of blemishes as long as there is that admirable quality to long for.

Marie is a financial officer for a large corporation. As a young adult she imagined herself to be Jacqueline Kennedy Onassis. She tried on Jackie's life and considered herself as the First Lady. Later, when Jackie became Jacqueline Onassis, Marie had another lifestyle to incorporate. Jackie, in her multiple incarnations, provided Marie endless material for trying on: appearance, clothes, dinner parties, husbands, different lives.

As Marie viewed it, she didn't take just parts of Jackie's life into her imagination. Instead, she became a whole-body Jackie, imagining herself organizing a White House dinner party, trying on an evening gown, talking to a head of state. Best of all, she could do this without risk because it took place in a pretend world.

What, if anything, carried over into her reality as Marie? She found some parts of Jackie's life that appealed to her (the glamour and the wealth) while other parts didn't appeal (the constant publicity and gossip). Her imagination revealed to her that life could be too complex, too rich. Through the trying on of imagination, she found herself more in tune with a simpler life. And that is what she continues to practice.

Another, perhaps more important carryover, also came with the pretend game. Because the real Jackie's life contained so many facets, Marie's fantasy also took on more than a single way of life. Yet continuity arose from her identification with one person—Jackie—over a period of years. As Marie discovered, the underlying unity is not actually Jackie's different lives but her style in fitting into those lives. Jackie always seemed to be her own person, someone who knew what she wanted. Ultimately, that style is what Marie identified with. She is intelligent, independent, and open to new experiences, all characteristics that she believes her identification with Jackie helped achieve.

A different form of identification is afforded by Earl, a successful professor of biochemistry, whose story is about heroes and nonheroes when he was growing up in a New Orleans housing project.[2] Most of his neighborhood idolized Joe Louis, the heavyweight boxing champ. Whenever Louis fought, every radio in the project would be tuned to the fight. Yet Earl did not think of Louis as his hero. He was put off by Louis's rough speech and his constant difficulties in his business affairs.

Instead, Earl was attracted to Jackie Robinson, the first man to break the color barrier in major league baseball. Robinson was everything that Louis was not: confident and articulate in his public appearances, deft in handling his business affairs, concerned about his community, and courageous in the face of racism. Robinson became Earl's hero and a formative role model for his professional life. Later, when Earl was a student, he had the chance of a lifetime: He got to meet Robinson in person. He was awed and gratified. Here was a hero that warranted his respect, admiration, and emulation.

In this process Earl identified with Robinson, but unlike Ralph's Tarzan and Marie's Jackie, he didn't become him in imagination. He wanted to be like Robinson only *in certain ways* but still remain himself. This is a very different kind of expansive identification, one in which we retain our own identity and borrow only certain characteristics of another person, grafting them on to our own identity. Earl later took on some of Robinson's characteristics. He became a spokesman and activist for civil rights and liberties. He successfully sued his state government for compiling a secret database of so-called troublemakers. During this time of unrest, he showed great courage and forthrightness in pressing his cause— the very characteristics he had earlier admired in Robinson.

A further variation in the nature of the identification process is provided by Laura when she was a high-school student who wanted to be from England. She liked the accent and sophistication of English people, as portrayed in the movies. She even practiced speaking with an English accent—a perfect upper-class English accent as she demonstrated. She had never imagined talking like someone from Liverpool or someone with a cockney accent, so she identified with only a particular class of English people. But that is natural because some identifications are incompatible with others—we cannot simultaneously speak with an English accent that's both upper-class and cockney.

Another aspect of her identification process warrants comment. She didn't want to be a specific person but rather a member of a class, someone from England with an educated accent. This is similar to the young person who wants to be an actress, a doctor, a cowboy, or a writer. It is an abstract want, perhaps starting with particular people but soon centered in no particular person at all. These wantings of class involve a longing for a set of skills and a style of life. For skills, it might be talking like the English or knowing how to be an actor. For lifestyle, it may center on the imagined glamour of being a doctor. In either case, the reality is almost always something different. For the actor, disappointment often erases years of discipline, anticipation, and hope. For the doctor, endless hours are spent in treating the suffering of others, people who frequently are far from grateful and may complain about medical care when their bodies will not heal their own self-imposed excesses.

But reality is not the concern here any more than our heroes having flaws we cannot see. In fact, ignorance may help the process of identification by lubricating the fit between a present reality and the reach for what we might be.

The process of expansive identification assumes still other forms. This one focuses not on a person but an ability, so in some ways it is related to Laura's wanting to be English, but it is independent of geography and is instead a mental capacity. Alfred, a man in his fifties, wanted to understand abstract mathematics because the content, the wild concepts, and the distant thought connections drew him to them. No particular mathematician had come to mind, but he wanted to have that mathematical aspect of the brain that allows for thinking in sublime abstraction. The ability of any fine mathematician would have served him. This form of wanting differs from Marie's constant identification with Jackie over her many lives. Alfred's yearning is almost the opposite: no loyalty to person, only loyalty to an abstract unvarying human capability.

Here is a less mental and more physical variation on identification. At times we wish we were more attractive so that we would not always have to succeed in life on the basis of character and ability. It would be nice to occasionally coast by on good looks. Or would it? I once had a student who wanted a better grade because she was physically stunning. She didn't say it in those exact words, but that was the message she sent: Let me by on the basis of being a beautiful person. Obviously it had worked for her before, and she couldn't understand why I insisted that she engage in honest effort. I hoped that when she got into the subject matter, she would enjoy it. But that never came to pass. I at once envied the power of her attractiveness and what she was able to get away with as a result—a positive identification—and at the same time thought of her behavior as a model of what not to identify with— a negative identification.

Identification is not just a matter of shifting, expanding, contracting, borrowing characteristics, or becoming a whole-body other. It also requires the resolution of seeming contradiction. Barbara, a massage therapist, wanted to be more like Mother Teresa, with her compassion for human suffering. Barbara is already a compassionate person, and wanting to be more so is a real longing for growth, a playing to one's strengths and stretching to the edge. But Barbara also wanted to be more like the movie star Sharon Stone because she was so naturally sexy.

An interesting combination and seemingly irreconcilable: Mother Teresa and Sharon Stone. Perhaps Barbara meant that sometimes she wanted to be like Mother Teresa and other times like Sharon Stone? Yes, she explained, that's true. It's time-sharing, like having a condo only at Christmas while someone else has it over New Year's.

That made sense because the two people who were part of her fantasy life would not occupy her consciousness at the same time. But Barbara pushed it further, saying that she could be both at once. To be compassionate requires passion. While we normally think of passion as something sexual, it is much broader. It is intensity for life. Mother Teresa has that kind of passion—and Sharon Stone does, too. So it is possible to be both at the same time.

Barbara's dance with contradiction made the fusion of Mother Teresa and Sharon Stone seemingly easy. But the problem of integrating identities is often difficult. It led the theorist of human development Erik Erikson to the idea of the identity crisis, a common stage in adolescence in which a youth is trying to determine a suitable identity, one simultaneously composed of past dependency on parents and the need for future freedom. For Erikson, it is not enough to try on new identities. One must make the new ones fit with the old ones and vice versa. That fitting can be difficult and lead to a despairing crisis or to a higher synthesis.[3]

Building an Alter Ego

Sometimes we want to be someone else, but we don't know who. This is certainly an abstract want but one worth exploring. To further clarify the self's nature, it is helpful to put a frame around not only its present form but also its range of possibilities. No better framing device can be found than in the construction of an *alter ego,* a sort of mirror image of self. The exercise of building an alter ego is a particularly useful form of centering the self because it quickly identifies an extreme self, one we could have become.

We know the process of alter-ego building is working when we have the distinct feeling of "Yes, that is possible. I could have turned out that way." We then have the option of picking a self somewhere between the present one and the reversed image in the mirror. The construction of an alter self is the prose equivalent of a cubist portrait. The light falling on different facets reveals separate virtues, separate truths, about the varied angles of refraction.

The idea of an alter is a familiar one as exemplified by Dr. Jekyll and Mr. Hyde and by Clark Kent and Superman. Dr. Jekyll is a dedicated, earnest man, while his alter in the same skin, Mr. Hyde, is cruel, snarling, and murderous. By contrast, Clark Kent, a mild-mannered and benign person, has as his alter Superman, someone of admirable and heroic proportions. Another difference is that Jekyll-Hyde involves split personality and pathology, while Kent-Superman intentionally transform into one another.

Both fictional pairs are imaginative literary constructions, and they suggest the idea that everyone might have an intriguing alter ego toward which the identity may expand. We want to find a way of creating an alter-ego self in which, metaphorically, the alter will reveal a left side as a right side, and vice versa, while being a realistic or understandable possibility. Let us illustrate, then, a method for building an alter ego by using Sam, a man in his late fifties.

A good place to start is with his relationships. The woman he is married to is a small Hispanic woman of passionate convictions, fine intelligence, and left-leaning politics. Now in his mirror self, we will construct an alter mate, one he dated in his earlier life. She is a tall blond woman, perhaps Scandinavian, whose politics are fervent right wing. She is quite different but not in every way because she also has a fine intelligence, albeit of a different kind.

Having constructed his alter mate, we look back on his major decisions in life, recollecting the important choices he might have made but didn't. For each such decision point we will try to construct a mirror opposite. A few years ago Sam became disillusioned with teaching. He needed an alternative. One option was to pursue a writing career, endure income uncertainty, lots of false starts, and loneliness. Of these he was certain, and no doubt other negatives would also reveal themselves. His other option was to see if he could get a state or federal job, where he would work hard but get home by 6:00 P.M. and relax on the weekends. He decided to get more serious about his writing. So his mirror occupation, the one not chosen, was to work for the government.

Moving back in time, he remembers that in college he switched majors many times. First elementary education, then history, then philosophy, and finally psychology. So his mirror self will reflect one of those other earlier choices—say, history.

His philosophical orientation in college was that of a pacifist. He believed that nonviolence of the kind advocated by Gandhi was the only way for the world to solve its problems and soothe its hatreds. But earlier he had been a fighter, so that is the temperamental extreme he will use for his alter self.

Further back in his life, he couldn't afford to both drink and smoke. He decided to drink, so now his mirror choice is smoking.

Still earlier in life, when in the eighth grade, he thought about not going to high school. Instead, he would become a carpenter like his father. Because he did go on to high school, his mirror choice is to be a carpenter.

Putting all of this together, and now going in a forward chronology, we are ready to construct an alter life for Sam. After finishing the eighth grade, Sam needed money for cigarettes and other things, so he became a carpenter's apprentice. His fellow workers were action guys, and he grew fascinated with their talk of firearms and explosives. He started going out with them on the weekends, where they'd set off explosives that they had stolen from the construction site. He got very good at knowing just what charge to use and how to place it to destroy something.

One day on the firing range he met an older radical-right woman, a tall blond, outgoing and persuasive. She was a college student, and that increased her allure for him, since he had never been around college women. Soon, she recruited him into the militia movement and talked him into going to college. There she urged him to study history because then he would be able to see the recorded abuses of government before doing something about them.

After college, he knew what he needed to do. He would go to work for the government. Then he would be in a position to undermine it from within. And when the time came, he knew how to use explosives.

That's Sam's alter self, a reversal in almost every way of his present identity. He found it surprising as it began to unfold, a self that looks back from the mirror with almost every feature reversed. To be sure, there's nothing unique about it. On another day of the week it might well have ended as a quite different reflection, with different left and right parts. Still, he learned something from it because it enabled him to see his own choices, his own development, as less rational and more contingent than before. With a few changes in circumstance and decision, he believes he could have been that crazy person in the mirror.

Masking the Self

If constructing an alter ego provides one means of extending the boundaries of self, trying on a mask serves as another. Masks create not just another appearance; they also reveal alternative selves within us, selves that may frighten us or selves to which we resonate. Masks also give us a license to be someone else, hiding the usual self. As such, they are different than makeup, tattoos, and the like. With these forms, we are not hiding who we are, just changing some aspect of our appearance, perhaps to perfect it. But with masks we become someone or something else, and at the same time we hide who we are.

We humans have an endless fascination with masks. We wear them on special holidays—or we may even create holidays for their use. Halloween and Mardi Gras bring out the chance to try on other selves for a brief time. Masks blend easily with the theater. With a mask I take on a role for a little while, become lost in it, and begin to see the world through my character's eyes. When I take on a role, I begin to speak with my character's tongue and say his words. Then my ears hear his voice, and my eyes see his face in my reflections, especially on ritual days like Halloween and Mardi Gras.

I'm watching a group of children in a Halloween setting, trying on masks. Jeannie has a wolf mask. She pulls it over her face with impatient excitement and then runs to the mirror. "Grrr," she growls as she works her hands in front of her like paws. "Grrr, look at me, grrr." She moves the mask back and forth to note the changes in the mirror. I can see her from the side, so I can tell that she is trying to make faces under the mask, to make the mask take on her expressions. She needs a better, smarter mask to do this, one that responds to the muscles of the face and the ultimate control of the mind behind those muscles. But she has made a good start at becoming the wolf she portrays. Perhaps because of her wolf role she will even grow into an advocate of wild creatures—or she may become a woman who runs with wolves.

Greg pushes her aside so that he can see himself. He is Batman and flourishes his cape. "I'm out to beat the forces of evil," he intones, "I'm going to get the Joker." He pulls down the mask so that he can see his real face in the mirror. He does this several times, alternately revealing and concealing his own face, rapidly swapping faces with Batman and Greg. He seems to be studying just what it is that makes him different from Batman and vice versa.

Fawn dances over in ballerina costume, touching a magic wand to Greg's head. "You're a frog," she says. "No, I'm not," he answers. "I'm Batman." He is confident in his assumed character, but Fawn doesn't like it and is trying to use the magic of her costume, her mask, to have him change into something else.

In another place, Cliff, an eighty-nine-year-old man, is getting ready for a Halloween party at the local senior center. He has on a GI surplus olive-drab jacket. I ask him who he is going as. "Bob Dole," he says. "See, here's where I got shot." He points to a hole in the jacket arm. Now he puts on a knit hat onto which beer can art is sewn. To top it all off, he also has a Batman mask. A bit of the ridiculous blended with folk art at the same time. "Tell me about the idea for your costume," I ask. "It's easy," he says. "Dole is the scariest guy I know." His eyes flash; he is a dedicated Democrat. He has transported himself, transmuted himself, into another person: a presidential candidate he doesn't like. This is a different kind of becoming, not that of an admired one but a parody of one not admired.

June is a former student of mine. She made her living as a New York artist before coming to New Mexico. Her specialty is mask making—wonderful, fantastic acrylics of colors and spangles and feathers and beads.[4]

For June, a mask takes people to a different place. Not just in the world but in yourself. Some place you've never been to before. A mask can surprise even its creator. One time June was selling her masks in New Orleans, inside a theater where the actors were wearing masks she had designed. After the production she started back to her hotel. She took a shortcut through an alley, which she probably shouldn't have. She heard a noise off to the side. A man was crouching in the darkness underneath a window. Her heart jumped up in her throat. He turned in the shadows, sprang up, and faced her, and fear turned to mystery and awe. His eyes were green, and his face was goatlike—Pan. He was wearing one of her own masks. They stared at one another. Then he turned and walked away. The power of her own mask had staggered her.

That is the point. Masks fascinate because we cannot predict their effects on our appearance or on the others who view us. According to June, we wear a mask because with it we enter another realm of existence, another state of mind, and for a while we impersonate the gods. But when we're lonely, a mask also acts as a friend, an imaginary companion, one who helps fill the loneliness. An artifact that transports us to the gods and acts as a friend—how could we ask for more?

Each age has its own masks. In our time a mask may take on nonphysical forms. In the privacy of his office, George sits in front of his computer screen, peering deeply into electronic space, looking for someone with whom to jointly resonate electrons. Simultaneously, he is in a virtual space, an Internet chat room, where numerous keystroke conversations take place. A person who calls herself Poet interests him. He invites her into a private room where they can talk on the screen without the interruptions of others. She is twenty-four, an editor for a big publishing house that does romance novels. She has mixed feelings about her job. On the one hand she thinks fantasy is important, but she is not entirely sure about the value of romance-novel fantasy. She hates science, loves rock music, and is a sensual dancer.

Since George wants to continue the conversation, he begins to assemble a self to fit the occasion and be of interest to her. He says he is twenty-five (a big lie), a stockbroker with a big salary (an even bigger lie), who shares her interest in poetry (true), and rock music (false—he hopes she doesn't call him on this). As he spins out his character to her, he begins to get into it. He talks about his favorite poet, Rilke. But when she asks him about his favorite rock lyrics, he hedges by telling her that he's trying to compose a song of his own. He makes up one on the spot: "I'm a poet lost in numbers. I'm yearning to escape the covers of my spreadsheet. I'm wrapped tight in it. I'd like to open an account with you. . . ." Bad stuff but done off the cuff, and it seems to deflect her question about rock lyrics.

Along the way, she says something in text that makes him wonder. Is this really a woman he's sharing electrons with? He asks a question about feminism that a person such as herself ought to know. She disappears from the screen. This interesting, passionate, smart young woman was probably a fifty-year-old truck driver with a beer gut and a slightly philosophical mind. Deceit knows no bounds. What is the world coming to? He, too, logs off.

Sherry Turkle, a psychologist and philosopher of Internet connections between people, points out that deceit is easy on the Internet because everything about you is typed text.[5] You are an abstraction of text. No one sees your body, hears your voice, senses your hesitations. You can portray yourself as anything, provided that you are believable in the typed word. Is this deceit, or is it only a trying on of other selves? After all, deceit is harmful, while trying on another self is just a harmless thing to do, an entertainment of the moment or perhaps a way of growing. And when I do it, I'm growing. When you do it, you're trying to deceive me.

Masks provide a good way of trying on another self for a short while. They transfigure identity briefly, and it is an easy matter to take off a mask and return to your previous self. The only lasting effect might be someone else's memory of your own silly behavior while you were wearing the mask. Hopefully you haven't done anything too disgraceful. And if you have, maybe no one will know it was you. The mask acts as a license to be different. Instead of traveling to a far-off land to act out and try on different selves where you will not be known, a mask is a cruise of the imagination here and now. Easy and reversible.

Constructing one's own mask is a way of seeing into other windows of the self. Consider the construction of a Janus mask. As the Roman god of doorways and gates, Janus had a double face, one that looked forward and another that looked backward. For present purposes, the backward-facing mask is what I have been; the forward-facing mask is what I want to be. Using clay, I try to fashion my self as I appeared in the past and also as I will appear in the future.

If I am not good at clay or sculpting, I can make my Janus mask from words. I go through a thesaurus in the section on personal characteristics and list words that most applied to me in the past (perhaps separate listings for ten years ago, five years ago, presently). And then I pick the words to describe myself in the future (say, five years from now, ten years from now). For example, in the past I was: shy, unconfident, gangly, stubborn, musically skilled, and snobbish while being unsure of myself. I want to reverse these characteristics to find a mirror self for my new persona. For my forward-pointing face I will be: friendly, confident, graceful, open to ideas, uninterested in music, a sympathetic conversationalist, confident, and thoughtful.

Noting the difference between my back- and forward-pointing faces, I may wish to describe and analyze the shifts between the two. What will I need to do to get from the one to the other? Will this be easy or difficult, silly or worthwhile, valuable or foolish? As I do this, I think about how masks function to connect my past, present, and future. Janus comes to life as I see myself in him, first in one face and then in the other. In the words that began this chapter, Janus has become part of my expanding, distributed self.

CREATING ANOTHER SELF

Whose happiest days were far away through fields, in woods,
on hills, he and another wandering hand in hand,
they twain apart from other men. . . .
Another self, a duplicate of every one, skulking and
hiding it goes. . . .

— WALT WHITMAN, *Leaves of Grass*

The empathy and personification systems make their presence known in early doll play—by which I mean the broad
category of teddy bears, rag dolls, toy firemen, Barbies, and Tamagotchis. A child playing with these inanimate toys projects human
feeling into their forms and embodies them with human characteristics. In addition, imagination constructs the stage on which a
doll performs.

In a typical scene, a little boy is playing with a toy fire truck in
the living room. The truck is a wooden one, and only by the most
generous interpretation does it look like an actual fire truck. The
firemen on the truck are wooden pegs with painted faces that are
inserted into holes. They don't look much like real people, either.
The boy is moving the truck with one hand, and with the other
hand he is pointing a hose held by one of the wooden firemen at
the furniture, all the while making hissing sounds as he squirts
imaginary water on an unreal fire. While the boy's muscles propel

the truck and his imagination pumps water through the hose, his voice gives sound to the water streaming over the raging fire and the cries of the other firemen as they point the hose at one part of the cushion and then another.

In his small corner of the living room, the little boy has created a microworld, one of reduced scale where the edge of the rug is a road, several couch cushions on the floor are a building that is burning, and he is the master fireman projecting his thoughts and excitement into the wooden peg fireman on the truck. But more than that, there is an entire created world of flames and firemen, the parts of which fit with one another. All are the projections of this little boy's imagination.

To create an entire world out of a few pieces of personified wood and living-room furniture is a remarkable human ability. The true philosopher's stone is not the one that medieval alchemists thought could transmute lead into gold. It is the imagination that converts simple props into fantasy and story.

What makes this possible? An easy answer is physical resemblance. According to this explanation, a good toy and its context should closely resemble the real situation, as perhaps a lifelike doll resembles a real infant. The resemblance strategy of toy manufacturers—and the parents who buy the toys—is to make the raw materials of imagination ever more like those of the real world. Thus the fire trucks now in stores are likely to be close replicas of real fire trucks. The firemen on those trucks must also look like real firemen. The same holds true for lifelike dolls, which have become increasingly realistic. This is, in fact, too bad because with close resemblance the imagination does not get a true workout. The more the surface resemblance, the less imagination required.

By the resemblance standard, the little boy's wooden fire truck and peg firemen are poor analogs, indeed. This point is underscored by noting that the same boy can transform a clothespin into an airplane, a car, a doll, or almost anything—a common ability of the mind at play.

Historical rag dolls and corncob dolls do not closely resemble real infants, nor do teddy bears closely resemble real bears. In fact, near resemblance is a product sold by manufacturers and marketers not to children but to parents. That imperfect forms like rag dolls have served to enchant children for centuries should tell us something: Close shape similarity is not required by children in their toys. The required resemblance is of a more abstract form, one of roles and functions. These the child often provides from imagination, an observation that suggests another approach to the construction of dolls and stuffed pets.

Forget physical similarity and instead take role and function as the primary facets of imagination. The result is a new class of dolls, as exemplified by an exciting Japanese import. The Tamagotchi is an electronic flattened egg shape with a key chain to hang from the wrist, a small display window, and three control buttons.[1] Nothing about its form remotely suggests life. It is as far from a lifelike form as one could imagine, neither human nor animal in appearance.

However, a Tam, as it is often called, simulates a number of functions of life. Its back story has it as a visitor from another planet, originally as an egg. When its human owner receives it, he or she uses the buttons to set its clock to coincide with earth time. About five minutes later the Tam hatches: An abstract creature form appears on the tiny display screen. Soon after, it begins to make visual and aural demands (via beeps) on its human owner: It must be electronically fed, given snacks, played with, cleaned up after a mess, administered a shot when sick, and when it gives a false demand—like crying when nothing is wrong—it can be disciplined.

To satisfy these demands, judicious button pressing is required. Thus when the Tam announces hunger, the right button press combination will sate it. The owner may also check on its health by selecting additional button combinations to see its current weight and make sure it is growing or how happy it is. If the

Tam is neglected for a period of more than five or six hours, it will become ill, and it may even die (in the Japanese version) or return to its home planet as an angel form appears on the screen (in the American version).

Of course, it is always possible to restart the Tam and begin the process over again with a new incarnation. But the object of the simulation is to keep the virtual pet alive as long as possible. As a time measure, one human day translates into one year of life for the Tam.

The Tam interests because this minimal abstraction of roles and life functions has a profound effect on its owners. Teenagers—that cold and heartless lot—develop intense attachments to their Tams. Lisa, a thirteen-year-old, was disconsolate and cried when her Tam gave up the ghost and went back to its planet. In contrast, Kevin, another teen, wished aloud that his "damn Tam would die and be done with it" because he was tired of its demands and didn't want to take care of it anymore. But—surprise!—he continued to care for it, all the while resenting doing so.

These are very human reactions to a real pet or a real infant. A Tam's sparse simulation of life takes a firm grip on people. We are prepared for this by our evolution, to invest emotion and care in helpless life forms—or quasi life forms, in this case—with behaviors like those of the Tam. In the language used here, we readily personify the Tam because it strikes a resonant chord deep within us.

Once the Tam has been personified, the empathic reactions required to serve it are so compelling and attention consuming that many teachers have banned them from classrooms.[2] As a result, some students ask a parent to assume the role of Tam caretaker while they're in school, providing their parents with a premature introduction to grandparenting.

Partly to avoid such problems, Tam owners have taken to "cheating." In one form, the owner returns to the time-set screen and stops midway in the process. The Tam may then be left in suspended animation and brought back to life after school. This is like having a sitter take over for a parent to allow respite. Future models of Tamagotchis are rumored to have an explicit pause function for this purpose. For now, it is worth noting that people rarely resort to cheating unless they care about an outcome. That they cheat to keep their Tam alive reveals their caring.

To sum up, the Tam exerts such a strong power for identification and obligation that it provokes real grief when it inevitably dies or returns to its planet. It is a toy that requires continual attention and interferes with a child's other ongoing activities. It has been banned in schools. It leads children to cheat to keep it alive. Ironically, the emotional power of this small electronic package suggests practical applications: Use the Tam as a test for seeing if a child is ready to take care of a real pet. If the child can handle, say, for two weeks the programmed level of care required by an equivalent real pet, then the child earns the pet. At the high-school level, psychologists are already suggesting that the Tam be used to teach teens about the obligations of childbearing and rearing.[3] Imagination has the power to teach.

Our Monsters, Our Selves

Imagination also populates consciousness with monsters and ghosts. Recently I was at a family gathering in a high-rise apartment house in Chicago. We were out exercising four-year-old M and two-year-old D at a nearby playground. When we returned, we found that the elevator had failed—unfortunate since our home base was on the twenty-second floor and a plane schedule had to be met. We retrieved a flashlight from the car and started to walk up those twenty-two stories. Fortunately for us we had the flashlight because at least half the battery-powered safety lamps in the stairwell didn't work. Apparently urban apartment houses don't seem to take fire codes very seriously.

We were concerned that M and D would be frightened by the darkness. In fact, they were delighted. Here was a great adventure, a great exploration on a darkened stairwell with immense shifting shadows to excite them. "Monsters," M said as he directed his flashlight on a shadow to make it go away. "No, dinosaurs" was D's answer as another shadow loomed ahead. Their voices rose in awe, their little bodies leaned forward in anticipation at each shadow. As we worked our way up the stairwell floor by floor, other people were coming down, and their sounds gave rise to the anticipation of moving monsters. To me some of the people looked scarier than the shadows, but that was probably my own imagination filling in ghosts and demons, the denizens of shadows from my own childhood.

These monsters, dinosaurs, and their relatives were the easy illustrations of imagination. They came without work or effort, and they had a reality all their own for both children and adults. They were benign for us, but under other circumstances they might have been more malevolent. I find it peculiar how easy the vivification process is. A shadow becomes imbued with life and takes on the characteristics of a never-before-seen monster. The noises of people coming down the stairwell become its cries, growls, and sounds of appetite. Instead of being perceived as other natural forms like mountains and trees, these shadows are interpreted as animals, as monster life, and every environmental support from moving shadows to stray sounds is incorporated into their being.

We did not think about it at the time, but we were part of a grand tradition: the telling of ghost stories. One of my favorites is Mary Shelley's *Frankenstein,* which she wrote at age nineteen while she, her husband, the poet Percy Shelley, and friend Lord Byron were on a holiday in Scotland. For amusement, they took turns telling ghost stories. Mary Shelley's Victor Frankenstein is the original mad scientist, and he fashions a monster out of miscellaneous body parts. The monster comes to life and for a while is Victor's servant. But then the monster becomes lonely and wants a mate, and Victor refuses, realizing the danger of a monster with a mate and all the population problems that would entail: "I behold the wretch—the miserable monster whom I had created."[4] In pique, the monster wreaks revenge by going on a killing spree.

A monster, like a human, wants love and a mate. Moreover, he will kill to get what he wants. Mary Shelley's monster is the ultimate personification of evil. The source for her idea, the source for her monster, is within the human breast. Our monsters are ourselves, the projection of our own fears.

Imaginary Friends

Created monsters are not the only companions of a society-seeking mind. Imaginary friends also proliferate consciousness and provide us with companionship. And not even external supporting shapes, such as shadows and sounds, are needed. Imaginary friends may spring entirely from the weave of the storytelling brain, yet they may take up physical space. Ben is five, and he has an imaginary friend named Oscar. Ben holds earnest conversations with Oscar, and when it's dinnertime, he sets a plate and silverware for him. At first his parents worried, but then they got into the spirit of things. "Ben, when you have a dinner guest to the house, it's important for you to take the lead and help prepare dinner. A responsible host does that kind of thing." Oscar persisted for a year, and then one day he was unable to come to dinner. Why? "Oh, he had to go on a long trip." Oscar never came back from his trip.

Imaginary friends are far more common than adults think.[5] They are usually nothing to be worried about as long as the child has other social relationships. They provide a confidant, a way of talking out problems and options. Furthermore, as Ben's mother discovered, they can be recruited for turning a child into a genuine helper in the family. Yes, a good host prepares dinner for his guest.

Imaginary friends go beyond the workings of the young child's imagination. Teenagers and adults often have a counterpart in an imaginary lover. The entire genre of romance fiction may be built on the foundation of imaginary lovers. In their best form, these novels help us imagine what an ideal romantic relationship should be. The reader constructs an illustrated fantasy as she reads and projects herself into the tale. In their most positive expression, these stories and their accompanying imagined illustrations fill the void of loneliness and show the way to overcoming natural shyness. All told, much can be learned from these loves of the imagination.

More at the fringe of culture than the romance novel are the sex catalogs and ads of adult bookstores and the similar Internet Web sites. They reveal a rich variety of objects for aiding erotic fantasy and facilitating the creation of imaginary lovers—adult teddy bears for the erotic imagination.

Like any invention, like any capacity of the imagination, a potential downside hovers close by. If the sexual teddy bear and the creative scripts that accompany it replace a normal adult connection between two people, then imagination draws entirely into itself instead of reaching out to others. More optimistic is the possibility that these devices serve as benign teddy bears, and as such they give confidence to the user and a chance for building a foundation from which he may reach out to others. In that case, the devices are part of a bridge that connects imagination and community.

Imaginary Escapes and Journeys

Sometimes the imagination needs neither monsters nor friends— it needs escape. When work becomes overwhelming, I imagine being somewhere else. My body is transported to a desert island, to a mountaintop, to a rafting trip down a white-water river. I am escaping the *here-now* to enter a *somewhere-else.* If reality is all we have, then we don't have very much. When creating a self, we also need to create places in the imagination to flee to.

Imaginal escape not only occupies daily life, it has expression in literature and art. My favorite example is James Thurber's "The Secret Life of Walter Mitty."[6] A hero self is cloned from the body of an everyday self who lives a boring life. The story opens as Commander Mitty pilots an eight-engine navy hydroplane through a dangerous storm. Ice is forming over the plane. It's nip and tuck as to whether they'll get through. At this point Mitty's fantasy is fractured as his domineering wife yells at him that he is driving too fast. It becomes clear that Commander Mitty is an imaginal creation, an alter ego escape artist for a man who leads a humdrum, browbeaten life.

Mitty drops his wife at her hairdresser's and goes on to run errands. Soon he has once more embarked to the land of fantasy, where he is now a surgeon performing a difficult operation. A life is in his hands. Then . . . once again he is interrupted by something more pressing in the world of the waking. He bumbles through it as he does with all that is real. And when the real becomes too intense, he again becomes a pilot, but this time one in combat. He is about to begin a suicidal mission. He tosses down a glass of brandy and takes off on a death-defying mission. Suddenly Mrs. Mitty pokes his shoulder, and he is forced to land quickly. His final escape begins with him leaning against a wall as he once more waits for his wife. As he presses his weight against the wall, he realizes he is about to be shot by a firing squad. Gallantly, he refuses a blindfold. The firing squad takes aim. . . . The ultimate escape from the real world.

Here is another tale of imaginal escape, this time from the pictorial arts. Remedios Varo, a contemporary Spanish-Mexican artist, is known for phantasmagoria.[7] For example, in the painting *Celestial Pablum* she has the crescent moon inside a birdcage. Outside the cage, a woman grinds starlight and spoons it up to feed to the caged moon. As I interpret this work, a human—the woman— tames and nurtures the moon as a natural form. In another work, *Solar Music,* a woman covered with a fern cape stands in a forest clearing. In her right hand she holds a violin bow while the other hand fingers rays from the sun. She is working the bow across the sunbeam strings. I read this work as an advocacy of human harmony with nature, but I am sure many other interpretations are possible.

Still another wonderful work of Varo's art, *Embroidering Earth's Mantle,* is an example of the community-seeking imagination, a self creating other selves. An autobiographical triptych painting shows the development of a young woman. In the first panel a number of women on bicycles move outside a building that looks like a nunnery. The women look straight ahead, no deviation to the side— except for one woman whose eyes are exploring, perhaps seeking an escape, as she looks discreetly toward the viewer.

In the second panel the same woman is in a tall tower. She and other women are embroidering a large cloth; the result is a tapestrylike form, a narrative on fabric. All the women are presided over by a stern-looking monk. The young woman in question has her tapestry flowing over the edge of the tower. Close examination reveals that the design of the tapestry contains trees and a house. In fact, the tapestry itself forms the landscape around the tower. The woman is creating a world outside, and in one corner of her tapestry is the image of a young man that she has embroidered into the cloth.

In the third panel is the young man, the imaginary lover of her creation. Now she stands next to him hand in hand as they float away together in what resembles an upturned umbrella vessel. Out of a humdrum existence the young woman has created an imaginary landscape and world, populated it with a mate, and they escape together. We all need ways of escape, imaginary places to go to, and a friend to hold our hand as we leave the here and now. Imaginary friends are not just for children.

To summarize Part II, when we lose social connection, we become aware of self in new ways. We preserve self by constructing membranes around us, and in the face of rampant change we do well to be steered by the unity system. Our memories, dreams, and other experiences are not pure and raw; instead, they are crafted, altered, and fit by the tailoring of an interpretive capability or system. To confront a changing and stressful world, to seize the opportunities it offers and avoid some of its damage, we have the capability of contracting or expanding our sense of self, once more to fit the occasion. Empathy, another great system of self, connects us to others. Personification, a close relative of empathy, enables the construction of models of the inanimate world that are based on human characteristics. At times we all want to be someone else, but there are different modes of doing this, for different motivations. We can also do this by constructing an alter ego or a Janus mask. Finally, we sometimes need to escape to the imagination where we create an imaginary friend or lover.

PART III

Creating a Spirit

[I]t is absurd for science to say that the ego-tistic elements of experience should be sup-pressed. The axis of [subjective] reality runs solely through the egotistic places. . . . To describe the world with all the various feel-ings of the individual pinch of destiny, all the various spiritual attitudes, left out from the description . . . would be something like offering a printed bill of fare as the equiva-lent for a solid meal.

—WILLIAM JAMES, *Psychology: Briefer Course*

How do I fit in the universe? Where am I going? What am I ultimately connected to? The answers to these questions coalesce within us and create our sense of a spiritual self. *Spirit* comes from the Latin *spiritus* meaning "breath." As such, it is the animating force, somehow separate from the body but of it, too. Figuratively, we take in spirit by breathing in and pass on spirit by breathing out. These elemental acts associate us with the sacred and the mysterious of the larger cosmos. That part of us that senses the sacred, something that is not easily reducible to matter and flesh, something more than body and more than the persona we construct for ourselves and for others—that is what is meant here by spirit, this direct experience of something more.

The spiritual self is present in religion: a need for a set of beliefs regarding contact and blending with the unseen that sometimes takes place in prayer, ritual, or in communion with the symbols of mystery and the infinite. But the spiritual is by no means limited to manifestation and belief in traditional forms of religion. Often, spiritual forces within us show themselves through a sense of purpose. The spiritual self is evoked and filled with awe by sunsets or the birth of a child. To create a spiritual self, we seek a meaning in life. We may find that meaning in everyday pursuits or in totems and fetish forms or in communion with nature. We may construct meaning and a spiritual self by selecting among the beliefs and practices of the world's religions, inventing new spiritual beliefs and gods. Finally, we extend ourselves beyond body and persona by creating a conception of afterlife or what I have termed the *afterself.*

BELIEVING IN SPIRIT

The thin red jellies within you or within me, the bones and the
marrow in the bones. . . .
O I say these are not the parts and poems of the body only,
but of the soul,
O I say now these are the soul!

—WALT WHITMAN, *Leaves of Grass*

For many people, the absence of spiritual belief is like a missing identity; there is a void, something to be filled or restored. Belief itself runs a gamut, from the fiery prophet to the reasoned position of an agnostic or an atheist, all of them committed to some view of the world. Off the spectrum of belief altogether is the person of unkempt purpose, one who has no conviction to guide life. The nature and justification of belief are our immediate concerns, where we will contrast the views of the evolutionary biologist and cultural provocateur Richard Dawkins with those of William James. Later we will address the transformation of belief as it occurs in conversion.

Richard Dawkins argues that religious belief is a virus of the mind, analogous to viruses of the body and computer viruses. In his view, a belief in god is like a computer virus, except that it inhabits the mind.[1] Just as computer viruses are harmful to useful programs, so, too, is the god virus harmful to the mind. Explaining why religion has a powerful hold on the mind, Dawkins argues that it is due to the natural processes of evolution. To live, a child must readily absorb information from parents and culture; in a dangerous world rapid learning is the road to survival. "So it's understandable that Darwinian natural selection would have built into the child's brain the rule of thumb, 'Be fantastically gullible; believe everything you're told by your elders and betters.' "[2]

Dawkins sees no useful social function for religion. Children are "easy prey to Moonies, Scientologists, and nuns. Like immune-deficient patients, children are wide open to mental infections that adults might brush off without effort."[3] Being gullible presents its own pitfalls. It makes one susceptible to mental parasites, false beliefs like: "You must believe in the great juju in the sky." Viruses of the mind undergo their own selection, and like all successful viruses they have a way of avoiding the defense mechanisms of the organism. The religion virus whispers to the child, "If you don't believe in this you will go to hell when you die." The religion virus also has a way of propagating itself: One gets special points in heaven by converting other people to orthodox beliefs. Thus the virus succeeds by duplicating itself and then carrying out its instructions for false belief in a new mind.

For Dawkins, faith is the primary symptom of a religion virus having taken over the mind because faith asks for acceptance without evidence. To protect ourselves we must embrace science because, in contrast, it draws on vigorous standards of "testability, evidential support, precision, quantifiability, consistency, intersubjectivity, repeatability, universality, progressiveness, independence of cultural milieu, and so on." The virus of faith spreads in the absence of these standards.

This is a strong indictment of religion, one that must be placed in historical context. To counter similar reasoning in the late nineteenth century, William James developed a contrary thesis in *The Will to Believe* and related writings.[4] James claimed that many choices must be made in the absence of compelling evidence, that these choices are consequential in their effects on our lives and to not make them is its own form of folly. For example, what is wrong with thinking that one will recover from an illness, even if there is no evidence directly supporting such a belief? What is wrong in thinking through years of marriage that one's beloved will persist as the most admirable person in the universe, a belief for which there is also a lack of evidence?

From examples such as these James goes on to argue for the right to religious faith, a belief that need not be founded on evidence of the senses. Admittedly, this is a large step away from his other examples, which seem more grounded in experience, but for James the criteria of belief are not correspondence to evidence but to the pragmatic consequences of those beliefs: Do they aid in one's conduct? Do they help guide one through illness and the travails of life? If they do, the faith is justified. James's pragmatism seems closely linked to the universal folk psychology that guides us all through life.

James knew of these issues firsthand. After finishing medical school in his late twenties, he slipped into a deep depression replete with suicidal thoughts. The path out of his affliction came from an argument for freewill, from the French philosopher Charles Renouvier:

> I think that yesterday was a crisis in my life. I finished [reading Renouvier] and see no reason why his definition of free will—"the sustaining of a thought because I choose to when I might have other thoughts"—need be the definition of an illusion. At any rate, I will assume for the present—until next year—that it is no illusion. My first act of free will shall be to believe in free will.[5]

While free will is contrary to many scientists' view of the world, the self seemingly operates as an agent who reaches decisions and freely makes choices based on volition. If so, this raises the conundrum of why an evolutionary process—itself a mix of deterministic and chance events—would lead to the development of a mind that is quite convinced of its own volitional freedom and control. James was well aware of this seeming paradox. His observation was that any complex philosophical question afforded so many viewpoints and so little basis for choosing one over the other, the only way to proceed with life is to make a choice based on something with no better designation than faith. Once the choice is made, life begins to fall into place and have meaning.

For counterclaims such as Dawkins's—one ought to believe only where there is perceptual evidence, and science is much more appropriate for coping with the world than religion—it is useful to consider how that presumed best arbiter of reason, science, is arbitrary. Many people think of science as the self-evident way of approaching nature and problems, but it has not always been so. Modern science, as distinct from craft and technology, is a mere twenty-five-hundred-year-old infant with Greek parentage. When looking to science's structure, what is revealed is a series of components cobbled together, each with its own ancient tradition from outside science. The following list indicates each component with a likely origin:

- Description, from narration and storytelling.
- Counting, from the commerce of livestock and coins.
- Measurement, from agriculture and surveying.
- Explanation based on unseen entities, from magic and religion.
- Prediction, from practical affairs and soothsaying.
- Causative action, from the immediate action-reaction experiences of the everyday world.
- Experiment, from a blending of perception and the logic of sameness and difference.

These ancient ingredients blended together form the basis of modern science. To be sure, science has abstracted from them, generalized on them, made great improvements and where necessary added and deleted features to them, and fine-tuned them to near perfection. Together they have given rise to a set of methods that generates knowledge at an unprecedented rate. Is science therefore an arbitrary structure, just like religion?

Yes and no. While science is itself a cobbling of other procedures, there is more to science than just combining the different procedures because in combination those procedures give rise to emergent capabilities, not present in the components, that allow for:

- Deeper understanding of the basic building blocks of nature than surface perception can possibly yield.
- Discovery of unanticipated phenomena and causes, particularly those beneath everyday perception.
- Predictive power undreamed of by magicians, soothsayers, and storytellers.
- Applications that are beyond the imagination of an earlier generation.
- A beauty of theory and result for which theologians would pray.
- A centering of us humans between the universe of cosmology and the microuniverse of atomic matter.
- Powerful new weapons for killing one another, from spears to mustard gas to nuclear bombs and biological warfare.

Most of these emergent capabilities speak for themselves and promote our understanding of the world. The last one—better methods of warfare—falls out of a deeper understanding of the world just as surely as science's more benign forms. The lesson is an important one: What is powerful enough to change the world for the better is likely to be powerful enough to change it for the worse. These new capabilities, then, take modern, systematic science far beyond the ancient origins of its components. And at some level of abstraction science and religion share a basic structure: a composite of ancient ways of knowing and acting that seek to understand the universe and our position in it.

In fact, religion is much older than science. Just how old we do not know, but possible ritual burials date to one hundred thousand years ago. Certainly such burials were taking place by fifty thousand years ago.[6] And the great cave paintings, beginning more than thirty thousand years ago, may well have had religious significance. These observations indicate that what we now call religion is a cobbling process of its own, with ingredients such as:

- Sensations and feelings of the sacred and mysterious; apprehension of holiness as distinct from the profane nature of the everyday world.
- Origin stories that center the self in the universe and provide a context of meaning.
- Unseen forces that shape life and the universe, either as gods or impersonal forces.
- Purpose in life, values.
- Unity and harmony.
- Ritual and ceremony.
- Moral systems.
- Social control and community organization.
- Prayer or supplication in different forms.
- Aesthetic elements, art, sculpture.
- Passage rites for birth, fertility, death.
- Sacred texts.
- Priesthoods.

Like science, when all of these are blended together, they exceed the sum of their parts and create an emergent form that shows resilience and personal grounding that help people:

- Dedicate their lives.
- Heal their wounds and salve their pains and loss.
- Reach out to help others.
- Fight, die, and become martyrs to defend their beliefs.
- Kill others with different beliefs.

Again, most of these emergents are self-explanatory. As with science, the last aspect again indicates that any invention powerful enough to do good is also powerful enough to do harm.

When we compare the cobblings of science and religion, noteworthy differences become apparent. Science generates knowledge and builds upon itself in ways that religion does not. Yet from an evolutionary perspective, religion is a more natural and more successful structure than science. It is more natural because it has existed for a much longer period than science, and it is culturally universal whereas science is not.

In addition, religion may be more successful in evolutionary terms. If religious people have more children than scientists, they get more of their genes into the next generation and come out ahead on evolution's scorecard. So when the evolutionist Dawkins—good scientist that he is—decries the superstition of religion, its irrationality, banality, stupidity, and gullibility, he may be ignoring the primary move in evolution's game: the passing of genes to the next generation.

As with any surprising result, the interpretive mind wants to contextualize it. The scientist will claim that the apparent genetic advantage of the religious person is terrible and the seed of a decaying civilization; the religious person will claim that his or her genetic advantage just proves that religion is a superior system to science. The rest of us may wish to step back from the fray and note the common truism that evolution does not make right, that civilizations have developed other means of keeping score: money, power, social recognition, morality, and justice, to name but a few.

With the perspective of both science and religion as cobbled enterprises, it is now time to look more closely to one key ingredient of religion, belief—in its most stark form, religious conversion.

Transformations

Spiritual belief is brought into relief by a loss of faith and an ensuing process of conversion. Conversion is a shift in beliefs, often ending in a markedly different state of mind than what one started from. The motivations vary but often are tied to a loss of unity and a subsequent effort to regain it. Thus a crumbling belief system leaves one in a troubled state. The solution is a new belief system and a restored harmony in both inner life and in relation to the ongoing world. Pooling across various dictionary definitions, we find:

> A conversion is a *fundamental change* in which one takes on a new religion, faith, or *belief.* It is the *process or result* of giving a different form or appearance, a change, *transformation*, translation, transmutation, metamorphosis, transfiguration. Closely akin ideas are of rebirth or regeneration. [Italics added.]

And as William James defined it:

> To be converted, to be regenerate, to receive grace, to experience religion, to gain an assurance, are so many phrases which denote the *process, gradual or sudden*, by which *a self hitherto divided*, and consciously wrong inferior and unhappy, *becomes unified* and consciously right superior and happy, in consequence of its firmer hold upon religious realities.[7] [Italics added.]

Putting the two definitions together, one may see that conversion is a fundamental change in belief; it may be a process or a result, it is motivated when the self is divided or coming apart, and the result is a new set of beliefs, a new unity of self. In addition, it is a process that may be gradual or sudden.

Conversion is an interesting mental species, without any clear counterpart among our animal brethren. As James said, "[M]an's liability to sudden and complete conversion . . . [is] one of his most curious peculiarities."[8] Conversion also is related to the identity crisis that is common to youth, but it may occur at any age. Like the process leading to conversion, the identity crisis involves a belief component and a powerful emotional aspect consisting of doubt, lack of self-worth, oscillation of choice, and the feeling of drowning and sinking and rising and going down again.[9] In this regard, religious conversion builds on the processes of a troubled transition from adolescence to maturity.

But other conditions also motivate the process of conversion. When we wonder about the deep questions—Why am I here? Where am I going?—our queries may be prompted by a loss of present faith or by a realization of some deep emptiness, an incompleteness. Conversion's answer is to seek an already existing system of beliefs to be embraced fully, just as drawing in the spirit by inhaling in front of a fetish is thought to bring in the whole animus of another. In its limiting form, a conversion is an acceptance of *all the new beliefs* and a leaving behind of *all the old beliefs* that in any way conflict with the new.

Quite apart from the new beliefs accepted and the old ones left behind is the strength of those tendencies, because in practice conversion ranges from superficial—mouthing the words—to deep—believing with all one's heart. If my conversion is superficial, I may move from being a zealous Marxist who believes that the world works by the force and logic of dialectical materialism to becoming an extreme Christian traditionalist who believes that everything that happens in the world is due to God's will. Of course, that may be simply trading one form of absolutism for another, as the chronicler of ideology Eric Hoffer pointed out.[10] For Hoffer a conversion from Marxism to a hellfire Christianity, or vice versa, is a simple change in surface beliefs while an underlying authoritarian viewpoint is maintained.

The advantage of conversion over forging one's own beliefs is that we find not just a few new answers to old questions but a new system for seeing the world as we acquire a new spiritual self. Indeed, a deep conversion takes place when an old way of seeing and responding to the world undergoes a seismic shift in content and in depth of commitment.

The mark of a profound conversion—one that is both broad in content change and deep in conviction—is a seeker who comes back with a different echo in the footsteps and a different vision before the eyes. The experience may reshape the rest of one's life. A new unity of self, a new focus of energy, is evident. Life now moves in one direction—a sharp contrast with the divided person whose each part is in discord with the others.

Unity of beliefs is the ideal, but sometimes people backslide to their old system. Often backsliding is taken to mean superficial belief, shallow commitment. But it need not, any more than a love once sincere can diminish in strength or a political belief can shift over time. Few things human are permanent, and it is unfair to insist that conversion has value only if it is fixed in amber.

The conditions of conversion warrant scrutiny. They may seemingly come from nowhere, but they are often precipitated by crisis. Perhaps I have been a dissolute drunk, say, or a debaucher of the innocent. Then one day I look in the mirror and decide that the face staring back at me is a stranger, one that I can no longer abide or live with. I seek help, find a god, and convert in the process. Or I may be a soldier in combat, starting the night as an atheist in a foxhole. As the battle wages, I begin to bargain with fate and tell whatever gods may be that if I live through the night, I will believe and never again doubt.

In truth, the path of religion and spirit is but one way out of drunkenness, self-loathing, or fear. Many who change their lives do so in ways that are not spiritual, but for various reasons the religious ones seem to acquire more prominence in social memory and the media. In the same way, a soldier in a foxhole may curse a god's existence for putting him there, and on surviving to the morning lose his faith. For similar social reasons, his experience doesn't make it into the spiritual account books. Nonetheless, he, too, experiences a conversion of a sort—albeit a negative one.

What are the precipitating conditions that underlie a deep conversion? As seen from the various accounts, they certainly include prior departures from a unity standard, ones that cry out for restoration:

- A sense of *inconsistency*. I cannot stand myself anymore. Too many contradictions build up in my old life and begin to push me away from it. At the same time, the promise of a new life beckons and pulls. If I just believe X, many of my problems will disappear.
- A sense of *incompleteness*. Disquiet, distress, a sense of imperfection about life are likely initiating points of conversion. If my life is aimless, lacking focus or purpose, a slow impetus builds and projects out the fingers of reaching and seeking. Or I may be plunged into a new experience and find that my existing beliefs are inadequate.

Bridging the chasm between the two lives, old and new self, now becomes my problem. Perhaps I don't completely believe in the new; the old is all I know. The old way offers money, attractions, power but perhaps betrayal of others and self, bad health, and bad conscience. The new way offers promise, but it is interlarded with uncertainty and proffers its own doubts. The gap between beliefs often strains my mental life for an extended time.

A struggle between the old and the new ensues. Push and pull threaten to rend the flesh through the fault line of the body. A battle wages for body and spirit. The opposing forces gather on the field of awareness. First the beliefs of the new are in ascendancy, and then the beliefs of old counterattack. The battle may rage through many sleepless, sweaty nights. The outcome is uncertain, and the stakes are vital. The result is high drama, momentous for the self, as William James would say.

If these are my experiences, I am not alone in the push from an old life and the pull toward a new one. The great Russian writer Leo Tolstoy experienced something like this.[11] A man of wealth with a large estate, he determined that he could no longer live a life covered with a civilized veneer, so he set out to give away his wealth to serfs, simplifying his existence by wearing only the clothes of the peasants. His wife tried to raise their children on the dwindling income of their vast estate. Oh, to have been a fly on the wall during a possible conversation:

He: We must get rid of our wealth to get closer to God.
She: God does not want our children to grow up destitute.
He: Only the simple life is worth living.
She: Your first duty under God is to your family.

Whether that was the conversation, we cannot know, but it was likely a dramatic, conflict-filled one, pitting different visions of faith and duty against one another.

As may be gathered from these varied accounts, belief conversion is not of one species alone, so classification is in order. In the traditional view of complete conversion Figure 12.1a, the procedure is out with all the old, in with all the new. William James described it as being *twice born*. With the new religious experience, usually the acceptance of some god and faith, one's life is thought to be transfigured and a religious rebirth takes place.[12]

The changes in belief may be slow or sudden. Religious fundamentalists and movie directors like the sudden, discontinuous form of conversion—an illumination from on high followed by spiritual rebirth—because the sudden is dramatic while the slow is not. To be sure, a movie representation of sudden conversion may depict doubt leading up to the change, one doubt tugging at another. But the final result is a clear break with the past self, and after the conversion all uncertainty is removed. No problem is seen in adjusting to the new life, in fitting the old self and the new self together.

Yet evidence is lacking to support the idea that sudden, complete conversion is more lasting than a hard-worked-for gradual change in beliefs. Moreover, jettisoning all of the past to accommodate the new means that everything is built on sand; the anchors of personal history and prior practice are absent. The resulting conversion is likely to be precarious. Whatever new wind blows may also blow away the new unanchored beliefs. Indeed, we see this in people who flit from one belief system to another, always in thrall of seeing the one true way—for now. Evidently their conversion is more a matter of style than of deep belief. For these rea-

(A) A COMPLETE CONVERSION

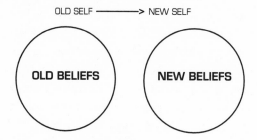

(B) A MINIMAL CONVERSION

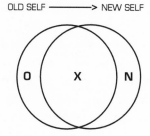

(C) A HALF-WAY CONVERSATION

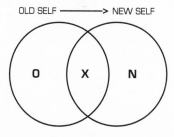

FIGURE 12.1. *The varied forms of conversion. (A) A complete conversion. The traditional view of conversion is that of a discontinuous process in which there is a sharp break with the past; previous beliefs and practices in conflict with the new are left behind. (B) A minimal conversion. One leaves behind a little of the old self O as the new self N takes on new beliefs and practices. But most of another part of the old self X comes along, too. (C) A halfway conversion. Large parts of the old self O are left behind, and other large parts of the old self carried forward X. The problem then becomes reconciling the old and the new so that they may live together in the same mind with a semblance of harmony.*

sons we should be suspicious of sudden, complete conversions, whether in the movies or real life.

Minimal conversion is probably the most frequent form as depicted in Figure 12.1b. A few old beliefs slide away and a few new ones come on board, but most of the old beliefs X persist. This is a minimal conversion because most of the self X is continuous from its old to new forms. Many people would hold that changes such as this should not be considered as true conversion. They are slight, gradual changes in spiritual belief, lacking the criterion of a fundamental shift as suggested by dictionary definitions. Nonetheless, it is useful to have a full classification of changes, and this is likely to be conversion's most common one—bereft of crisis and high drama but important in the gradual growth and change of self. Certainly, tent preachers and Hollywood producers will find little of interest here, even though it probably accounts for most spiritual change.

The halfway form of conversion, of Figure 12.1c, is in many respects the most intriguing. At first glance the complete conversion in 12.1a in the top diagram seems like the most difficult form of change because every important belief and spiritual practice is left behind. But that may be ultimately easier than having to decide what to leave behind and what to bring, as in this intermediate form, which provides the additional difficulty of how to fit the old with the new. The fitting process may well be an agonizing matter of horse trading between two different belief systems. Here is real doubt, and the drama is not just to the point of decision. It may last all of one's life.

In the halfway conversion of 12.1c the daily processes of casting away and incorporation are unlikely to be swift and irrevocable; instead, they promise a slow and agonizing trial with much backsliding. Doubt and uncertainty fill the mind every step of the way, and no sharp point in time marks the conversion. During periods of movement toward the new self, difficulties of incorporation with the old self present themselves. Priorities must be set and values plumbed to determine those priorities. If part of the new conflicts with part of the old, which should be jettisoned? Can one be modified to suit the other? If so, how? During times of backsliding, the comfort of the old ways may beckon.

A deep conversion is a difficult labor, partly because a belief system usually comes in a package, not all of which may be to one's liking. It is also difficult when it requires leaving much of one's past life behind. The package behind exerts its own pull and repulsion while the one in front does so, too. The perplexed soul may unravel in the middle, carrying the two belief systems, one on each side, each pulling the fabric of self its own way.

Other Conversions

If a conversion is a shift in belief, then not all conversions are in the direction of increased spirituality. Sometimes people fall out of faith, as James noted, and other times the same feeling process of conversion is toward more secular ends.[13] This process may be called a counterconversion, or a negative conversion. It, too, may lead to peace of mind.

Here is an example. Roberto, a thoughtful and serious man in his sixties, remembers vividly the moment when he lost faith in conventional religion. He was sitting in a mainline Christian church listening to a sermon when he was eleven years old. All at once a feeling came over him, almost like a revelation, that the minister didn't know what he was talking about, that the sermon was sheer hokum. Up until that time Roberto had considered himself a Christian, knew as many Bible verses from heart as anyone in his Sunday school, and prayed regularly. After this experience he never again returned to his faith. His was a sudden conversion, away from the religious toward the secular. He now believes in a vague kind of humanism, usually devoid of doctrine or large philosophical assumption. He seems as happy and fulfilled as most people. From that point of view, his counterconversion was successful.

Other secular, conversionlike experiences must be noted. The act of falling in love bears a number of resemblances to religious transformation. It may be sudden, deep, and forever, just like the complete religious conversion. To be sure, there may be hesitation in the courtship, but once the arrow of commitment penetrates the heart, there is no looking back. Once again, this is the love story of movies.

Or love may be something that occurs slowly, gradually, with a building of trust and mutual dependency over time. This form of love seems at least as lasting and fulfilling as the sudden outbreak of passion and bonding, just as the slow acquisition of beliefs may be more lasting than a sudden spiritual conversion.

One may also fall out of love, as in a counterconversion. That experience, too, may be sudden or gradual. A woman wakes in the morning and looks at her partner sleeping in the other half of the bed and wonders what she ever saw in this person. How could she have been so dumb? She must get out of this relationship as soon as possible. Then she assembles reasons as to why the relationship has gone sour—but this is after the fact of feeling, a sudden counterconversion of love into something else.

Or the counterconversion in love may be more gradual. The proportion of times spent together subtlety shifts from enjoyment and enrichment to fighting and unease. Or maybe it is a gradual drifting apart without overt conflict. In any case, love does not end suddenly, but it slowly looses prominence and sinks amid the details of everyday life.

The parallels between spiritual and love conversions are suggestive in indicating that the conversion process is not just limited to matters of spirit. That should be no surprise by now because the self is a construction from all the processes and mental materials available to us, cutting across the divisions of body, persona, and spirit.

While it is normal to associate belief and faith with the spiritual experience, there are other vital ingredients. We now turn to one of those, a sense of purpose that gives rise to a feeling of energy and direction ranging from the secular or profane to the profoundly sacred.

Chapter 13

PURSUING PURPOSE

Scaling mountains, pulling myself cautiously up,
holding on by low scragged limbs. . . .
And such as it is to be of these more or less I am,
And of these one and all I weave the song of myself.

—WALT WHITMAN, *Leaves of Grass*

We humans are purpose seekers, more defined by our ability to pursue purpose in diverse ways than by almost any other human trait. Our varieties of purpose constitute one of our more distinguishing characteristics. Almost anything will interest someone. In fact, one of William James's main philosophical principles was pluralism, a recognition of the immense range of human purpose, interest, and valuing. James made that very diversity a sought-after human value.

To be a pluralistic creature, one with many purposes, is to be human. The capability for being purposive may well have evolutionary significance. A striking difference between the human-protohuman line and the apes such as chimps and gorillas is global distribution: Historically, the human line has covered the earth—every continent, every climate, except Antarctica—while the apes are limited to a narrow equatorial belt. This remarkable difference in dispersion points to huge adaptive differences, at least some of which may be due to the ability to take on almost any goal, any food, any landscape as one's own prize, one's own resource, one's own reason for being.

Being purposive is our natural state, made evident by the

unusual circumstance of being without purpose. The evocative and exotic-sounding French word *ennui* means a state of listlessness and dissatisfaction resulting from a lack of interest, a state of boredom and tedium. One who is afflicted with ennui has a hesitant and aimless step. The foot does not come down firmly, the eyes do not look straight ahead, the heart beats faintly and without passion.

But if a person is filled with purpose, she also has passion, direction, and a gaze that points straight. The foot comes down decisively and moves the body toward an object; the hand shows no hesitation in what it grasps. An image in the mind illuminates the path ahead.

Most of us know the value of purpose, but we are not altogether clear what that purpose should be. Some take their purpose from parents or an existing faith. Others must find it on their own. In the latter case, before we have purpose, we may be purpose seekers. Our purpose may be no more than to have a purpose. We may be consumed by the search because we reject the state of ennui and want the decisiveness of those with direction, those who fit themselves into a larger context of life. We want that firm step and fixed gaze, but we are not sure of the way to look, the direction to step.

If being purposive is metaphorically embarking on a journey, then a lack of purpose is equivalent to having a vehicle with inadequate propulsion, its engine defective or short on fuel. Or the steering may be at fault, with the wheels pointed simultaneously in incompatible directions. Also, there is no value in the journey itself, no feeling of well-being associated with it. But when we have purpose, those conditions are reversed. The engine is powerful, there is abundant fuel, all the wheels point toward the destination, and the occupant is joyful because there is value in what will be seen at the end of the journey. Purpose acts as motor, fuel, and steering for the human vehicle.

What is the underlying nature of purpose? To answer this question, I have borrowed a number of concepts from William James's treatment of truth and faith. Then I freely adapted them to the idea of purpose, the most distinctive characteristics of which now follow.

Purpose seizes us, binds us rather than being deliberately crafted by us. It knocks often, and we should be open to it. While we seldom create it, we can fight it off or nurture it. If we are without it, life feels meaningless, unconnected to other things.

Purpose is selective. Because the possibilities of the world and the mind are so rich, we cannot begin to explore them all. To attempt to do so is to wander aimlessly. Selection sets us on track and enables our journey through life.

Purpose should be pragmatic; that is, it should hold out the possibility of practical effects on one's life; it is more than just an abstraction. A purpose faithfully followed should change a life. Pragmatism—the practical—is based in craft, where truth is established in how well a method or technique works in the assembly of a work. The ideas that give rise to a useful work have pragmatic truth; those that are not useful lack that truth. An important corollary comes of this: The criterion for judging a belief or a purpose is not its origin but its result.

Insofar as the self is a work in progress, we must not be obsessed with mistakes, which are inevitable in craft. They are less dangerous than the conservative stance of inaction. As James put it, "Dupery through hope is not worse than dupery through fear."[1] Nonetheless, we want to engage in this craft of the self so as to minimize large and irreversible mistakes. Unlike an improperly fired vessel that is misshapen and cracked and can be discarded, we have only one body and must take care to avoid the worst mistakes.

Purpose is prospective, something we reach out to, that pulls us, rather than a cause in the past that is pushing us. The meaning of life is not the image in the rearview mirror of our ancient past; instead, it is to be found on the road ahead where possibility resides. This is a conclusion in contrast with the evolutionary view, and it is a paradox at the same time. Our evolutionary origins have built a nervous system that focuses on the future.

Purpose is emotive. It commits and focuses emotional energy. Once committed, a subjective vitality and effervescence fills us. To borrow William James's words from another context: Purpose fires us with an acute fever rather than being directed by dull habit; the passion of purpose fuels zest and action.

Purpose is tied to desired emotions. States of well-being and happiness often come as a result of achieving a purpose. Indeed, implementing significant purpose may provide the most direct access to these frequently sought for states of mind.

Purpose places value on actions and results. The strongest purpose is likely to be connected with values: to alleviate suffering, save lives, honor traditions. Value and purpose intertwine to remove indecision. Deep, value-based purpose puts us in touch with the unity system that we have repeatedly called attention to. When things work as intended, we feel a sense of harmony and happiness, almost as if we are part of an unseen order.

Purpose allows us to forgo immediate whims and temptations, eschewing short-term gain for long-term interest. The immediately pleasurable is conquered by the lasting; temptation is vanquished by the valuable.

Having said what purpose is, we should distinguish it from near contenders. Purpose is not necessarily the same as having a goal. Wanting to go to my car so I can get to the post office is a goal. But it does not usually involve the inner seizure and thrall of purpose; its scale is too small and too short-lived, the emotions it arouses too insignificant. Few temptations intervene that must be resisted.[2] In addition, a goal is usually outside of us, while a purpose is inside—to be sure a representation of what is outside but one that is combined with feeling, motivation, and value. For reasons such as these, I think it is useful to separate purpose from goal while admitting that some usages show more than a little overlap.

In summary, purpose is much more than an intellectual process, more than a goal, encompassing as it does inner states of deep feeling, energizing emotion, and the placement of value on actions. All are likely to have effects in life.

The Monomaniacally Purposeful

At one time or another, most thinking people ask themselves: What is the purpose of life? What is its meaning? How do I fit into the larger fabric of life, earth, and universe? On a grand scale, we may go on a quest that becomes all-consuming. More commonly, we try one major purpose at a time until some niche we fit into is found. Or if we are not monomaniacal, we may simultaneously string together many small purposes, like beads in a necklace of pluralistic forms.

We begin our examples of purposive people with an extreme case, someone driven by one overriding monomaniacal purpose, someone who never deviated from a purpose chosen early in life. Throughout history, the wilderness, caves, and mountaintops have provided solitude for those who seek meaning. In these places we experience awe, reverence, wholeness. It is as if the isolation of unusual environments acts as a mirror to reflect our deepest thoughts and bring them into the open. Unusual places stoke the spiritual impulses within us. By seeking them out, we become lost in the wilderness, and we find ourselves.

Reinhold Messner, mountaineer extraordinary, serves as a compelling example of a single-minded purpose quest in unusual environments.[3] From the earliest age, Messner found his life associated with climbing. His father was his initial teacher and source of encouragement. As a child Reinhold sought out rooftops and other high places. His brothers also showed strong interest in climbing, but Reinhold's fascination was extreme. As an adult he has climbed every significant mountain in the world, including all of the fourteen eight-thousand-meter peaks in the world.

Often he chose the most difficult path of ascent, using ropes and other equipment only as safety devices. When standard challenges no longer held his interest, he became a solo climber. He was the first to climb Mount Everest alone, which he did without oxygen. He commonly imposed time tests on himself by beginning a climb at night, with the constraint that he had to reach the summit before the sun struck the ice, melted it, and sent boulders crashing down on him. The time window of safety that he allowed was often exceedingly narrow. Any difficulties whatever and he would have been stranded in the middle of a near-vertical rock face with boulders dislodged by melting ice hurtling toward him.

Why did he do this? Because it gave him a feeling of complete freedom, one that seemed to have a spiritual component. Indeed, the title of his autobiography is *Free Spirit*. Messner is a man who has discovered his purpose: to free his spirit through ever greater challenge and risk. In his devotion to climbing, his dedication and compulsion seem almost religious. Climbing is everything—it guides his life, directs his step, and fixes his gaze. He is most alive in the face of danger, in his case extreme physical danger.

Yet his heroic quest for freedom of spirit has also had its downside. Two of his brothers died in mountaineering accidents, Gunther on a joint climb of Nanga Parbat and Siegfried on a climb of his own when he was hit by lightning. On the fatal climb with Gunther, Reinhold lost four toes on his left foot and two on his right. Nonetheless, he returned to climbing. In addition, Reinhold's wife divorced him because of his compulsion: "Perhaps it was impossible for a woman to live with a madman like me."[4] He returned to climbing. His father told him he had transformed a sport into an "illness."[5]

Is that true? Yes and no. If he were a Mother Teresa who ruined his health through humanitarian devotion by helping the dying, we would not call his devotion an illness. A purpose that becomes an illness is defined by another person's assessment of a goal's worth. The world both needs and suffers from the monomaniacal.

In his own terms, Reinhold Messner's quest was directed toward defining or discovering a spiritual self. To do this, he had to find his personal boundaries, what he was capable of, what his limits were. Then he played at the edge of those limits, constantly pushing them by crossing the boundaries. For the most part he did not do this recklessly but carefully, thoughtfully, with calculation and precision, a variation on the theme of pursuing perfection. Always a greater target was aspired to, a higher peak, a more difficult climb, a more personal way to achieve it by doing it alone and with fewer climbing aids.

The significant point to draw was that he was seemingly monomaniacal in purpose. Everything else was subordinate to climbing. We see other examples of individuals consumed by a single overwhelming purpose. The child prodigy in music who does not wash out but becomes a mature artist is a likely counterpart. Mozart serves as an example. In art there is Picasso, who showed great talent and dedication from the earliest age. But let us turn to the more common case, someone who enters into a series of monomaniacal purposes.

The Serially Purposeful

A more common experience than that of Messner's is afforded by the serial purpose seeker. Such a person may be no less monomaniacal but like a serial monogamist has only one great passion at a time. Jim, a thoughtful, handsome man in his forties with some miles on his face, illustrates this form of pursuing purpose. His account is of interest because it closely blends both secular and spiritual purpose seeking.

Jim's first awareness of purpose was when he prayed as a child. His parents were deeply religious and encouraged and required the daily practice of religion to find one's way. It was a consuming activity for him. However, he remembers little of the details; the content of the prayers and rituals are all lost. What comes back to him are the emotions. He prayed because of fear—God might punish him for getting into the cookies, as he put it. He also prayed because it made him feel good. On a few occasions he even had a state of ecstasy or exultation that seemed to illuminate his path. His life revolved around prayer. It was the guiding purpose in his childhood years.

Then his dog became sick, and he prayed it wouldn't die—but it did. After his dog's death, prayer started to lose its hold. This phase of his life ended—there wasn't any sharp breaking point— at age ten or eleven, maybe. At first he continued to pray because his parents had taught him that that was his reason for being alive, but it became more and more mechanical. Then he stopped doing it altogether. Afterward he remembered being listless and undirected for a while. His parents kept telling him to get interested in something. But he couldn't. He was waiting for—not searching for—his next big purpose in life.

Then it came to him: baseball. He was good at it and practiced for hours every day. He played catch all the time with another boy, each one trying to throw harder than the other. Saying prayers, that was his parents' purpose imposed on him—but baseball was his own first real purpose, one that he chose himself. He wanted to be a ballplayer more than anything. He easily made the team and was some sort of kids' league all-star.

Baseball did much for him. It structured his time and filled his waking hours, both indicators of an effective purpose. Even when he was sitting at his desk in class, he'd think about baseball—how to do a particular pitch, how to pitch to a particular batter, what part of his opponent to overcome. He'd make sketches in his notebook of bats, balls, caps—anything connected to baseball. He'd listen to every game he could. He badgered his parents to get a TV so that he could see the games. He'd dream about making a perfect pitch—a really fast pitch that nonetheless seemed to hang in the air just in front of the batter. Then, just as the batter started to swing, the ball would curve to the inside and drop suddenly.

That was the perfect pitch. He never actually threw it, but he dreamed it often. It was like a prayer—wanting something unreachable just beyond his grasp, wanting it more than anything but not quite having it. Yet baseball was more than a driving purpose. Like any calling, it also involved suffering. His practice was serious, so serious that his whole body hurt much of the time. He pushed himself to the limit and beyond. As he looks back, he describes the experience as a mortification of the flesh to draw on a higher strength.

Notice that his terminology is religious: a calling and suffering to get in touch with a transcendent state, to establish a connection with a higher power, with perfection. He wanted to get better and better. Perhaps it was egotistical, but he didn't think of it that way. The perfection had to be sought; he had to do it. It wasn't egotism—at least not most of the time. He was simply compelled to do what he did.

His fascination with baseball lasted until he was a freshman in high school, maybe age fifteen, and then he dropped it completely. But he didn't experience that old feeling of ennui again. His new interest just pushed baseball out of the way: girls. He simply couldn't get enough of them. They filled all his thoughts. In geometry he'd spend time thinking about the curve in the neck of the girl sitting in front of him, the shape of a leg belonging to the girl across from him. In English he'd compose poems of specific desire to abstract girls. Everything he did was for biology. Girls were like God and baseball multiplied together. Biology took over his mind and emotions.

In college he still had his share of desire, but it came more under control. His purpose now was sexual conquest but not so driven—more like a game. He became a master gamesman. "The dating rituals in college I played out on an imaginary game board—like an erotic chess board. I drifted ever more deeply into the game, moving the pieces with exquisite timing and skill. I thought of myself as a chess master of desire, on a board where I made my own rules."

Then other purposes began to intrude. He worked part-time for a land developer and learned he could make money on land speculation. Soon he ventured out on his own. Before long, he realized that he had a new god called money. His waking hours were devoted to thinking of ways of making more. How could he buy up an orange grove at its agricultural value, plot it with a contractor partner, and then sell it off at many times its cost as a real-estate development?

He became wealthy at an early age. The purpose of making money shaded into the purpose of a game; his conversation filled with game metaphors of scoring and beating the other side. He entered into a land deal not because it was a good investment but because it involved high risk. He craved the danger as much as the money. At about the same time, he started doing risky things like fast driving, bungee jumping, and sky diving. He wanted excitement because he felt most alive when in danger. Danger just enhanced everything and made him feel vital, just as his parents felt when they talked about God, with that inner light in the eye. A little risk or fear helped bring on a heightened feeling, which produced a spiritual overtone. "Risk and fear make you really aware. You push that awareness to the absolute edge. You find yourself by charting your limits or boundaries and then crossing the boundaries into your next self."

An intriguing phrase: "your next self." It reminded Jim of another aspect of himself, his personal relationships. He had always been so consumed with one purpose or another that he'd had no long-lasting personal commitments. One night a girlfriend told him he was selfish and afraid of any kind of human commitment, that he was just a game player. He hadn't looked at himself that way before.

Something that he describes as a revelation came to him. He really knew for the first time how much he had missed by making every passion in his life a game, whether prayer, baseball, sex, or business. He promised himself that he'd change. He would lead a new life, and it would start by sorting through his different purposes, his different compulsions, and trying to achieve some balance among them: They should not be directed only inwardly; they needed an outward focus too. Soon afterward he began to use his financial resources and acumen to help raise money for local charities. He invested in clubs and after-school activities for children. "If you can get kids into art, music, athletics, then you weaken the pull of the gangs and the gravity of an aimless life."

The result of his epiphany was "finding himself." Over a period of several months he experienced joy, awe, suffering, exultation, and a little bit of fear from this new commitment to life and community. "Now that I look back on it, I definitely see this revelation as a kind of religious experience. It connected me with other people and other generations. It made my life purposeful."

The emotions Jim described are the ones that mystics talk about as happening during a religious experience. A nun may speak of being the bride of Christ with similar language. Definite parallels hold between the religious and the secular purpose quest.

Common to all of Jim's different purposive acts is the way they focused and invigorated his life. A sense of purpose gave him direction, made his footsteps firm, occupied his thoughts, and provided a sense of anticipation. This was true no matter how diverse the different purposes, whether praying, playing baseball, or the pursuit of sexual experience, or the making of money. What made the difference was that his last purpose connected him to others.

Another conclusion also stands out: The purpose of a given act can change dramatically over time. For Jim, making money changed from a game and a conquest to a tool for helping others to a genuine commitment to community. The same kind of behavior—say, financial dealing—can have many different purposes, from self-aggrandizement of wealth accumulation to a moral and ethical commitment to children and another generation.

The Pluralistic in Purpose

Purpose does not have to be grand and serious. Sometimes it shades into small things: tending a garden, growing a beautiful rose, learning to play the guitar better. It is in these miniquests for small perfections that most of us find the meaning of life. These are simultaneous purposes in rough harmony with the major parts of life—work, relationship, and personal development. Instead of being monomaniacal in purpose, we find purpose in many small things at once. We are pluralistic in purpose.

Before purpose, the self is receptive to many forms of experience, open in numerous ways at once, both penetrable and permeable. After purpose, the interests of the self narrow necessarily because of focus and direction as we select and intensify some things while completely blocking others. Most of us are time-sharers and cycle between these states. After a period of intense directed activity, we relax and become expansive, open to multiple directions of experience. Then, after too much openness, we once again feel the need to focus, to exercise the searchlight of a purpose that leaves everything else in darkness.

The pluralistic in purpose endure a risk opposite to that experienced by the monomaniacal. They may have too many forces pulling at once. To avoid multiple tensions, one needs a guide to order these many small purposes and quests. Once more the unity system directs us with its questions: Do our actions fit in with our other purposes? Do they link us to a longer time perspective? Do they focus our life in a consistent direction, one that is coherent and directed toward a complete self? Ideally, our purpose quests will be somewhere between improving our tennis backhand and answering Mother Teresa's commitment to the dying. We want our multiple purposes directed not just inward toward ourselves but also to a wider community of caring and love.

These are the broader purposes to build on, whether small or large, to weave with one another into a still larger texture. When we do this, we avoid the narrow extremes of Jim's early obsession with sexual conquest and Reinhold Messner's search for danger and altitude. We may also act as Jim did, redefining a present passion into something deeper and grander in its experience and reach. In the process, money and power may become the spiritual.

What, then, is the meaning of life? It may be a grand purpose: writing a great novel, transforming an area of science, composing a timeless opera, triumphing in a great battle. But for most of us that meaning is pluralistic: trying on dozens if not hundreds of little purposes—discarding some, shaping and holding others—and then threading the survivors together in some coherent, consistent whole. All of it is done with the idea of being as complete a person as possible, one who lives in a present body, a present persona, and with a present sense of spirit, where all parts work in concert and grow together in a more unified way. Sometimes the sense of purpose from these small weavings becomes so broad and so bright that it allows for a spiritual vision of self and the universe.

The Inner Light of Purpose

Purpose is not the end-all of life but a lens providing focus. Like a physical lens, one can look through purpose from different directions, turn it on different objects, hold it at different distances from the eye or from the object. Purpose sometimes comes first, before we do something, and in its most extreme form it comes last, a situation in which we look back over our lives and try to find or establish meaning after the fact.

Most often, purpose is found somewhere in between. We do not start with it, we do not end with it; it comes to us slowly as we work through the complexity of our actions and thoughts, just as understanding gradually comes from the intertwining of action, thought, and feeling.

There is much more to purpose. It also involves finding boundaries and crossing them, seeking limits and then exceeding them. And it clearly involves transformation—in Jim's case a slow kind of conversion of purpose, moving from the sacred to the secular and then back to the sacred.

In an evolutionary setting, human purpose is much broader and changeable than the wired-in motivations we see in our animal kin. No other organism has purposes that range from the biological aspects of reproduction to the sport and thrill aspects of bungee jumping and hang gliding to building a nation or founding a faith.

Where does human purpose come from? As a conjecture, let us see if human purpose seeking shares common characteristics with another biological structure such as passion. The beginning of passion is often felt as a vague nonspecific arousal or desire. This is followed by the search for an object of desire, usually for someone of the opposite sex with undefined physical characteristics or personality. The object of desire is recognized and becomes a specific person when something clicks in place, or there may be a gradual attraction that deepens over time. Romantic pursuit follows. With acceptance there is a persisting commitment to the desired person.

Notice the comparison with the development of purpose. The beginning of purpose is also often felt as a vague nonspecific arousal or unfilled need, followed by the search or quest for an object of purpose, usually for a goal or activity with undefined characteristics. The object of purpose is then recognized and becomes specific when something clicks in place, or there may be a gradual appeal that deepens over time. Intense dedication follows with a persistent commitment to the desired object or task.

The parallel between the two systems—passion and purpose—is substantial, but it may be no more than surface similarity as with the convergent evolution of bird wings and insect wings, which have no common origin. Nonetheless, evolution often uses existing systems to model other ones. A double copy of one system randomly takes place. Then the first maintains its usual function while the second is free to develop on its own. In this scenario, the purpose system splits off from some more biologically based system of passion and takes on its own unique properties over time.

Furthermore, while each system—passion and purpose—is shown to have a sequence of steps, a stage theory is not warranted since one can enter the sequence at different points. For example, no vague nonspecific stage of arousal must precede attraction for either passion or purpose. The principal differences between them seems to be the response system aroused (sexual or nonsexual) and the arbitrariness of the target. Regarding target or object, the purpose system is much more general than that of passion, with targets ranging from the biological to the completely arbitrary, whether golf, gardening, or climbing Mount Everest. It is this very flexibility that has contributed in no small part to our success as a species and our spread across the surface of the earth.

While undoubtedly a biological foundation exists for purpose, a more psychological one is rooted in the storytelling mind. The basic storytelling schema says that someone we care about wants something and has to overcome obstacles to get it. That is a shorthand description of what human purpose is all about.

We can also step back, take an outside perspective, and see our own actions as those of a character in a story. Why did we do what we did? What was our purpose? This is a line of questioning that seeks to understand our own past actions. If we are more systematic, we may keep a journal and intermittently pour over it to discern patterns, meanings, and larger trends behind our actions. Once we see a purpose in our past actions, it becomes easier to recognize in our future actions. We have engaged in an act of tense shifting, moving from understanding our past acts to understanding our future ones. Our reflective capabilities enable us to see ourselves in the story of our life, as a character in an unfolding drama. We are writing our own story.

Chapter 14

FINDING THE SACRED

As I see my soul reflected in Nature,
As I see through a mist, One with inexpressible completeness,
sanity, beauty . . .

—WALT WHITMAN, *Leaves of Grass*

A glorious sunset does more than strike the eyes. Its colors suffuse deeply within the body and mix on the palette of feeling. With the sun and clouds, a sense of the sacred is stirred. As spirit-seeking creatures, we want more of that feeling. And later, when the sun goes down, the moon will rise to present its mysteries and further our awe.

The sacred is characterized by such feelings of mystery and awe—a mixed emotion of reverence, respect, dread, and wonder. The sources of these feelings may be beauty, sublimity, and the extraordinary—something other than the natural or usual order. Finally, the sacred is characterized by feelings of holiness or sanctification, a pervasiveness of spirit, a force infusing objects and events. These feelings have no precise counterparts in the physical world, as would the perceived brightness of light or loudness of sound.

Along with purpose, these experiences of the sacred seem to be the elemental and formative ingredients of the spiritual life. Like purpose, which is secular as much as religious, the sense of the sacred may have both secular and religious origins in the emotions provoked. Recent work on the adaptive nature of emotion in relation to environmental preference sheds some light on the secular side of the mysterious and awesome. Students of environmental preference, such as Stephen Kaplan, Gordon Orians, and Judith Heerwagen, have shown that people possess marked aesthetic preferences for environments that likely coincided with those in which our distant ancestors evolved.[1] Thus the African savanna landscape of scattered trees and surrounding grasslands has both *refuge* and *prospect* dimensions: When danger presents itself, the broad view allows quick evasive action—by fleeing or climbing trees—and it makes visible such prospective resources as game and plants. Of course, the particular balance of refuge and prospect may also hinge on inner states like hunger and confidence in one's abilities.

The emotions surrounding landscape, environment, and seasons—mystery, awe, reverence, apprehension, and terror—likely had survival value in selection of a given environment for living, whether to stay and when to leave. These same emotions may then find other uses, perhaps in religious devotion. We know that an evolutionary adaptation for one function may also take on others. In fact, a very common form of creativity is purpose shifting, or exaptation—employing an existing structure or process for a new use—and this occurs in both evolution and technology.[2] Thus fire might begin by keeping us warm or fending off predators and later serve for inducing the formation of chemical reactions, as in cooking.

The suggestion, then, is that these emotional states induced by the perception of select environments were gradually brought to bear for new uses, particularly spiritual or religious ones. Notice that this is not an argument for reductionism. To the contrary, it is one for a new synthesis, one using existing emotional processes for something altogether different. The sacred as a mysterious property of the world and self becomes a force, an emanation, an energy for which people will dedicate their lives in religious expression. That is certainly not a reduction but rather an expansion of human capability.

According to the historian of comparative religion Mircea Eliade, the sense of something being sacred or holy as opposed to being commonplace or profane is a fundamental distinction that separates the religious life from the everyday life. All objects, events, and actions are sorted into these two classes, the sacred and the profane, with correspondingly different treatments.[3] The sacred is filled with mystery and value while the profane is all of the commonplace that does not arouse similar impulses of value. For Eliade, the sense of the sacred is universal across cultures and across known time, if not for all individuals. This sensitivity is built into the human mind, but its triggering forms vary greatly. When experienced, the sacred enhances or values certain perceptions and their causes, making them more prominent and deserving of attention. As such it may be adaptive, even if we do not always know the precise nature of the adaptation.

Contrary to this argument is the apparent fact that what is regarded as sacred differs dramatically from one belief system to another. But some perceptions seem close to universal in their ability to arouse the feeling of the sacred, the mysterious, the awesome, the holy: sunsets, storms, the birth of a child. Whatever the cause of such experiences, the institutions we call religions carefully cultivate them and embed them in their larger structures.

To add to the puzzle, almost anything can be endowed with the feeling of the sacred—and has been by some religion at some time: mountain, cave, tree, rain, moon, sun, animal, plant, stone, cloud. Moreover, different cultures have varying proportions of experience divided between the sacred and the profane. Modern secular society explains mountains, caves, trees, rain, and so on in physical and scientific terms, with little labeled sacred. Yet Pueblo Indian people—at least the traditional ones—place a large proportion of objects and events in the sacred category.[4] Whole areas of land may be sacred—mountains, rivers, regions. Certain animals and plants are also sacred. It is almost easier to say what is *not* sacred.

Yet the sacred is not outside the self. It is more like color or beauty—an awareness that may be triggered by outside events but is itself a property of mind. Others disagree. The theologian Rudolf Otto employs a concept he calls the *numinous,* closely related to what we have here called the sacred. The numinous, according to Otto, is in the external world. Still another view—one that I prefer—is that the sacred, the numinous, is the result of a fit between the properties of the mind and the world, just as beauty is a fit between the properties of an external form and the characteristics of the mind, just as valuing is a projection of mind onto object.

In any case, once something is classified as sacred, certain actions commonly follow: respect and veneration, devotion and prayer, sacrifice and offerings, rites and rituals. Usually the sacred form is something other than its literal existence, so myth and tale elaborate and contextualize it in the life of the culture. Symbols may also be constructed as when a rock cairn or tree becomes the *axis mundi*—the center of the earth. Places become sacred and are not interchangeable with other places. For tribal peoples, a wilderness area is analogous to a cathedral in Western culture. The emotional life is elaborated on with respect to the sacred forms and takes on new depths of veneration, fear, ecstasy, mysticism, and love. Together these feelings and actions make for active worship. Together actions and symbols serve to consecrate objects and events and make them ever more sacred.

Vision Places

The sacred sometimes manifests itself in a waking or nocturnal dream, in the geography of the imagination.[5] In the Judeo-Christian tradition this is a revelation; in Native peoples' tradition it is a vision. The vision of Black Elk, an Oglala Sioux holy man born in 1863, is well-known but little analyzed for its interpretive and inventive richness. It serves as the counterpart of William James's secular dream, with the difference being that the content is interpreted by Black Elk to have great spiritual significance. Once more interpretation takes the raw forms of experience and imposes value on them. Black Elk spent his entire life making sense of his vision, drawing out its meaning, fitting the pieces together, linking them to his people's experience, interpreting the whole.

At the age of nine Black Elk began to hear voices when he was alone. One day when he was eating, a voice told him, "It is time; now they are calling you."[6] Almost immediately his lower body began to hurt, and soon his legs, arms, and face swelled up. While he was lying down in a presumably waking dream, two men descended from the clouds, each with a spear from which lightning flashed toward him like shooting arrows. They then tell him that his Grandfathers are calling him and beckon him to come. A cloud swoops him up, and the men introduce him to his steed, a talking bay horse. "I looked, and there were twelve black horses yonder all abreast with necklaces of bison hoofs, and they were beautiful, but I was frightened, because their manes were lightning and there was thunder in their nostrils."[7]

The bay horse then takes him to a council of six Grandfathers, one for each compass direction plus one up to the heavens and one down into the earth. The tepee of the Grandfathers is built from a cloud and sewn with the thread of lightning; its door is a flaming rainbow. Various prophecies are put forth, including a predicted difficult time for his people as the bison are lost and the winds of the world fight with one another.

The Grandfathers—the Powers of the World—call him for instruction. Various sacred objects are introduced: a wooden cup full of water that is the sky—so that Black Elk may use it to create life—and a bow that has the power to destroy. He is given a charge: "Take courage, younger brother. . . . [O]n earth [there is] a nation you shall make live, for yours shall be the power of the white giant's wing, the cleansing wind."[8]

The Grandfathers give him a peace pipe from which an eagle stretches; Black Elk is to use it to make the sick well. One of the Grandfathers, the Spirit of the Sky, turns into a spotted eagle and exclaims: "[A]ll the wings of the air shall come to you, and they and the winds and the stars shall be like relatives. You shall go across the earth with my power."

Black Elk mounts his horse in the sky: "I was the chief of all the heaven riding there, and when I looked behind me, all the twelve black horses reared and plunged and thundered, and their manes and tail were whirling hail and their nostrils snorted lightning."[9] "I had been riding with the storm clouds, and had come to earth as rain, and it was drouth that I had killed with the power [of the Six Grandfathers]."[10]

He returns home from his vision: "Then I saw my own tepee, and inside I saw my mother and my father bending over a sick boy that was myself. And as I entered the tepee, someone was saying: 'The boy is coming to; you had better give him some water.' "[11]

Let us examine some of the creative elements of the vision. From the beginning it is interpreted as a sacred experience, a calling rather than as hallucinogenic. The elements are partly based on the real and partly on the phantasmagoric. Men and horses—real objects—descend from the sky, and their spears are flashing lightning, an unusual blending of elements—human, tool, storm—all fitted precisely together on the same size scale, quite different from their normal occurrence on many different scales. A cloud takes on a new function, being able to lift Black Elk to the skies, and a horse talks, blending human and animal characteristics. The Grandfathers are blended with the coordinates of the earth and possess superhuman powers. Lightning becomes the mane of a horse, in a juxtaposition of different forms with different scales of magnitude. In fantasy, the horses wear necklaces of bison hooves, a humanlike adornment on a horse-sized scale.

Magic prevails, once more, with thunder coming from the nostrils of horses and a rainbow acting as a door.

Sacred objects such as the cup of sky, the bow, and the pipe are symbolic tools for the charge given him to fix a drought, to make the sick well, and to fight for his people. Transformations from one form to another take place repeatedly; a Grandfather turns into an eagle, and Black Elk turns into rain—the first from one life form to another and the second from a life form to an aspect of climate that is essential to all life. Building materials are fashioned from clouds, lightning, and rainbows. Throughout, there is a marvelous fusion of human, animal, natural materials, and elemental forces.

Reactions to Black Elk's vision may vary. What William James refers to as the "medical materialist" would see the vision as the result of fever and illness inducing hallucinatory effects.[12] James himself laments such a view and counters that the materialist confuses possible origin with the pragmatic truth of experience. Does an experience shape one's life for the better? Does it ramify into the larger community by helping others? For Black Elk the vision was formative for his entire life, and it aided him in ministering to his people. Even years later he was still interpreting aspects of it: "I know now what this meant, that the bison were the gift of a good spirit . . . but we should lose them [in the time to come]."[13]

Another reaction is that the vision is partly the work of the poet John Neihardt, who edited and saw to the publishing of Black Elk's experience. The claim is that more than Black Elk is speaking here.[14] That claim involves a questionable line of reasoning, with the seeming presumption that Black Elk was untutored, so he could not have produced such a work by himself. Even if true, the result would be like any other religious document that passed through many hands and minds before it touches us in the present. Any rich tradition is likely to suffer or benefit from the joint action of more than one mind. Interpretive elaboration is an ongoing process, one in which new connections and emotional truths are continually sought.

The Navajo Creation Story

The environmental preference studies of evolutionary psychology reveal another fascinating truth. People want orientation; completely homogeneous environments are disturbing, whether featureless deserts or uniform forests. Getting lost or disoriented must have been life threatening to our ancestors, and it still is disturbing nowadays. Expand on that idea: The absence of being lost is being centered, being located in some place. Expand on it again: Being centered also means having a place in time. And still again: For the ultimate centering, a creation story provides for the origin of a people and an explanation of the landscape that surrounds them and how it came to pass. Even more, a creation tale centers a people in the earth and the universe for all time.

The Navajo creation story satisfies all of these needs. It locates a people in a time and place, and in so doing it explains the source of the environment. The Navajo Reservation and close-by areas contain many creature fossils, lava flows, mountains, desert, red cliffs, and a diverse culture of flora and fauna. These are carefully woven into the Navajo creation story.[15] For example, the black lava beds around Mount Taylor in western New Mexico are the blood of ancient monsters. Here the storytelling mind is at work to make sense of one's place in time and geography. The area contains many dinosaur fossils—ancient monsters by almost any reckoning—that must have had blood. There is also a Navajo deity called Monster Slayer. Perhaps he is the one who shed the blood of the dinosaurs, the manifestation of which is the dark volcanic lava flows.[16]

In this account we see an explanation for a landscape feature—lava beds—for fossil remains—dinosaurs—and the creation of a personified deity—Monster Slayer. The entire description is part of a larger belief system of the Navajo's, one emphasizing *hozho,* a blend of beauty, balance, and harmony—not that different from the unity system we have discussed. Inherent in the Navajo creation story is the fundamental idea of relationship, as modeled between the male and female First Man and First Woman and, in later manifestations, Changing Woman and the Sun. Because First Man and First Woman argue, evil is created in the form of Alien Gods or monsters. Then Changing Woman and the Sun unite to destroy the monsters. The harmony between Changing Woman and the Sun ultimately leads to the creation of the Navajo people.

The storytelling mind is pulling together a disparate set of physical features and family relations to make a coherent explanation of the whole. That account centers people in their environment and tells them how to relate to one another.

The Roswell Creation Story

The sacred, the numinous, is valued. People want mystery and awe in their lives and reach for those states when they can. Sometimes that reaching finds an object partway between the sacred and the profane. Let us examine such an instance and then show how it might become a closer approximation to the sacred.

In July 1947 some debris from the sky came to ground near Roswell, New Mexico, not far from a vast military complex, White Sands, where missiles are tested.[17] There is some dispute over the nature and disposition of the debris. The military later claimed it was a weather balloon with an attached platform, part of a top-secret sensing system to monitor nuclear explosions in other parts of the world. At the time of the crash there was a national fascination with flying saucers and aliens. Over the years the event has been elaborated on by memory, imagination, and commerce. Now a significant number of people claim that bodies of strange-looking creatures (aliens?) were taken from the crash. The military denies all this, claiming that later crashes of test planes and crash dummies were the basis for public claims about aliens. To be sure, the time sequence is wrong, but people often mix events together in memory in less than veridical ways.

In short, the government denies anything like aliens, and its denial is taken by the believers as a cover-up. The rationale for the cover-up is less clear—supposedly that the government wishes not to panic people, as would surely happen if genuine aliens came to earth.

Fascinating events surround the Roswell crash, not the least of which is the eager willingness of many people to jump to the conclusion that aliens landed there. Their logic is intriguing. Certain inconsistencies are evident in government reports, and some of the official records are missing—therefore, it must be a vast cover-up, hence it must have been aliens. Lots of logical slips abound in this chain of reasoning. There are numerous inconsistencies on the part of the believers, as well, but for them only the government inconsistencies count for evidence of aliens.

There is a mild plausibility to some of their claims. Certainly Earth is unlikely to be the only planet in the universe with life forms, and governments often lie. But the inconsistencies of the government do not begin to make the case for Roswell aliens. Why would the military cover this up when it would be an incredibly great opportunity for a bigger military budget? One can almost see the headlines: ALIENS ARRIVE, NEED NEW DEFENSIVE WEAPONS. And new defensive weapons would require a larger Defense Department budget, larger armed services, more opportunity for promotion—almost everything that zealous career officers could hope for.

The likely explanation feels somewhere between the two extremes of alien visitation and government denial: The military was engaged in secret tests, and they did not want to talk about them. Or the record keeping and missing records just reflected the normal screwups of a large complex bureaucracy, and they were so embarrassing that no one will admit to them.

By definition, random events are uncontrollable, whereas dealing with another intelligence that plans, schemes, and assembles military forces—like we do—can be dealt with by co-opting, coming to an agreement, or killing. For this and other negative reasons, people want to believe in aliens and their brethren,

246 Creating a Spirit

angels, ghosts, devils, and the like, because a personification can be handled while the random cannot. To put this in more positive perspective, people want myth, mystery, and magic in their lives, and events like the putative alien visitation provide them. When other people try to take away these same inner states, resentment is sure to follow.

Still, important questions remain: Is the Roswell case an example of misplaced awe and mystery, conferred lightly and squandered like love on an unworthy object? How could the Roswell experience be elevated from mystery and awe into something sacred?

The problem in investing in conspiracy theory is one of negativity. We draw into ourselves, fanning the fires of suspicion and hatred, instead of expanding our horizons and feeling the flush of life. In that sense, the mystery of Roswell is definitely misplaced. Of course, if one is a vendor selling alien paraphernalia, then a different perspective is in order: Promote mystery and conspiracy because they naturally appeal, and product sales are in the offing.

The Roswell experience currently offers mystery and perhaps a bit of awe but nothing approaching the feelings of veneration and openness that are often associated with the sacred. Something more must be implanted in the awareness of Roswell for it to approach spiritual significance. How can the storytelling mind amplify this event to make it more ennobling by adding an element of the sacred?

To start with, those aliens need to have a moral message—and an uplifting one, at that. Roswell needs another alien visit in which someone is told that to save humankind we must clean up the environment, love one another more deeply, and lend a helping hand to those less fortunate than ourselves. Only with some strong moral message can we begin to get past the negativity of conspiracy and travel toward more life-enhancing stories. Of course, more factual mooring would also help.

More of the Sacred

If mystery and awe are so important, how can we get more into our own lives without being born into a rich Navajo tradition or journeying to a New Age Roswell happening? Is there a way of getting more of those emotions at the deepest level of feeling? Perhaps. We could start by writing down the triggering events of such experiences: sunrises, sunsets, skyscapes, mountain vistas, the first cry of a newborn, the calm face of a loved one sleeping next to us, the marvelously lined face of a wise old man or woman. These are experiences that connect us with nature and with one another in a long line of history; perhaps they are the original patterns that evoke the sacred.

If so, we can try to amplify the feelings of the sacred by combining separate experiences in varied ways to construct our own sense of a larger sacredness with its own potentially ennobling characteristics. The idea is simple enough, although untested: Just as joining enough bricks can build a cathedral, so may joining small experiences of the sacred produce an even larger sense of it. Perhaps we carry the newborn outside and lift her gently before the morning sunlight in a greeting—a ritual of nature and life blending with one another. In the process, two mysteries combine: new life mixed with new light. We may also have words of our own to add to the occasion, a third element, and our own statement of connection with light and life.[18]

Community and closeness also enter into the sense of the sacred. The experience just described, of baptizing an infant with new light, can be done in a small setting: one infant and one adult. Or it can be expanded in scale to include both parents, the larger family, and perhaps a community of friends, as well. Now we are connected with nature, life, and one another. Together we form a context, and all of us in that collective unit reach out to the flow of nature and time.

Or we might compare the lines of the mountain and the lines

in a grandfather's face. As we do so, we realize how much of the moment called "today" is surrounded by ancient flows and mergings, events and meanings.

In all of these cases, we start with events that singly provide some sense of the sacred. We then build or compose on that sense and seek to amplify the sacred by combining the related experiences. If we are successful, we will gain a greater appreciation of the sacred and of our own role in creating it. Then we will no longer need Roswell because mystery, awe, and the sacred are within us and between us, as nature mixes with us and the people we care for.

QUESTING FOR SPIRIT

*I think I could turn and live with animals, they are so placid
and self-contain'd. . . .*
They do not lie awake in the dark and weep for their sins. . . .
Not one is respectable or unhappy over the whole earth.

—WALT WHITMAN, *Leaves of Grass*

What is the spiritual? It is when we view the world and
ourselves as consisting of unseen and ununderstood
forces that we nonetheless feel deeply. These forces are associated
with our old friends, mystery, awe, and the sacred. Probably we all
experience these qualities, but we interpret them differently. Some
of us equate them with what is most valued, others with what is
superstitious and silly. In the latter group are extreme reduction-
ists, holding that the world should be explained only in physical
terms. Nonetheless, these feelings for the spiritual are real and valued by most people, so whatever their origin, they warrant respect
and the work of understanding.

The spiritual self may not find an existing religious system that
satisfactorily answers its questions. Then the self will have to seek
its own answers. On such a quest, one goes on a journey alone into
the wilderness, getting lost to find the way. The ties of the old ways
are weakened by the isolation and reorganized during the journey.

The quest for sacred or holy forms takes varied paths. Traditional Native peoples often seek a totem or guardian animal spirit to guide them through life. Writing in the last century, the anthropologist Frank Hamilton Cushing sketches the underlying logic.

> [The Zunis] suppose the sun, moon, and stars, the sky, earth, and sea, in all their phenomena and elements, and all inanimate objects, as well as plants, animals, and men, to belong to one great system of all-conscious and interrelated life, in which the degrees of relationship seem to be determined largely . . . by the degrees of resemblance. . . . [A]ny element or phenomenon in nature, which is believed to possess a personal existence, is endowed with a personality analogous to that of the animal whose operation most resembles its manifestation. For instance lightning is often given the form of a serpent, with or without an arrow-pointed tongue, because its course through the sky is serpentine, its stroke instantaneous and destructive. . . .[1]

Just as the shifting of purpose from the secular or profane to the sacred is a kind of conversion, so, too, is taking on the attributes of a totem animal as a guardian spirit. Admittedly the matter is not usually thought of that way, but there are strong reasons for doing so. A package of properties and beliefs is taken from an animal model into one's own system of perceptions and reactions to the world. Any animal species that has survived millions of years cannot help but teach us something of the way of the world and self. The deer teaches of beautiful and agile motion; in a kind of empathic reach, we can imagine being in its body and moving as it does. The hawk instructs in the patience and joy of soaring. We can almost feel the lofting currents of air push us over the landscape and imagine being able to see for miles with a detail unrealized by the human eye.

Here are thoughts related to animals from the Sioux, cited by the ethnologist Joseph Epes Brown:

> Brave Buffalo: Let a man decide upon his favorite animal and make a study of it—let him learn to understand its sounds and

motions. The animals want to communicate with man, but Wakan-Tanka [the Great Spirit] does not intend they shall do so directly—man must do the greater part in securing an understanding.[2]

Lone Man: I have not much to tell you except to help understand his earth on which you live. If a man is to succeed in a hunt or the warpath, he must not be governed by his inclination, but by understanding the ways of animals and of his natural surroundings, gained through close observation.[3]

In such examples the animal acts as a metaphor of flesh, a living model of relationship to the world. As such, that metaphor grows with knowledge of the animal's adaptations and life cycle. Because every existing species has a successful adaptation to nature, much can be learned from its fit with the earth. The animal metaphor of fit, adaptation, relationship, and meaning grows with the study of the animal. The animal becomes a guide to living one's own life. Insofar as the metaphor is an instructive one for humans by showing us useful insights into making a living, it is on its face also an adaptive process.

Unlike the stereotypical religious conversion that occurs all at once and forever, the assimilation of a spirit animal's capabilities come more gradually and build on one another. Only as we observe over time do we begin to appreciate the subtlety of an animal's relationship with the earth, its wisdom and understanding of nature. The spirit animal's powers and ways come to us as we read its characteristics into ourselves and project our own hopes and longings into it. Once again the work of empathy reaches to a non-human form. We extend ourselves as we take in the wisdom of the spirit animal's fit with nature.

The Questor is not passive in this endeavor. He or she must select and interpret animal actions that are appropriate for human use. Later, after the quest, one's sponsor will also interpret what has been experienced, thereby furthering community beliefs and cohesion. Finally, the Questor reenacts the vision through dance, song, acting out, and employing a small object called a fetish—usually a carved stone that is a rough facsimile of an animal such as a bear or a deer. The result is to reintensify the experience, shape it through the reactions of others, and make it a shared communal event. The process allows for individual experience, new information for the group, and a continuity of knowledge and understanding through the group process of reexperiencing and interpreting.

The journey may culminate with the making of the fetish, which is believed to possess characteristics of the corresponding spirit animal. But the characteristics of the fetish must first be projected there by the Questor and the community. The fetish then acts as a mirror from which the user draws a reflection, and its characteristics are employed by the possessor of the fetish to aid in a hunt or for other religious purposes. For example, belief has it that by breathing in deeply as a deer fetish is held to one's lips, the user incorporates into his own body and mind the deer's speed, hearing acuity, and spirit. Like religious conversion, these characteristics of a fetish come in a package, and taking them in is like a large act of receptive empathy—or like a deep receptive mind reading of the deer and its capabilities.

Models of Spirit

Citizens of the industrial world do not believe in fetish animals whose powers reside in a stone facsimile, but, in fact, our modern lives in complex societies are filled with fetishlike equivalents. When we pray to Lady Luck and kiss the dice of chance before rolling them, when we pray to a religious icon asking for relief of suffering or forgiveness from an indiscretion, we are engaged in fetishlike behavior—albeit not based on an animal fetish but on a personified equivalent. In each case the processes and assumptions behind such practices are that of a thought model. Somehow the model embodies aspects of a real thing, and by knowing the model, we also come to know, understand, or influence the hidden reality behind it.

At the very least, the fetish and personification act as a central unity for remembering and organizing thought and action. We have seen that the fetish object is believed to incorporate properties of the animal it resembles. In this sense the fetish is a model. Voodoo dolls are also related to fetish use in their employment of a figure or other model. Once again, a concrete representation—perhaps a model that resembles the person who is the target of a curse or a piece of hair from the person—is employed.[4] Then thoughts and actions of vengeance are projected into the doll, and, according to belief, travel from it to the person it represents. In effect, one's wishes are converted into the body of a victim or oppressor through the intermediation of the model.

The underlying rationale for both fetish and voodoo representations is a kind of animism. Life processes such as intention and hope are thought to inhabit the inanimate—a stone bear or a doll—and then intentions and hopes are thought to pass through the model and influence the target animal or person.

As citizens of the modern industrial world, we do not believe in any supernatural power for fetish objects or voodoo dolls or religious icons. Yet the matter is not so simple, as the following example illustrates. John, a senior professor, found the rationality of his own beliefs called to question several years ago while engaged in a delicate negotiation with a university. The provost had said that his visiting contract was to be renewed, but he received nothing in writing. Then the provost publicly announced his own resignation to become the president of another institution. Despite repeated inquiries, John still had nothing in writing, and he was becoming uneasy. Soon he'd have to return to his regular university, even though he wanted to visit longer. Then a new provost took over—and he knew nothing of the previous negotiation. But if the matter was as represented, he said, there would be no problem. Despite repeated inquiries, however, there was still no word. The new fellow was clearly dodging the issue.

John's wife, Gloria, noticed his escalating unease and arrived at a solution by employing a voodoolike tradition. She bought a small troll doll, put it in a grass basket with a lid, and gave him a supply of stickpins. She had drawn a large *P* on the doll's chest. For every day that John didn't hear from the provost, he got to stab a pin into the doll.

At first he thought this silly, since he was at the skeptical end of the superstition continuum, definitely not believing in voodoo or anything like it. Nonetheless, jabbing pins into the doll gave him an intense feeling of satisfaction, almost exhilaration. After a week of pin sticking he received a letter from the new provost announcing his reappointment. So a little voodoo worked? Yes and no.

John's skeptical mind said this was a lot of nonsense, but it could not quite override the deep-seated idea that the doll functioned as a symbol of the provost and as a connection to him. Hence what happened to the doll also happened to the man: Stick a pin in the doll, and the man will grab his shoulder. But an additional assumption was also needed: The provost would realize that his pain came from not keeping his word and not doing his job. Lots of assumptions here with no basis in scientific fact, yet the quicksand of these assumptions was firm enough for John's hopes to stand on.

The tendency is to dismiss such thinking as silly and superstitious. That is fair at a specific level, but it is a premature judgment when the thinking process is carried to a higher level of abstraction. Far from rank superstition, these same thinking processes make possible an identification with the characters of storytelling and literature. We feel a character's pain and send out our hopes or hatreds to her, even though she is only a fiction. These are powerful processes and form the basis of the story-listening mind that learns so adeptly through fictions.

At a deep level, voodoo dolls also share *some* characteristics with a good scientific model.[5] Push the small, convenient model to influence it and find out what it does, and we can expect the same outcome when we push the large, real thing. Of course, many steps span the difference between the predictions of voodoo and those of a scientific model, so I am in no way saying that voodoo is just like science. But common to both is the deep-rooted notion that a model has a strong connection to reality, that by working with models we can come to understand and influence the course of events in the world. Voodoo may even have an advantage over science in one respect: Feeling good about the actions taken on a model is not officially included in scientific thinking.

Prayers to the Spirit World

Fetishes and voodoo dolls act as concrete intermediaries in communication to a spirit world. Like their more interior cousin, simple hope, they are a mode of communication by which spiritual forces are summoned to one's aid. The prayer of Western religions, absent an icon, is simply a more abstract verbal means of communication because instead of having a model to work through, a fetish or a doll, the practitioner appeals directly to a higher power. That power is usually a personified one, a godlike form with definite human characteristics such as a sense of fairness and an ability to right wrongs.

Prayer itself comes in varied forms of address to the deity. We are all familiar with the relief prayer when we address the higher power to seek alleviation of our afflictions: "Dear God, stop the pain." This is the normal process of hope hitched to a belief in something sacred and powerful. Another common variant is the give-me prayer where we ask for some desired object—a sports team, say, may pray to win before a game: "Dear God, let me win this one for the Gipper." Again, hope is present, but this time it is also hitched to greed and a sought-for personal power as well as team solidarity.

Still another form is the revenge prayer, where we ask the gods to get even for us, to punish our oppressors. The example that follows comes from folklore collected in the 1920s by Zora Neale Hurston, a black woman who knew about oppression; it is a powerful negative prayer, a hope once again but this time for revenge, justice, and a return to balance in the world:

> To the Man God: O Great One, I have been sorely tried by my enemies and have been blasphemed and lied against. My good thoughts and my honest actions have been turned to bad actions and dishonest ideas. My home has been disrespected, my children have been cursed and ill-treated. My dear ones have been backbitten and their virtue questioned. O Man God, I beg this that I ask for my enemies shall come to pass:
>
> That the South wind shall scorch their bodies and make them wither and shall not be tempered to them. That the North wind shall freeze their blood and numb their muscles and that it shall not be tempered to them. That the West wind shall blow away their life's breath and will not leave their hair grow, and that their fingernails shall fall off and their bones shall crumble. That the East wind shall make their minds grow dark, their sight shall fail and their seed dry up so that they shall not multiply.
>
> I ask that their fathers and mothers from their furthest generation will not intercede for them before the great throne, and the wombs of their women shall not bear fruit except for strangers, and that they shall become extinct. I pray that the children who come shall be weak of mind and paralyzed of limb and that they themselves shall curse them in their turn for ever turning the breath of life into their bodies. I pray that disease and death shall be forever with them and that their worldly goods shall not prosper, and that their crops shall not multiply and that their cows die of starvation and thirst. I pray that their houses shall be unroofed and that the rain, the thunder, and lightning shall find the innermost recesses of their home and that the foundation shall crumble and the floods tear it asunder. I pray that the sun shall not shed its rays on them in benevolence, but instead it shall beat down on them and burn them and destroy them. I pray that the moon shall not give them peace, but instead

shall deride them and decry them and cause their minds to shrivel. I pray that their friends shall betray them and cause them loss of power, of gold and of silver, and that their enemies shall smite them until they beg for mercy which shall not be given them. I pray that their tongues shall forget how to speak in sweet words, and that it shall be paralyzed that all about them will be desolation, pestilence and death. O Man God, I ask you for all these things because they have dragged me in the dust and destroyed my good name; broken my heart and caused me to curse the day that I was born. So be it.[6]

The first paragraph is a bill of indictment—what injustices have been incurred. Noteworthy here is not just the physical harm done to the victim but also the harm to reputation and self-image—the persona. Most of the remainder asks for remedies of varied forms, ones to be carried out not on just the purveyors of the injustice but also on their progeny. The final two sentences summarize the whole, emphasize the damage to one's name, and ask for the execution of justice, a restoring of the world to balance.

A question arises: Does prayer have adaptive value? Does it aid in our survival and ultimate reproductive success—or at least our perceived sense of well being? The revenge prayer is closely akin to James's argument for faith. We believe we will get well even though we have no proof of it. That belief may indeed work to our advantage. We believe that our prayer will be answered even though we have no proof. Believing strongly is an act that bestows strength. The revenge prayer collected by Hurston speaks as loudly for catharsis as any of Aristotle's arguments. It is a magnificent indictment and tirade. Just saying it makes explicit the different grievances and their respective priorities. For others in the community, it calls forth sympathy, and it may organize for action. At the least, as any teacher knows, we do not really understand something until we say it aloud before a class. Maybe prayer works in the same way. It helps us to understand ourselves.

In all of his journey, the Questor works through varied forms. He seeks out holy places where the self is lost so that it may be found. He seeks kindred animal spirits through the finding and study of a spiritual guide. Then he projects animal properties of courage and speed into a stone fetish and breathes these back into himself during inspiration prior to the hunt. He has visions and places spiritual interpretations on them. He prays through his models and his spirits, projecting hopes to gods through fetish and prayer. And, he believes, the great powers will answer back in the bounty of the hunt or in relief from affliction. These are just a few of the remarkable capabilities of mind as the Questor embraces the unseen world, the world of spirit. Through it all, from a vision within the mind of the Questor, the stem cells of fantasy, interpretation, and hope send out emanations to practical action.

BUILDING A FAITH

I have said that the soul is not more than the body,
And I have said that the body is not more than the soul,
And nothing, not God, is greater to one than one's self. . . .

—WALT WHITMAN, *Leaves of Grass*

God—a word that is worth a thousand pictures. Deep inside the self is some process that reflects vague thoughts and performs the most audacious act of creation, the making of a god, a faith—a supreme extension of the self. And in this act of creation, we often use human characteristics to personify an entity called god. This process has occurred at different points in history, all over the world, to answer the enduring questions: Who am I? Why am I here? What should I do? In our attempts to answer such questions, we go beyond the physical self, trying to understand the mystery of life, death, and our place in the universe.

The idea that gods and faiths are human creations is not new. In the last century the philosopher Ludwig Feurbach claimed that deities are the constructions of imagination. He found it lamentable, a superstition-ridden act. Sigmund Freud had similar views. Carl Jung thought of gods as projections of the human imagination, but he regarded the result as quite wonderful and rooted in archetypes of the mind, roughly equivalent to William James's earlier notion of instincts.

If we are to craft faiths, it is necessary to keep in mind the requirements that should be satisfied. Any god or faith should help us in a time of trouble, provide us with guidance and direction in our quests, help us relate to others, place us in the universe, and teach us some meaning for the mysteries of life and death. If it does this, its origins are of secondary importance.

To say that faith is a human construction does not diminish it. To the contrary, it places it on the same pedestal as our most exalted works of art and invention. Imagination has always been the architect of our greatest works. Often we select from previous work and freely combine ingredients to form a new product of the imagination. We do this readily in technology and art, but we have been less likely to do so in religion.

For religion there is an exclusivity of devotion that has prohibited deliberate intermixing of faith, especially in the Western tradition. Islam cannot mix with Christianity nor Judaism with Buddhism nor Catholicism with Hinduism. In fact, over long periods of time religious mixing has usually taken place as the result of migration, proselytizing, and the sword.

What is missing from religion is the voluntary, intentional mixing and innovation that characterizes invention and art. Religious exclusivity has prevailed because people seem to believe that only one form of spiritual experience can be true, and it is theirs alone. Any other is a contaminant that must be eradicated. Why this is the case is difficult to understand, but its effects are written in conflict and blood. Perhaps exclusivity has adaptive value for groups. Any mixing, then, threatens their conception of how the universe works. A world view is not easily come by, and religion provides just such a view. Those who question a world view are destroying the one way the people of a culture have of thinking about creation. Because of this threat, nonbelievers must be converted or killed. One's view of the world—no, the world itself—is at stake.

Mixing Bowls of Faith

One great mixing bowl of faith is not intentional invention but the marriage of partners from different religions. Such unions become increasingly frequent as higher education becomes more universal and travel and migration more common. A recent *Newsweek* article sketches these unions, and their complexity.[1] Claudia grew up as a Roman Catholic and married Richard in 1978, with a rabbi officiating. The couple has three children being raised as Jews, and Claudia herself converted to Judaism eight years ago. But every Christmas they have a Christmas tree—neither a Jewish nor a Christian symbol historically but something that Christians have long since assimilated. Now Richard is beginning to worry that his rabbi might see the tree.

Here is a clear example of fusion and conflict produced by interfaith marriage. A tree has become a matter of contention, even though the major issues have been resolved, at least since Claudia's conversion. Once again the past intrudes because conversions are rarely one hundred percent.

This couple's mode of accommodation, one partner converting to the other's faith, is not the only way. Often both people will compromise by rejecting each of their faiths. Perhaps he a Jew and she a Catholic will together become Unitarians—or perhaps nothing at all, a secular family in a secular culture. Or each may retain their own faith, but the children will be raised in only one, hers or his, a decision often reached on the basis of grandparent influence or intrusion. Or they may try to raise the children in both traditions, going one week to one house of faith and the other to the next.[2]

Still other forms of blending occur. Tom, raised a Methodist, and his wife, Amy, raised as a Jew, had a ceremony for their son, Graham, that was neither the ritual Jewish circumcision nor the Christian baptism; instead it was a dedication with a rabbi and a minister in joint attendance. The parents intend that Graham, when he becomes old enough, will make his own choice as to faith.[3]

However, some religions refuse to instruct a child in both faiths at once, perhaps because they feel that the child will be confused. Or perhaps they do not like the idea of competing. Also, for a child to choose between a mother's and father's religion means that at least one of those faiths will be rejected. The wonder is that most families resolve these delicate issues and most children survive them. That is a good thing because such mixes are becoming more prevalent as the world becomes ever smaller.

If marriage is one mixing bowl for faith, college is another. There is a large difference, however. The fusions of faith resulting from marriage are the result of one person trying to accommodate another. In college, choice may be much more direct because the student is sampling from different faiths to build his own—a deliberate construction engaged in freely. The spiritual self creates its own system by selectively accepting or rejecting pieces of different faiths, so one may accept beliefs from a variety of faiths rather than accepting or rejecting an entire faith.

Thus far this sounds like a less radical step than conversion, but in fact it may be more so because the aspects of different faiths are then blended with one another much as a master chemist prepares a new compound, a chef creates a new dish, or a writer builds a novel. For example, a Christian may take on the practice of meditation from one of the Eastern religions or become immersed in the idea of the Hindu cosmic soul.

More and more, people are engaging in this form of mix, match, and blend theology that is sometimes referred to derogatorily as syncretism, or cafeteria religion.[4] Many theologians resist this development because of its inherent tendency to impurity and its freedom from organized religions and priesthoods, but the movement is nonetheless accelerating. Its power rests on combinatorial explosion, just like the inventions of technology and story and most recently the fusion dishes of cosmopolitan cuisine. The result is an endless blend of ingredients and an entirely new range of spiritual nourishment.

New Ideas of Spirit

More radical than mixing and blending is the deliberate construction of an entirely new religious concept. The analogy to invention would be the first occurrence of stone tools or lasers: something new under the sun. To illustrate such a construction of spirit, we examine retrospectively the Buddhist notion of Nirvana and how it may have come to be. I have chosen it because it is quite far from my own beliefs, so I can consider it abstractly. Of course, my understanding and explanation of it may present it in ways that Buddhists themselves would not approve.

Loosely translated, Nirvana is the absence of desire, striving, achieving, and sensory flow. Such experiences are to be avoided because they represent only the ephemeral and the transient. These conditions in turn engender the possibility of afflictive states and their attendant suffering: sorrow, grief, sadness, and despair. By entering or achieving Nirvana, the transient is escaped and with it the sufferings associated with birth, age, disease, and death.[5] Much of Buddhist thought and practice is accordingly devoted to escaping the hold of sense and desire as a means of avoiding suffering. The cessation of these states results in Nirvana.

So far we have been trying to define a concept, but the matter is more complex because Buddhism emphasizes that Nirvana cannot be captured as "to its form or shape, its duration or size, either by simile or explanation, by reason or by argument."[6] However, according to Buddhist scripture, it can be characterized by its qualities:

> Nirvana shares one quality with the lotus, two with water, three with medicine, ten with space, three with the wishing jewel, and five with a mountain peak:

- As the lotus is unstained by water, so is Nirvana unstained by all the defilements.
- As cool water allays feverish heat, so Nirvana cools and allays the fever of all the passions. Moreover, as water removes the thirst of men and beasts who are exhausted, parched, thirsty, and overpowered by heat, so Nirvana removes the craving for sensuous enjoyments, the craving for further becoming, the craving for the cessation of becoming.
- As medicine protects from the torments of poison, so Nirvana protects from the torments of the poisonous passions. Moreover, as medicine puts an end to sickness, so Nirvana ends all sufferings. Finally, Nirvana and medicine both give security.
- And these are the ten qualities that Nirvana shares with space. Neither is born, grows old, dies, passes away, or is reborn; both are unconquerable, cannot be stolen, are unsupported, are roads respectively for birds and Arhats [a high saint exempt from future rebirth] to journey on, are unobstructed and infinite.
- Like the wishing jewel, Nirvana grants all one can desire, brings joy, and sheds light.
- As a mountain peak is lofty and exalted, so is Nirvana. As a mountain peak is unshakable, so is Nirvana. As a mountain peak is inaccessible, so is Nirvana inaccessible to all the passions. As no seeds can grow on a mountain peak, so the seeds of all the passions cannot grow in Nirvana. Finally, as a mountain peak is free from all desire to please or displease, so is Nirvana.[7]

Nirvana is a rich, complex religious concept, particularly in its construction. The question we consider: How would anyone think of such an idea? How might it have been created? Two approaches come to mind. In the first, one attains the internal state of Nirvana and then tries to characterize it by numerous metaphors and analogies to the outside world. After searching memory and experience, one finds similarities to the lotus, water, and so on.

The second approach begins with noteworthy characteristics of things that allow for personification—lotus, water, mountains—and attempts to internalize them as analogous mental states. Just as cool water allays fever, Nirvana allays desire, where fever is a bodily state and desire is mental. So the search is on for a mental state that alleviates desire—the road to all suffering—just as water alleviates fever. Once found, we remember that state. Just as space is not born and does not die, so it is with Nirvana. We find a mental state that does not speak of beginnings and endings and remember it, too.

Proceeding in this way, one strives to combine the varied remembered states and then builds from them an exceedingly complex composite state called Nirvana. This path of construction is itself an invention that, like physical invention, combines varied elements, builds on them, and seeks to fit them all together in a difficult to construct but exquisitely beautiful structure. Of course, that state is not easy to realize, but it is worth working toward, even if it takes a lifetime.

Whichever method is used to build Nirvana—from mental state to external analogy or from external objects and processes to mental state—it is clear that powerful religious concepts can be created in this way. Whether the Buddha did it in one of these ways, I do not know. But in reading the Buddhist text, my impression is of a carefully crafted, invented theology designed to meet distinct human needs. I imagine that the Buddha did a little of both, working from inside to outside and from outside to inside. In either case, Nirvana is a beautiful construction of spirit.

Constructing a Spiritual Self

Anna, a twenty-four-year-old painter, decided to build her own religion. She began by examining ingredients from the world's great faiths and then selected those aspects that she needed for herself. Later she tried to fashion the result into a coherent whole.

She found that this wasn't an easy task, but she didn't have to start from scratch. She was reared in one of the traditional Protestant faiths, and some parts of it still appealed to her while others did not. She resolved to change one thing at a time. First, she rejected selected aspects of her family faith, such as the part about people of other faiths going to hell. It demeaned others and didn't enrich her own beliefs, so why keep it?

After she became comfortable with what remained, she began adding things one by one such as a meditation routine. She reasoned that if meditation was used as a technique, it would have little if any doctrinal implications for her own faith—unless she was so careless as to tell her minister what she was doing. In that case she could expect an argument from him: "You can't just pick and choose your beliefs as if religion is a cafeteria of practices." But why not?

To guide her in making sometimes seemingly arbitrary decisions, she used an abbreviated unity standard. Were her constructions of faith reasonably consistent, and did they move her toward being a more complete person? If not, she'd back up, just as she would when painting a still life and finding that the colors were wrong or the perspective wasn't the richest one to pursue. Whenever she was satisfied, she continued on her course. After all, the whole wonderfully rich panoply of world religions was available for her to select from.

As success in her spiritual construction became palpable, she grew more daring. She'd try a belief for a week—perhaps the reincarnation of the Hindus—much as she tried on different masks in anticipation of Mardi Gras, to see how the belief affected her. At this point she knew her minister would tell her that she was destroying the foundations of her faith, so she carried on an imaginary dialogue with him, in which an inner voice asked the questions he'd ask if he knew what she was up to. If his questions were persuasive and her own emotions agreed, she backed up. A pattern soon emerged, with his imagined voice telling her that trying on these beliefs just makes religion arbitrary—anything becomes as good as anything else; it's all relative; there are no eternal truths when one follows the dangerous path of experimentation.

She always rejected that argument. Just as a still-life painting of a bowl of fruit is arbitrary in the sense that there are many ways to compose it—some of which are uninteresting, if not wrong—judgment was needed throughout to produce the best work of artistry. Besides, there were many ways to build a faith, each decision requiring its own judgment if the result was to be a work of art.

et us now consider in more detail objections that Anna's minister might raise. Each objection is then followed by a rejoinder.

The design of faith creates wanton freedom. If gods are designed, the minister might say, then belief is arbitrary. Religious people are properly disturbed by the idea of constructing gods because if a god is invented, then it could have been otherwise; it could be anything. How can a god have any meaning if it is not absolute but always open to an alternative nature?

Rejoinder. Reflection places that arbitrariness in a larger context and also separates it from value. Most artifacts of the made world—the products of human culture and human technology— are arbitrary because they could have been otherwise. Different musical scales exist across cultures, different forms of hand tools are found among the peoples of the earth. Different games capture the imaginations of varied cultures.

But such observations in no way detract from the idea that some structure, such as a scale, is necessary to make music; some tool, such as a hammer, is necessary to do a certain kind of work; some rules, such as those for a game, are necessary for play. Whatever the musical scale, tool, or game, some works are better than others.[8] Once more we see that values can exist alongside arbitrariness: The creative process flourishes halfway between complete constraint and complete arbitrariness. The value of a creative work is not to be confused with its origin.

If faiths are designed, then moral systems have no foundation. If morality is not anchored in religion, then conduct becomes seemingly arbitrary, and moral rules lose their authority and potential for governance of wayward passions. Constructed moral codes run straight into a relativism that makes any conduct possible. Any moral system becomes as good as any other.

Rejoinder. The answer to this objection is to consider the bedrock of moral systems. The most effective are built on a firm foundation of biology and mind, tapping into innately experienced categories of moral feeling such as justice and guilt, good and evil, right and wrong. To be sure, the content that excites a feeling varies substantially from one culture to another. But no civilization ignores with impunity the fixing of content to moral categories. Indeed, culture may be impossible without the binding of content to intrinsic feelings of a moral nature.[9]

Nor is the fit between content and category entirely arbitrary. We are much more inclined to associate guilt with betrayal than with successfully resisting torture, more likely to pair courage with self-sacrifice than with self-gain, more likely to couple shame with cheating than with winning fairly. There seems to be a rough sort of preparedness for what kinds of experiences excite what emotions. While the fit is not exact, it is a constrained correspondence somewhere between being completely arbitrary and tightly bound. This kind of middle fit is exactly the situation best suited for the work of design and creativity.

In addition, moral and ethical rules can occur independently of particular religious systems because they are rooted in the practical experience of community. This is true at a rudimentary, pre-rule basis in chimpanzees, where reciprocity, consoling, and mutual defense are regularly practiced.[10] While chimpanzee conduct is not rule mediated, their helping behaviors are the foundations on which moral rules must build to generate regularity and generalization, all of which may occur independent of theology.

To take a human example, the Golden Rule organizes human relations, and it does not need religious underpinning at all.[11] Probably its surface origins come from the simple reciprocity required in communal life:

Don't kill my goat and I won't kill yours. (Negative form)
I'll treat your goat as I would want you to treat mine. (Positive form)

Similar injunctions may also develop for the treatment of chickens, children, and spouses. As the common form underlying the different specific rules becomes apparent, the general rule takes on its modern and highly abstract form:

Do to others as you would have them do to you.

Underneath the surface origins is an emotional grounding, as well, one associated with a sense of fairness and unfairness, justice and injustice, inborn categories of reaction open to and readily fitted with particular cultural content. When the practical aspect of reciprocity is paired with an emotional sense of right and wrong, we have fertile ground for a powerful moral rule.

While the relations of community living and emotion may well be sufficient to establish such a rule, it is undoubtedly strengthened by being embedded in a religious system, where natural guilt and shame reactions can be grafted to violations of moral principle. The point is not to make religion and deity irrelevant to moral rules. Rather, it is to show that moral systems are grounded in biology and community. While there is some freedom in the expression of rules, such a system is far from one in which any conduct is justifiable. So the design of a faith may include within it a moral system that is far from arbitrary, and is based on our natural emotional responses of justice and guilt, right and wrong, good and evil that come from community living.

If deities are constructed, then revelation—the traditional standard of religious truth—has no place. Deliberate design would take away from revelation and place the gods on the same level as other products of the imagination: hammers, dishwashers, and cars. Instead, when one has a vision, hears voices, or experiences a miraculous cure from illness or affliction, the result is a revelation—something beyond the self that is controlling experience and the world about me, telling me something wonderful.

The truth of my revelation is not from argument or design but from immediate and compelling experience. Afterward I am charged with faith, energy, and direction. Religious experiences just come to us, like Black Elk's visions and voices. If the gods are inventions, then there is no place for the visions and the voices that may appear in the darkest of times. Black Elk's vision will be rejected, and the burning bush of Moses will be extinguished.

Rejoinder. That is simply not true. A designed faith need not exclude visions and voices. As with revelation, they are simply another source of material for potential incorporation in the construction of faith. Some of us have unexplainable visions, and some of us hear voices and receive messages through prayer. But the resulting experiences must be interpreted and fitted into the overall structure of a spiritual self, just as with Black Elk's rich vision of calling and William James's dream. Such experiences are but one source of ideas and can no longer be an exclusive source of religious inspiration. To be acceptable in a faith, they must fit into an overall system of belief, like any other inspiration.

We may ask why deities so often have their origin in imagination obscured by story, involving a source of revelation seemingly independent of the human imagination. Evidently a revealed god is no longer arbitrary and can become omnipotent, transcendent, something beyond ourselves—all characteristics that are more difficult to come by when an idea is issued from the deliberate workings of the mind.

Yet revelation has its own difficulties. A genuine experience of revelation (as distinct from conscious attempt to obscure a human origin) is specific, intense, and narrow—and rarely is it enough to construct an entire faith on. The solution in the past has been to await other revelations, which may never come. Alternatively, the supply of options is enriched by collecting revelations from many people and then having councils charged with accepting or rejecting revelation candidates. The acceptance process of councils then acts as a fitness selector analogous to a comparable process in evolution, with some things weeded out and others embraced. This is a decidedly slow process compared to deliberate invention and artistic creation where we engage in thoughtful generation of ideas as well as selection from existing experiences.

With conscious design, we need no longer wait for revelation to come; we can be active designers and crafters engaged in constructing an encompassing system of belief, a story to be lived by and told for ourselves and the human community. The designed faith must also be strong enough to take criticism and entertain shaping and elaboration, all to become a better work of art and inspiration. To the extent that the process of craft is understood, revelation becomes less necessary—remaining as but one source of inspiration for the whole process of creation.

Faith constructed by design is a cold, calculating process, providing none of the conviction, heat, and passion of the true religious experience and its accompanying mystery. If a deity and a faith surrounding it are matters of design, then the entire religious experience is an emotionally empty thing. Religious ecstasy, awe, reverence, and magic will be no more. The central aspects of faith have little to do with conscious, reasoning processes. They are matters of mystery and feeling. Conscious contrivance serves neither.

Rejoinder. Perhaps the conscious design of faith is too cold, too arbitrary, to create religious passion and martyrs for belief. We do not have enough experience to answer this objection with certainty, but surely a presumption of coldness, a vacuum of passion in design, should not be our starting point. In fact, design is exciting. As with any work of composition and artistic creation, a hidden form emerges before the eyes, materializing from a block of wood or stone or a blank canvas or page to reveal itself and its beauty to the world for the first time.

If one is a genius, the result may be an exalted work of art, a

Bach mass, a Leonardo painting, a Shakespearean tragedy or comedy, a Taj Mahal as architectural wonder. All of these are the designs of mind. All are arbitrary in the sense that they could have been otherwise. All involved conscious, deliberate creation. Yet each one's worth is in no way diminished by knowing this; each one's capacity for arousing passion is in no way eradicated. In the design of faith, we are engaged in just such a construction of our ideals and our spiritual selves. What could be more exciting?

A Constructed Faith

A constructed faith acts to focus and blend human reactions that are difficult to reduce to material terms. Good, evil, awe, mystery, and the sacred plunge us into the magic of life. Once we have assigned these most human attributes to the gods, the forces of good and evil are played out in great dramatic conflict. The human storyteller is making sense of experience by projecting the properties of the human mind onto the events of the world in a natural and profound way.

The use of human characteristics in the construction of the gods finds its resting point: Humans are not in the shape of gods but the other way around. We build them as reflections and repositories of our fears and our yearnings. This is a view consistent with the works of sophisticated theology such as *Models of God* by the theologian Sally McFague and *Satan* by Elaine Pagels.[12] In this perspective, God and Satan are religious inventions formed to answer the deep questions we humans confront. In the right balance, both creations serve human needs, to direct us toward or away from various acts, beliefs, and relationships—and above all, to fit our lives and the universe into a common framework of interpretation and meaning.

A good construction of deity is an idealization of what we want to be—or sometimes what we most fear or hate: a loving god or a stern god. Personified gods—those with familiar human characteristics—come from the same mental abilities and psychological processes that allow for seeking perfection in appearance, the crafting of imaginary friends and enemies, the seeking of extensions to the self, and the empathic identification with heroes and the loathing of villains.

As such, our gods and their characteristics are additional evidence of human thought expanding beyond the bounds of body and evolution. Biologically, no creature is immortal and all-powerful; still, our gods are. They are also much more than fictions. In the best sense, they are idealizations of the storytelling mind, our most audacious creations, our furthest expansion of the created self, one that goes beyond the body, beyond the persona, toward the far reaches of the spiritual imagination.

How, then, to escape the rigidity of traditional faith? Let us return to an idea of the biologist E. O. Wilson, the notion of consilience, or jumping together. Recall that he advocates that the arts and the humanities jump closer to the methods of the sciences so that they, too, may show more capacity for sustained growth. Specifically, he argues that the solution of problems in the sciences is much aided by the relatively free flow of ideas from one discipline to another, where different units, materials, and principles are free to combine to yield a needed result.

He is undoubtedly correct that the sciences have benefited from consilience. But let us use his idea differently here. We need a consilience of faiths for the wisdom of different religions and spiritual traditions to more freely jump together, so we can draw on the insights and values of many traditions. Here are some of the more deliberate forms of created faith, together with accompanying problems for each.

Many people turn to New Age alternatives. They want to know how the needs of afflicted flesh and yearning spirit find peace and a place in the scheme of things. While the New Age person is inclined to be open to a wide variety of beliefs and practices, constructing a new faith is a difficult matter. It is simple enough to put together the spiritual equivalent of a butter knife joined with a flyswatter—say, a crystal, a mantra, and a smoky candle to channel an inarticulate voice. Yet such materialisms are unlikely to succor our afflictions or settle our yearnings. Traditional religions have good reasons for resisting unmotivated change and the resulting hodge-podge of parts that gives rise to a pastiche of self. Skill is needed in knowing what spiritual changes to experiment with, what ideas or practices to combine, and finally knowing what to accept or reject of the new forms generated.

Another form of faith construction, one avoiding both the rigidity of traditional religion and the New Age problem of knowing what to combine, is to find a guru with an already designed system. Ideally, this is a person who has thought long and hard about spiritual matters, often taking a bit of this and a piece of that religion, then combining the result in a new synthesis that works for him. That is fine as far as the guru is concerned, assuming he has carefully blended the separate pieces into a reasonably coherent system. The problem is that his blend may not work for others. Frequently when one guru is unsatisfactory, the answer is to find another. Many people do just this, drifting from one belief system to another in an unfocused way, following a serial monogamy of faith.

Another way may be in order: finding a new kind of religious professional who is deeply conversant with a variety of the world's religions, one who can guide us in assembling a faith for ourselves. This professional would be a spiritual architect, a person familiar with the designs, aesthetics, building materials, and construction methods of many faiths, someone concerned with our individual needs and who helps us design a structure of faith that closely fits those needs.

This kind of architect will want to know about us as individuals—the fears, needs, aspirations, and mysteries that perplex us—before selecting ingredients from different religious practices to design a faith to fit us. We might even design our own deities with the architect's help. Such a modern-day teacher would be a true innovator of the spirit. I do not know of anyone who currently acts in the capacity of a spiritual architect—surely a new profession waiting just off stage in the fringe of our time's awareness.

Finally, we may decide to chart our own path, build our own spiritual fusion. If we are to do this with utmost seriousness, we are on a long path of finding what others have done through history. We will be selecting what seems best for us, trying to fit the puzzle parts together, and sometimes building our own ideas, practices, and rituals. This path requires study, understanding, and a depth of penetration that extends over a lifetime. In addition, it may be lonely, without the social support of conventional faith. It is what William James suggests as the bedrock of faith: a personal construction as opposed to an institutional package.

Nonetheless, we will certainly need guidance in our construction, require standards for knowing what to combine with what. Once again the unity system helps to focus our efforts. For any given combination of elements from different faiths we must ask: Will the result be consistent, compatible, and coherent while making us more complete? If it is, then we are most likely developing a faith that harmonizes with the human condition, that honors a core self, whether looking backward or forward, outward or inward.

We return now to the standards for a faith. Let's restate them for easy reference: Any god or faith should help us in a time of trouble, provide us with guidance and direction in our quests, help us relate to others, place us in the universe, and teach us some meaning for the mysteries of life and death. If it does this, its origins are of secondary importance.

Without such standards, it is difficult to know if a religion is doing what it should. To a degree, any faith that has lasted centuries will at least minimally satisfy these standards. The real issue, then, is how to do better. That is a question that cannot be answered until it is widely raised. But it is a vital one—for our time and for all time.

Chapter 17

CREATING AN AFTERSELF

And I say to any man or woman, Let your soul stand cool and
composed before a million universes. . . .
I bequeath myself to the dirt to grow from the grass I love,
If you want me again look for me under your boot-soles.

—WALT WHITMAN, *Leaves of Grass*

It is dawn, the light just visible over the Sandia Mountains. In the valley below, two women are on the ground in a balloon gondola. The burner is on low while they wait for something. A man closes a car door and brings a vessel. He hands it to the women. It is an urn, containing the ashes of a friend and fellow balloonist. The burner is turned to high, and the balloon slowly ascends, floating over the countryside. When it is above the Rio Grande, the urn is slowly emptied, and the ashes of a dear friend are scattered along the river as a last memorial. He can rest in a place he loved, as he had wished.

William James had intriguing ideas about an afterself. In a famous lecture on immortality in 1898 he had this to say:

> Immortality is one of the great spiritual needs of man. The churches have constituted themselves the official guardians of the need, with the result that some of them actually pretend to accord or to withhold it from the individual. . . .
>
>   It is a matter unfortunately too often seen in history . . . that

when a living want of mankind has got itself officially protected and organized in an institution, one of the things which the institution most surely tends to do is to stand in the way of the natural gratification of the want itself.[1]

James's intention was not to advocate a belief in immortality; instead, as he so often did, he wanted to provide an intellectual grounding for the belief if one was so inclined. His argument was designed to get around the reductionism of a medical materialism that holds the following: The only thing real is the body—in this case, the brain. Mental states are simply a function of that organ in action; they are the symptoms of the brain. When the organ dies, so do all of its states.

James began by assuming a continuum of cosmic consciousness, something like that of Hinduism, that links experience to religion and a wider consciousness. In this sense the brain is like stained glass that absorbs and reflects certain wavelengths of light. It is merely a portal for the entry of parts of that larger consciousness.

Few contemporary psychologists or philosophers of mind would have anything to do with such a claim. Of course, the much greater sophistication in knowledge we now have with respect to brain functioning does little to explain the experience that James was seeking to ground. How is it that a material organ like the brain gives rise to sentience, awareness, the *qualities* of experience such as good and evil, love and hate, beauty and awe—not to mention, the desire for immortality? We are still a long way from brain states represented by voltages and neurotransmitters to such experiences. And James sought to provide a basis for one of the most distinctive of these human experiences, a belief in soul and afterlife—a strong conviction and evident need for much of humankind.

James is certainly right that we humans do not much like the idea of just dying and being no more. Why else would we intermittently create the varied forms of afterself to send off our dead? Indeed, every culture—if not every individual—has some concept of an afterself, something that persists beyond the body. This belief, and the practices supporting it, provides one of the great expansions of self. The afterself ranges from an afterlife of the body or spirit to the transmigration of the soul to immortality through works and influence and to deliberate memorialization.

The soul and immortality are nonsense in terms of categories in the physical world. Try to find anything in a physics book that even hints of them. Yet they are strong human beliefs. Evidently evolution has produced a mind not constrained by the way the physical world works—at least in physics textbooks. Because of such a loose fit between nature and mind, we can imagine what may be, what will not be, what we desire. Perhaps it is because of that loose fit and light constraint with the physical world that we are human, that we construct an afterself.

The Immortal Self

Let us begin by considering an important special case of the afterself, that of an afterlife. It parallels the splitting of the persona into different components, as we saw earlier with varied masks and roles. But with the afterlife some essence is split from the body and survives it. The simple and naive logic of differences guides us. With death the body is still present, but something vital has disappeared. For many people that vital essence must be somewhere— perhaps a soul that exists independently of its physical container, the body, and has taken flight.

Whether one believes that this really happens is not the concern here. Rather, it is the capacity of mind and vision required to come to such a belief. The human idea of an afterlife separates us sharply from the rest of the biological world. For William James, the consequences of such a belief lend it pragmatic truth if it influences conduct. Even if it started out as only a tale, its effect on actions lend it a certain reality.

The oldest firm evidence for belief in a human afterlife comes from grave sites of thirty-five thousand to seventy-five thousand years ago, where tools and goods were buried with a body, perhaps to aid the departed in the next life.[2] Here were early manifestations of the idea of an afterlife, some form of existence that outlasts the body. The inclusion of tools and other artifacts in graves increased over time, with later burial sites of thirty-five thousand to ten thousand years ago much more likely to contain such relics. Some conception of an afterlife seemed to be growing over time.

Different conceptions of that next life vary greatly. The pyramids and the burial rituals of the ancient Egyptians suggest a self working to extend beyond the body and the present life.[3] A pharaoh spent his span of years, and a major part of his kingdom's resources, preparing for his afterlife. As put forth by the Egyptians, the very conception of an afterlife is a dramatic extension of the body self; it is the creation of a mirror self in an aftertime. From a modern perspective, one may argue about drawing resources from society that might have been better allocated to its growth and sustenance. Not all extensions of self serve life. But it is also true that the Egyptian culture of pyramids lasted a very long time.

In our time there is Billy Graham's early belief that heaven is a place where "we are going to sit around the fireplace and have parties, and the angels will wait on us, and we'll drive down the golden streets in a yellow Cadillac convertible."[4] Some facsimile of the body is preserved in another place, along with one's favorite toys, such as that Cadillac. This is a very direct projection of the treasures of the material world onto a concept of heaven. Perhaps it has its origins in those ancient tools placed in Paleolithic grave sites.

Much more abstract is the Hindu idea of transmigration of souls—or reincarnation, as it is also called.[5] The *jiva*, or individual soul, appears from nowhere, like bubbles in boiling water. A soul is first attached to a simple form of life, perhaps an insect. With that organism's death, the soul migrates to another body, then to another, and so on. When the soul reaches a complex animal or human, it becomes aware and knows itself. In our terms, a self is created.

The origins of this idea are unknown, but natural examples of seeming rebirth are abundant. A plant freezes, apparently dies, then sprouts again. Or it is cut back, and then with spring it is reborn with new shoots coming forth. Perhaps such plant models gave rise to metaphors and beliefs for a transfigured human existence. Transmigration is more complex, to be sure, but all the storytelling mind needs is a foothold, and it will do the rest by elaborating context and significance.

For the Hindus that story has great practical import. Karma, a process dealing with moral cause and effect, carries over the content of mind from one transmigration to another. The wages of sin or goodness in a past life are revisited in the present life, and current moral decisions will carry over into a next life, too. A moral universe places a heavy obligation on individuals to act properly, but the wheel of rebirth also offers the possibility of improvement and perfection, two deep human motivations.

People continually look for ways to prolong life or circumvent death. A New Age solution to extending the self, called cryonics, borrows indirectly from the embalming ideas of the Egyptians. Believers in the practice—sometimes called immortalists—leave instructions for their dead bodies or heads to be frozen. The thought is that biology and medicine will advance; then on some future day the cryogenically preserved will be unfrozen, the diseases that caused death will be successfully treated, and they will be resurrected as living forms. A fantastic belief, certainly, but the freezing process already works with embryos that, on thawing, can produce a viable pregnancy. Of course, bodies are not embryos. The technical and scientific barriers to freezing an entire body, without damage from ice crystals, are formidable. But one advocate of cryonics argues that while he would not bet his life on the procedure, he has no qualms about betting his death on it.[6]

Information and its possible downloading to the brain provides the newest approach to extending life, an ultimate in New Age thinking about an afterself. The idea is that the important part of self is not body, not persona, not spirit, but information. It then follows, via computer metaphor, that the information in your brain might somehow find residence in another brain. If so, you will have acquired a kind of informational immortality. The way to do this, according to Internet discussion groups, is to find a way of uploading the information in your present brain to computer storage. Then when a suitable recipient is found, that same information would be downloaded to the recipient's brain, and the I-that-is-you would take up residence in another brain. You would acquire informational immortality in the process. Note the abstraction: Self is only information, and that information could take residence in any brain.[7] Questions of fit, capacity, and emotional structures are not considered.

What interests here is the idea of afterself, albeit in different forms, extending from Neanderthal burials to New Age cryonics, from a body going on a journey to another land to the journey of information in the brain going from present body to computer memory to another replacement body and brain. The idea of immortality for self exerts a powerful hold on us. No matter its doubtful basis in fact, science, or technology. We construct endless stories about it.

Markers of Self

Closely parallel to the idea of an afterself is the way in which we memorialize ourselves and others. The spiritual self is extended through such acts of memorialization, literally becoming a part of the memory of others. Here are some forms and variations on the idea of memorialization.

Using a tombstone as a marker of graves is an ancient practice. Tombstones are an economy pyramid—yet they also differ. Each pharaoh built his own pyramid; now hardly anyone builds his own tombstone, and the task of selection is left to others. Pharaohs accepted death, even looked forward to it; we deny it and leave the details of our demise to others.

A physical memorial in stone provides an external memory and sign of respect to the dead. It functions as a reminder for the living. A memorial service is the corresponding ritual vehicle for memory fixing, selecting important aspects of the dead so that they may live on through our memories. In a memorial service I attended for a friend, people took turns recounting their experiences with him. They were getting their memories in order, fixing them in place, and establishing them as a community memory and influence. The stories were of kindness and whimsy, of a man with humor and compassion for others. One wonders if there was also a group censor in subtle play because nothing really negative made its appearance (never speak ill of the dead). Perhaps the man was always on good behavior. Or maybe our memories were undergoing a selective winnowing and cleansing in yet another manifestation of the interpretive mind doing its work.

Memories of the dead are also prompted by graphic displays. Old English manor houses with their gallery of ancestor paintings on the walls provide an example from the upper classes. Once again, these are all images of the stalwart in life's prime: handsome, attractive, and often made more so by the artist's flattering brush. In origin, the portraits were like the pyramids, commissioned by their subjects. They serve, then, a dual rite of celebrating a life during its time and remembering it after its passing. Now with photos and video cameras, resemblances of a loved one become another form of family gallery that serves to connect generations.

Goods of the departed also refuel memories, especially when they become symbolic. A social worker was charged with getting people out of their houses for an urban-renewal program, so a new highway could be built. The people were compensated for their homes, but one of the requirements was that nothing bolted down could be moved. An old woman agreed to the terms, except for one condition. She wanted to keep the toilet that her dead husband had sat on for forty years.

As the social worker explained it, the toilet acted as a symbol for the old woman—a symbol of having come out of a rural background, subsistence farming, and outhouses into modern civilization and economic success. It was one of the first marks of that success that she and her husband had enjoyed together. The social worker promised to look in the other direction to allow the toilet's removal. We never know when some object will acquire symbolic value for our lives, and we ought to be open to it when it occurs.

Many people live on through their works. My father is ninety and in poor health. At some less-than-fully-conscious level, I have been looking for ways to remember him after he is gone. During his life he was a skilled carpenter who took great pride in his work. I have several of his handcrafted tables, and they will be long-lasting memorials of his enduring influence on me. When I look at one of those tables or use it, my own life will be connected to his in this long chain of human existence.

Stories also connect us across the generations. My father recently told me of his growing up. As a little boy in Michigan, he remembers sitting on his grandfather's lap and listening to stories of the Civil War. His grandfather had been with General Sherman on the march to Atlanta. One day a great battle took place. The next day the army camped at a riverbank to do amputations. With mist rising and a red sun ascending, the amputated limbs were thrown into the water, and the river ran with blood, both shades of red swirling together in a mix of memory. As I listened to my father's story of his grandfather, the horror of the Civil War acquired a new reality for me, one deeper than from books, because of this tale of mayhem and death connecting generation to generation to generation.

Public works also serve as a memorial. The steel tycoon Andrew Carnegie used his wealth to build the Carnegie Free Libraries, over twenty-eight hundred across the country. In addition, Carnegie Hall in New York was built with his benefaction, a building and an institution that has given cultural enrichment to many thousands of people. In his charities, Carnegie advocated public benefit from the accumulated riches of individuals.[8]

Contrast the pyramids with Carnegie's libraries as a memorial. The pyramids emphasize the dead while the Carnegie Free Libraries celebrate the living and questing mind—quite a difference. Of course, Carnegie may have been atoning for past sins, since the treatment of his workers in the steel mills was neglectful and brutal. Memorials may be designed to ease the mistakes and abuses of a life. Whatever Carnegie's ultimate motivation, there can be no doubt that his libraries and concert hall are magnificent memorials.[9]

However exemplary the Carnegie Libraries are as a living memorial, few people have the resources for such a legacy; it is not a general model. Yet in a scaled-down form it provides its own possibilities. Dwight, an executive for a large local bookstore, recently died. He had been a friend to many writers in the area. As a suitable memorial, writers influenced by Dwight donated one of their own books to the public library, and a memorial sticker with Dwight's name was pasted into the front cover of each book. Whenever someone checks out one of these books, they will be reminded of Dwight's love of books and his influence on writers.[10] This is a fine memorial, a smaller, more affordable and personal version, of Carnegie's libraries.

Oral histories provide a way of constructing one's own memorial or writing one's own obituary. The last course I taught at the university was for the Law School and involved instruction in and the taking of oral histories from notable legal minds in New Mexico.[11] We concentrated on people who were of advanced years and who had made a significant contribution to the state's legal history, the results to be archived by the library.

After some initial reticence, a common reaction of interviewees was one of delight. Participants were pleased to share their personal histories; the interview provided a way of remembering their salad days and their significant deeds. It provided a kind of memorial in the literal sense—a memory of their accomplishments and not just for others but also a way of ordering memories for themselves. The standard objection to oral history is that it is often not fact but just story. I have no trouble with this, since story is often as important as fact. Where would we be without our personal myths? If the interest is solely in fact, then corroboration is required. Even then, when discrepancies occur and narration is shown as invention rather than report, the way in which people cleanse their memories of fact is of interest.

Our children constitute a biological memorialization. "You have your father's mouth, your mother's eyes." We see ourselves in our children. They are truly an extension of ourselves, a living memorial. Particularly in close-knit communities where the family name is something to uphold and be proud of, each generation is a memorial to the preceding one, a memorial not just of biology but also of character. More than one child has been told, "You are a Jones/Ortega/Lee, and our family does not do that. The family name means everything and you must honor it." The family and its name is a unit, not just here and now but extending across time, having an accounting with history. As William James expressed it:

> We must care more for our honor, our friends, our humanities, than for a sound skin or wealth. And the spiritual self is so supremely precious that, rather than lose it, a man ought to be willing to give up friends and good fame, and property, and life itself.[12]

The Internet provides a new and powerful form of immortalizing and extending the self. In particular, a Web page may function as memorials for cybernauts. The late Timothy Leary—psychologist and advocate of LSD trips—was a man of mythic proportions, extremely intelligent, an explorer of the reaches of consciousness, a self-promoter of grand dimensions, a social prophet, and a less-than-responsible advocate of the drug culture.[13] Wherever he went, controversy was sure to follow—up to, including, and even after his death.

One of Leary's final acts was both innovative and of potential use to many people. When he realized he was dying of prostate cancer, he constructed a Web page providing an account of his life, his writings, and his thoughts on death. For a while he even considered depicting his suicide on the Web—an idea he ultimately abandoned—as he died from cancer's cause. With his last words he said, "Why not? Yeah."[14] Leary left money to have his Web site maintained and updated on a regular basis, a memorial of ideas and works. A Web page is a powerful form for remembering, and, unlike tombstone inscriptions, it is open to revisions as survivor's memories expand, undergo refinement, and transmute fact into myth.

The Ethical Will

A final example offers a different kind of self-constructed memorial. The *ethical will* is a means of leaving a part of the moral self to others.[15] It is a document used to pass on not possessions but values and wisdom from one generation to another. Examples come to us from people who thought they were soon to die—those in World War II concentration camps and ghettos, about to go to war, or living in other extreme situations. Ethical wills are often chilling and gripping statements from those who have lost everything material and still want to leave something of themselves for the people they love.

Sometimes, as in certain Holocaust wills, what is passed on to children is an understandable request for vengeance. This is from the will of Zippora Birman, who perished in the defense of her ghetto in 1943:

All is lost. This is our fate. . . . Cursed is he who reads this, mournfully sighs, and returns to his daily tasks. . . . We call upon you: Vengeance, vengeance—with no mercy, with no sentimentality, with no "good" Germans. For the "good" German let it be an easier death; let him be killed last. . . . To vengeance do we call you, you who were not imprisoned in Hitler's hell; this is our summons, and you are compelled to fulfill it. . . . Our crushed bones, scattered to all corners of Europe, will know no repose and the ashes of our corpses, scattered to the winds, will have no rest until you avenge us.[16]

The ethic passed on here is revenge, an eye-for-an-eye, a memorial of bewilderment and hate, understandable values in the circumstances. But more positive values were also conveyed from the zones of death; in the words of Shulamit Rabinovitch, who died in the Kovno ghetto:

If I could only bequeath you the ability to get along with little and the ability to do everything for yourself then you, being free, could never be unhappy. . . . We were not useless here; in any way we could we tried to make things easier for those around us. I am leaving the world with almost a clear conscience. I lived my life. I have no complaints to anyone.[17]

The courage and the will to work with the hand dealt are palpable. It is hard to imagine a surviving child not being moved and partaking of a parent's values on reading a document like this. Finally, here is a deeply poetic will from the Israeli writer Dvora Waysman, written for her four children:

I am leaving you the fragrance of a Jerusalem morning. . . . I am leaving you an extended family—the whole house of Israel. . . . I am leaving you the faith of your forefathers. . . . I am leaving you pride. . . . I am leaving you memories. . . . [H]ow rich you are![18]

While the ethical will is a Jewish tradition, it is an idea that can be practiced by all of us. One may begin by filling in sentences such as the following:[19]

- The important events of my life were ____.
- The moral lessons I have learned are ____.
- My definition of success is ____.
- I ask your forgiveness for ____; and I forgive you for ____.
- I love you and I am grateful for ____.

The open sentences can be modified to fit the life and the occasion. The result is both a will and a memorial of a different kind, one that communicates across the generations a little of one's self and one's values. That is indeed a powerful memorial, a far-reaching extension of the self.

We humans want to leave something of ourselves behind after the death of the body. And the people we love and who we leave behind in life want something of us to remember. We accomplish both by extending the self beyond the body through works, hopes, information, story, and values.

Memorialization of the self takes both bad and good forms. Some of what we leave behind may be destructive of a society. Pyramids are a candidate for the destructive use of a society's resources. And heaven viewed as driving through an expensive development where the streets are paved with gold and everyone has a yellow Cadillac is another candidate. In these examples it is evident that the invention of an afterself is not unlike that of technical invention in one important respect: Any created form powerful enough to do good is also powerful enough to do harm or be used in a frivolous way. So it is with our conceptions of the afterself.

On the positive side, ethical wills attempt to leave to loved ones those thoughts and values that we view as most precious. When done with imagination, photographs, videos, oral histories, and Web pages all help to maintain cohesion and continuity between generations. What better immortality, what better expansion of self, than to be part of the best in the continuing human stream, united by value and hope? An afterself at its best contributes to the human continuity and unity that are the cornerstones of civilization and self.

DIRECTIONS OF SELF

W e humans walk on a high wire. At one end the wire is secured to the misty foundations of our evolutionary past, the nature of which we are just beginning to understand. The other end is tied to an equally obscure foundation of sentience and choice. For our most serious, compelling choices, we do not know if there is a net underneath. We are balanced at the middle of the wire connecting these two very different purchase points, halfway between evolutionary constraint and rough freedom. For just such blends of constraint and freedom, just such balance points, design and creativity flourish. No surprise, then, that as we walk the wire, we are shaping ourselves in ways yet unanticipated.

Some of us refuse to walk the wire, freezing in place. Then we may drop to the side of tradition, becoming static creatures in a changing world. Some of us walk too fast, hurtling along the wire. Then we may drop to the other side, becoming failed explorers. But most of us walk the wire at varying rates of speed, trying simultaneously for balance and forward movement.

We have walked a short expanse of that wire in these pages. The key idea is that the self is engaged in its own creation, often a voluntary, intentional creation. This is possible because the influence of tradition has waned, new technologies have given us new options, and we are developing new insights into the self. Insofar as culture is important in the creation of the self, we no longer select from one setting but a mix of world cultures. Traditional moorings like religion have also broken loose. For many of us there is no longer a central religious authority in control. Instead we choose religion, if at all, like culture—a piece of this and a piece of that to sculpt our spiritual selves as we go.

We may be guided in our choices by the three great systems identified in these pages: unity, interpretation, and empathy. We seek the feeling of harmony afforded when the unity system is in balance. The interpretive system helps us square new experience with existing beliefs and values. The empathy system enables us to reach out to others, sharing in their thoughts and emotions, sometimes borrowing for our own use as we extend ourselves in multiple ways. In concert with the powerful imaginal capabilities of mind, these three systems allow us to invent chimerical friends and lovers, models and heroes. All of these capabilities together make possible the construction of faiths and deities to guide and direct us, thereby crafting a self that extends far beyond the bounds of the physical body.

From the vantage of our high wire, we are now ready for preliminary answers to deep questions—first the general answers and then the more specific ones.

What am I? I am a body, an appearance, that is nominally biological but something more, as well. I seek perfection—and its relatives, preservation and restoration—for my body. I do this through surface manipulations such as cosmetics and deeper alterations such as the surgeries of appearance: liposuction, hair transplants, and all the rest. For my reproductive body, and the ultimate extension of self via the creation of another, I may use the assistance of cells gathered from others as part of the new biotechnology of birth.

Who am I? I am multiple persona, with different ways of thinking about myself and presenting myself. My persona, constantly shifting with the numerous roles and situations I find myself in, consists of different identities to assume. The boundaries between these identities are in ever-present flux, yet I try on the varied identities in the hope of creating an enduring self, one that grows and expands, one that is unified and enjoys a feeling of harmony.

Why am I here? I am here to invent spiritual meaning for myself and my condition, to create purposes, gods, and beliefs about my origin and my destination. It is these stories that implant and serve spirit. Their force guides my life and makes me an entire person. They act as inventions that tell me where I am and where I shall go. Over time, minds like mine have evolved and given rise to capabilities that enable me to ask questions like these.

Each focus of awareness—body, persona, spirit—reflects a different essence. And the nature of the sentient, conscious I-self is to monitor, perfect, and extend the three components of self. The task is a difficult one because the I-self must do all this while fitting together with the demands of the physical and social worlds. Although this inner I-self seeks perfection and extension, it must often compromise or balance between the ideal and the possible.

Our final task is assembly: The ecology of body, persona, and spirit must mesh. They are separate balls that we juggle as we move over the high wire. In our movement and juggling we try to create an overall presence that fits together while continually growing and sliding into new meanings and new worlds as we cross invisible boundaries on the wire.

Because we engage in so much self-creation, it is easy to think that we do not have a nature, a unified core. But that nature becomes more apparent not so much as a specific thing but as a collection of abilities and trade-offs. The constructed self is a compromise resulting from the pull of many tendencies and the press of many situations. It is more like a body politic, a neighborhood of competing influences, than a single physical body, with not one preference point so much as preference intervals for each of our underlying dimensions of belief and action.

In this miniature political system, complex trade-offs occur between the competing forms of body, persona, and spirit so that none of them is invariably most important. As in a body politic, the different parts of us must negotiate with one another as competitors, lovers, strangers, and enemies. From these negotiations of parts we sometimes reach unity. When we do, our spirit is fulfilled, if only for a little while.

Human nature, then, is not found in a specific concrete embodiment of cultural or religious practice but at a higher level of abstraction: not a specific appearance but a concern about one's appearance, not a specific character but a unity of character that may be achieved in varied ways, not a specific religious self but one that is built from purpose, a sense of the sacred, and the storytelling imagination that centers one in the social and physical universe of human experience.

These notions make more sense when we look closely at creation in technological invention. Historically, inventions of self have been slow coming compared to the rate of change in physical artifacts: Material culture is rapid moving, the self less so. If that is true, then why?

Largely because the elements of self are just beginning to be teased apart so that they can be recombined in new ways. While recombination is not the only route to creative forms, it is a very powerful one. All of Shakespeare and the Bible come from the permutations of twenty-odd written characters of an alphabet. The entire physical world of materials is made of the couplings of about one hundred elements. The immense variety in the fabricated world of invention and technology comes in large part from endless possibility for recombination.

Similar possibilities for self-creation are beginning to be offered as the self is split into elements that are subsequently recombined in their own endless ways. For body makeovers, our face is scanned and a copy of it split off into a computerized image, and then simulated cosmetic elements are applied to our digitized self on the screen. Many appearance cycles can be tried in a short time. The mix-and-match capabilities of the computer quickly yield images of a more or less satisfactory fit with our physical face. Yet no commitment is required to any specific image; any unsettling combination can be erased from the screen. Satisfactory ones can be transferred from digitized representation to our own face with increasing degrees of exactness. Years of appearance options are condensed into a single session.

For persona changes, a similar speedup is occurring. We try on different masks and borrow the personas of friends, acquaintances, celebrities, heroes, and fictional characters for possible incorporation. New roles—some demanded by school, others by work, and still others by relationship—press upon us. We seem to be involved in many more persona shifts than in earlier times and cultures. The difficulty is forging an underlying identity, one with some unity, amid these multiple surface forms that keep combining with one another.

For the changing world of spirit, variation and variety do not begin to approach that of the invented world of technology. An important reason is that little freewheeling recombination occurs among the elements of the world's faiths. Spiritual traditions do not harness the possibilities afforded by the intentional cross-mixing, combining, and permuting of different elements as happens in the world of artifact invention. If anything, there is a barrier to combining the parts of different religions, usually erected by the upper echelon priests of a faith who are concerned with constancy rather than change.

The rationale for the practice of mixing faiths is one based on an analogy from the world of artifacts. Suppose we did not allow mechanical and electronic elements to combine because that would be contrary to the wishes of the mechanical and electronic priests: Impurity—the mixing of the mechanical and the electronic—must be prevented at all cost. That would mean we can't have printers with our computers because the one is substantially mechanical while the other is electronic. We could not have modern cars because they inescapably mix the mechanical and the electronic. The conclusion of the modern spiritual seeker is to the contrary: Faiths must be allowed to freely mix their ingredients with one another.

The inventions and designs of the spirit are at least as complex as those of the technical world. That is why we also need another alternative to indiscriminate combinations of faith, one in which sophisticated priests and theologians act as architects of the spirit, architects who are willing to help us create the most promising new combinations of faith for our individual and communal needs. We need open religious expertise working on them. Vital elements are everywhere in the wisdom traditions of the world's religions. Those elements in combination will enable new experiences of spirit and the construction of new religious selves.

Compass Points in a Big Bang

Where is the changing self going? Clearly, toward more variety as an option. The overall universe of self is expanding, and we are on the leading edge of one of the biggest bangs ever. The subparts of body, persona, and spirit—and the resources for combining them—are becoming more obvious and more numerous as we parse them into smaller units. It is as if the number of elements in the periodic table keep increasing. With each increase in the number of elements, ever more permutations and combinations of self are possible to create. In the midst of this superabundance, no one can point to *destinations* of the self, but *compass directions* are emerging. Here are some of those directions in the shape of trends:

New technologies provide new options for body modification without guidance on how to use them. If a body part is not the right size or shape, an individual may decide to have it altered. Sometimes that will be a wise choice, sometimes it will satisfy only vanity, and still other times the result will be tragic. Exploration inescapably entails risk, and this is certainly true for contemporary explorers of the body.

The constraints of birth and our most elemental relationships—what it means to be a mother or father—are loosening. We can look to livestock breeders here for what is likely to come. If a reproductive technology can be used with animals, humans will also use it on themselves. Human cloning is now in the foreseeable future, and such new capabilities of reproduction rapidly outrun the slow historical course of evolution. Ethical and moral systems are also losing the race to technology. We can keep people alive even though significant parts of the brain have shut down.

Motives for self-modification span the full range, from experimentation to being unique to being similar to others to selfishness to love. Spread across different people, the same act can encompass all of these motivations. And then motives themselves may be combined and recombined, just as the other components of self. The motives of the heart enjoy their own blending and multiplication. Novelists know this well.

The demands of culture on the persona impose new requirements. We must produce more selves for newer situations because, in William James's sense, the number of social selves is growing rapidly. The self of work may differ radically from the self of home and the self of friendship. To some extent this has always been true, but we now find ourselves in more social contexts, more relationships, necessitating more selves, each with a briefer half-life. Integration of these separate selves cannot help but be difficult.

Because so much in the way of altering body and persona is new, we repeatedly need to place ourselves in the world of possibility, a situation that cries out for spiritual connection and unity within ourselves, between ourselves, and with the larger universe in which we find ourselves. Some of us find new centers by choosing varied aspects of different faiths to construct our own belief systems. Occasionally, we may even craft new religious forms.

Is any guidance in sight? Yes, what is needed now are new

constraints on the freedoms with which we sculpt our new forms of self. Proper constraints do not stop creativity; instead, they help to guide and focus the freedom to create. They act like scales and keys for musicians in providing structure while allowing variation.

Useful constraints on changes include fitting the self and its development into longer time frames and broader communities, the very things that faith and spirit emphasize. We also need to seek harmony on a par with power and beauty on a par with the application of force. There is no reason that these strategies should not find honor at least commensurate with our more aggressive impulses. And all of this needs to be done with an eye to the unity system, with its components of consistency, coherence, completeness, and community acting as a guide rather than an absolute. In fact, many guidelines are available for our use, and we will need them all because we are at the very beginning of this process of consciously creating the self.

While constraints can guide us, we inevitably encounter experiences that can make sense only through the workings of story. First, consider a thought from William James, and then we will elaborate on it:

> I firmly disbelieve . . . that our human experience is the highest form of experience extant in the universe. I believe rather that we stand in much the same relation to the whole of the universe as our canine and feline pets do to the whole of human life. They inhabit our drawing-rooms and libraries. They take part in scenes of whose significance they have no inkling. They are merely tangent to curves of history, the beginnings and ends and forms of which pass wholly beyond their ken. So we are tangent to the wider life of things. But, just as many of the dog's and cat's ideals coincide with our ideals, and the dogs and cats have daily living proof of the fact, so we may well believe . . . that higher powers exist and are at work to save the world on ideal lines similar to our own.[1]

Playing on James's idea, imagine now that you are a dog strapped on a surgical table and need to construct a story explaining why you are there. A figure in white, with a knife, begins to cut into your body. What do you make of your tormentor? Is he attempting to aid you in some way you can't comprehend—or harm you for reasons you can't fathom? From time to time, different observers wander through the operating room and offer commentary.

First, a figure who refers to himself as Satan nods with admiration. "It is so pleasurable to inflict suffering. It offers the delight experienced by a boy who pulls legs off a bug." You shudder. Based on this encounter alone, the story that makes most sense is that you are at the mercy of a sadist who is bent on destroying you.

Next, a man called Job enters. He looks you in the eye and speaks. "This is God testing you," he says. "Have faith, and you will reap great reward." He is holding out hope for your suffering, explaining it as part of a grand plan. But it doesn't really make sense to you why anyone would concoct such a test. In your story you would not have a god who imposes such arbitrary trials.

Then a bearded, exuberant man called Walt Whitman stands over you. "This is not evil; there is no evil in the universe, only the flood of sensation, the overwhelming richness and sadness of life pressing down or lifting up on you. Whatever it is, embrace, savor, revel in it, even if it is your own pain." An inspiring message, but you're not sure it helps you. It is an alien story with no discernible midpoint or end.

Now a woman who calls herself an evolutionary psychologist passes through. "You are in a real predicament," she tells you. "But be assured: If you survive, it will be a tribute to your strength and stamina. Then when you reproduce, those good underlying genes will be perpetuated. If you don't survive, then any weakness in your genetic makeup will perish with you—and the overall gene pool of dogs will be improved. So, you see, evolution wins either way."

Somehow this does not comfort you. It is a cosmic story, while you are looking for a personal one.

Finally, a man with kindly eyes who calls himself William James stands next to you, takes your paw, and begins to speak. "You live in a pluralistic universe. There is evil, although we don't know why. The varieties of experience, the varieties of religion, are legion and show that the mind is not uniform nor are the needs of the self. You must put together your own beliefs, guided by what works for you under these difficult circumstances. Don't rely on ideology. Be pragmatic above all. You have the capacity for your own dog stories. This white-coated creature with the knife may be cutting you up for dinner, or he may be a veterinarian making you whole again. Or—and I realize this is beyond your capacity for understanding—he may be a medical researcher who through your sacrifice will develop therapeutic procedures that will save other dogs or people such as your masters. Within your limitations, form your own story. A useful one will alleviate at least some of your suffering."

You begin by thinking of your white-coated tormentor as someone your owners brought you to for help. After all, they love you and wouldn't hurt you without a reason. But this is too abstract a thought for you to pursue further. You close your eyes, try to draw on your own resources for help, and picture yourself chasing cats. At least it seems to help—perhaps because it's your nature and the limit of your imagination, the very boundaries for which story is designed.

Changing Self Today

A contemporary Changing Self picks up the opening account of the handprints in Chauvet Cave. She has just completed her first year of college and is getting ready to go home for the summer. As she walks through a wilderness area, she reflects on her various changes of body, persona, and spirit during the year. At the level of obvious body differences, she now wears her hair much shorter because it is easier to care for—a practical and contractive reason; it isn't always necessary to be expansive.

She has a butterfly tattoo on her ankle and is thinking of getting another tattoo on her shoulder. These are not practical forms; rather, they are aesthetic expressions. She likes the way her butterfly looks, and oh yes it will bother her mother. So perhaps the butterfly is also a statement of independence. Life is so complex—it's hard to do anything for just one reason.

Her roommate had her navel pierced. Perhaps Changing Self will try that next year. She definitely doesn't want to go any further than that. There is such a thing as too much independence. A few of the women in the dorm have had breast augmentation. She understands why they have done it and respects their choice, but it isn't for her. Not just because of appearance but because of long-range effects such as making it more difficult to detect breast cancer. A very practical matter, since an aunt died of it.

Even more important this year than the changes of her body have been her changing sense of identity and self. She did an exercise in psychology class to find her mirror or alter self—simply looking back at the major decisions these last few years and for each choice point imagining the road not taken. At the end of the exercise, all of these roads not taken were then fitted together. Her mirror self turned out to be an extroverted, artistic woman. Changing Self liked that woman and decided to move her everyday self in the direction of her mirror self.

The idea of identity kept coming up in new ways. Her purse and credit cards were stolen, and she found out it was like being a nonperson. For a few days she almost stopped existing—no money, no drivers license, no student ID and corresponding privileges. To restore a sense of selfhood, she went to a costume party where she deliberately lost her real-life identity. She told one guy she was a poet and a writer. She told someone else she was a comedian. All of these were imaginative stories that she made up on the spot.

She became so good at constructing these masks that she occasionally wondered who she really was. She decided that her identity was best described by her good memories. She was moving toward her mirror self, anyway, and during a dorm skit she actually took the role of a comedian. When other people laughed at her routine, she felt a moment of discovery, almost as if seeing herself for the first time. The audience acted like a looking glass and helped her in the makeover to a comedic self.

One thing she still struggled with though—the contradictions between some of her different selves, especially the old and the new ones. She had been taught to be quiet and restrained, but that didn't fit with being an entertainer. How should she handle this uncomfortable conflict? Ignore it? Let one part win out over the others? Or time cycle, acting restrained on some days of the week and acting outgoing and exuberant on others. She'd have to work on her contradictions.

Beyond the individual notions of self-expression there resided a deeper yearning—a need for purpose in life. She'd sought it in some of the milder illegal drugs but quickly realized that the ability to sculpt mood was at best a control of transitory states, not the directing purpose she wanted—a purpose that, whatever its nature, would allow her to go beyond her body, herself, to somehow make at least a small part of the world a better place.

That kind of thinking sounded almost religious. She didn't know for sure what she now believed in, but it clearly differed from the faith of her parents. She remembered the family minister telling everyone that only people of her religion could be saved; others were destined for eternal damnation. It didn't make sense. At first she tried to keep her family's faith, rejecting only its exclusivity. Then she found fault with its prayers, and one thing led to another. She dropped out of the church. Growth sometimes requires the shedding of past beliefs.

Then her boyfriend asked her to his church. Everyone was friendly and accepting, but they wanted her to convert. She thought about it, but some of their beliefs bothered her. After her biology course she could no longer believe in an afterlife in a conventional sense, nor of a traditional God. Maybe what we are all evolving to is a new kind of god—or maybe it is our ideals that are the truly holy. But thoughts like this seemed too remote. She began going to meetings of different faiths. No one system of belief satisfied all of her yearnings, but each had something worthwhile.

She began to assemble her own beliefs from these bits and pieces. It was like a picture puzzle. Seeing the fragments of a face and reaching out to them, moving the pieces around to see how they fitted together, until a coherent whole face emerged. When she came back from a science class, she tried to fit in those ideas, too. Still, there were large gaps because the science courses didn't concern themselves with many of her questions: Who am I? Why am I here? What should I be doing? Where am I going? For that matter, in answering her questions, most of the different religious faiths she'd tried also came up short.

She began to construct a new faith for herself, almost without realizing it. Some days she believed in a god, and other days she didn't. When she first realized this, it shocked her. But soon it seemed natural and comfortable, like changing clothes to fit the circumstances. Sometimes she thought of god as community when friends and family reached out to one another during crisis. Other times, in the biology class, god was in the mystery of life, the code of DNA, and the direction of evolution. Still other times, like when a dorm friend died in an auto accident, she didn't believe in any kind of god at all.

Most of the time it didn't seem to matter. What she yearned for was a life, a world, and a spirit more concerned with harmony than force, more interested in beauty than power. Those seemed to be her directions, even if they didn't disclose her destination. She decided to spend part of each day thinking about harmony and beauty. Sometimes it involved studying a flower; other times, looking at the way a pond changed with the season. Those thoughts made her incorporate nature into her beliefs; without its preservation, there would be nothing else. That's what she believed for now—but perhaps not tomorrow. After all, she was Changing Self, each day creating herself a little more.

One day Changing Self wound her way along the path down a rocky cliff face and stood on a sandy beach. Waves slapped the shore, and the ocean breeze flowed through her hair. She had come to this beautiful place to leave a mark of herself, and she felt almost like a female Walt Whitman, wanting to sing praises to nature and to herself.

At first she thought about leaving a pigmented handprint on the rocks, like the thirty thousand-year-old marks in Chauvet Cave. Then she thought, What if everyone now alive did that? What a mess! She decided to do something different, to create her own ritual and mark of self. She slowly took off her clothes, feeling the warmth of the ascending sun on her body. Then, just by the water, she stretched out on the soft sandy beach, wiggling into it, making a deep impression. The sand conformed to her body and her body to the sand. Carefully, she sat up, rose to her feet, and looked at her image in the sand: a distinctive human shape. She moved back from the water, sat down cross-legged, and watched the incoming tide slowly advance and absorb her form. The image in the sand melted and became a part of the waves, the water, the ocean, the sky, and the universe. Yes, that was it. A sacredness that came from her own ritual—a Changing Self blending with the universe.

A postscript. Serious creations of the self, like the inventions of technology, have the capacity of transfiguring life and society. If you have transformed yourself in a new, creative way, please let me hear about it.

E-mail: bobweber@alumni.princeton.edu

NOTES

Preface

1. For a postmodern depiction of the self, see Gergen (1991), who thinks of the modern self as a pastiche of cultural influences that he does not care for, a fragmented self. My own view is different. As pieces of many cultures become available for choosing among, the role of any one culture necessarily diminishes. Yet as any chemist knows, the breaking apart of complex forms into elements allows for greater subsequent freedom of combination. Similar breaking apart and synthesis is also the heart of the novelist's powerful alchemy, particularly with regard to character construction. Fragmentation and recombining as such is neither deplorable nor commendable without consideration of the direction and context of change.

2. For example, see James (1890, 1892, 1897, 1902, 1907).

3. The psychologist Jerome Bruner (1990) makes this point with particular force as he details the storytelling capabilities of the mind.

Introduction

1. Other interpretations are also possible. The handprint may not be intended as a mark of individuality but of social or religious significance (Faulstich, 1986). Whatever its intention, it is a mark of self, created with foresight.

2. Mithen (1996) provides a thorough and exciting theory of the evolution of the mind, from the viewpoint of a cognitive archaeologist.

3. The critical essays are those on the stream of consciousness, the nature of the self, and religious experience. See James (1890, 1892, 1902). The 1890 versions are lengthier; the 1892 versions, more succinct. Usually I quote from the 1892 versions.

4. See also James (1902).

5. Tooby and Cosmides (1992) present a useful description and critique of an extreme position that they refer to as the standard social science model. Whether any scholar would hold to all its provisions is open to question. Windschuttle (1996) provides a similarly useful critique of postmodernism.

6. This idea is evidently from Leda Cosmides, as referenced in Mithen (1996). The Swiss Army Knife is actually more complex than it seems. In previous work, I have treated it as a prototype of innovation, involving at least four distinct forms of invention (Weber, 1992).

7. Mithen is not sure where linguistic intelligence falls in this chain of development.

8. Cosmides and Tooby. (1997).

9. Mithen (1996, p. 11).

10. Johnson and Franklin (1993).

11. Williams (1997).

12. Williams and Nesse (1991) provide an informative account of how evolution affects health.

13. Cosmides and Tooby (1997), Pinker (1997), Csikszentmihalyi (1993).

14. Wilson (1998).

15. James (1992, pp. 195–196). For another insightful view on harmony or unity, see Csikszentmihalyi (1993), where the basis of harmony is held to be a complex organism with optimal differentiation and integration.

16. For example, Mithen (1996) suggests that burial and other

group relations of Neanderthals were relatively advanced, while their technical culture of tools was quite primitive by *Homo sapiens* standards. By the way, it was once the standard to refer to Neanderthals as *Homo sapiens neanderthalensis* and ourselves as *Homo sapiens sapiens,* two closely related subspecies. With the recent preliminary work on Neanderthal DNA suggesting a very distant relationship, the appropriate designation is now *Homo neanderthalensis* and *Homo sapiens,* respectively.

17. For life as story, see Bruner (1990) and Turner (1996). A related variant is life as musical improvisation, as described by Bateson (1989).

Chapter 1: Trying on Faces

1. Carpenter (1975).

2. Gallup (1982).

3. Gallup (1982). This is but one test of self-awareness, and it by no means acts as a complete marker of self-consciousness. For criticism of it as a defining act of self, see Dunbar (1996). Probably no one test defines the existence of self.

4. James (1992).

5. Cosmides and Tooby (1997).

6. Of course, this is an imaginative construction. Nonetheless, there is sound historical basis for the instruments, cosmetics, and practice as described: Erman (1971), Tyldesley (1994).

7. Tyldesley (1994) talks of Egyptian mirrors and carrying cases.

8. These are 1996 expenditures from McArdle (1997). See also Smith (1996).

9. This assertion is based on one of Pinker's (1996) arguments.

10. Anonymous (1994).

11. Bell (1976).

12. Harris (1994, p. 149).

13. "Ran" is actually a composite of several people. This is frequently true of the other interviews, too.

14. For the modern spa experience and computer-assisted makeover, see Watkins (1990), Elmer-DeWitt (1986).

15. Now programs with similar functionality are available for the home PC. One scans in a video image of self and then uses the software tools to modify that image.

16. I am indebted to my colleague Vera John-Steiner for pointing out this line of reasoning to me.

17. Dennett (1978). Dennett also refers to belief-desire psychology as the "intentional stance."

18. Baron-Cohen (1997).

19. According to Premack and Woodruff (1978, p. 515), "An individual has a theory of mind if he imputes mental states to himself and others." It seems to me that "theory" might be the wrong term here. Usually when we think of a theory, we mean something that is arrived at as the result of intense mental effort. In contrast, the ability to read the reactions of others seems natural and not the result of conscious mental effort—although it can certainly be developed beyond its natural state. Similar points are made by Baron-Cohen (1997), Povinelli and Prince (1998).

20. Dunbar (1996).

21. *Time* (1993, 142, no. 21). The popular name for this kind of averaging is morphing.

22. Johnston and Franklin (1993). See also Johnston's Web site for an ingenious use of genetic algorithms in the construction and selection of ideal faces: www.psych.nmsu.edu/~vic/.

23. Gergen (1991). Of course, the ideas of variety and core are logically separable, as I will argue later.

24. Csikszentmihalyi (1993, p. 213).

Chapter 2: Painting, Tattooing, and Piercing

1. Rubin (1988).

2. Coe (1992, p. 219).

3. Mithin (1996).

4. Spindler (1994).

5. Roberts (1988), Rubin (1988).

6. This seems to be part of Princeton's informal oral history, and it may not be correct.

7. Coe (1992).

8. Rubin (1988).

9. The ideal waist-to-hip ratio is 0.70 or less; Singh (1993).

Chapter 3: Surgically Extending the Body

1. Haiken (1997). My account here is largely based on hers.

2. Haiken (1997, p. 1).

3. Diamond (1996).

4. Another possibility, one I think unlikely, is that the common ancestors of apes and humans six million years ago had large breasts or a large penis. These organs were then selected for reduced size in the development of apes, while they maintained their size in the line that led to modern humans.

5. Quindlen (1994). Others arrive at different dimensions when scaling Barbie up to life-size.

6. Quindlen (1994).

7. The quote is from a PPQ advertisement on the Internet: 12.27.98: www.best.com/~wking/ppq.html.

8. Barron Centers.

9. A good summary of these procedures is provided by Beeson (undated).

10. Spindler (1996).

11. American Academy of Cosmetic Surgery figures, quoted in Spindler (1996).

12. This section on Jackson and the associated quotes are from Honan (1997).

13. These quotes are from the interview with Honan (1997).

14. To put the analogy of self-exploration in the context of physical explorations, here is a quote from one of the great adventurers of our century, Roy Chapman Andrews, the man who discovered fossilized dinosaur eggs in the Gobi Desert during the

1920s. On returning to Peking in 1921 and finding himself in a dust storm, he entered into his diary:

> The yellow blanket reached as far south as Shanghai and hovered over the sea sixty-five miles beyond the coast. It came from a land parched by fourteen well-nigh rainless months. . . . Peking was certain to be attacked and looted . . . smallpox was raging. . . . So with dust, war, and smallpox we felt the summer was beginning rather well. (Andrews [1943, p. 179])

15. Schneider, Levitt, Morton, Yoo, Skolnik, Brooks, Jones, Arias, McNeil, Sugden, Sider, Salcines, Sandler, Nelson (1996). Presumably these figures are for a contemporary U.S. population.

16. Garner (1997). These figures are from a magazine poll in which predominantly U.S. readers responded. It is not a random sample of the population but a self-selected one, and it therefore should not be taken as truth carved in stone. Nonetheless, I see nothing in the results that strike me as unbelievable.

17. See Kiernan (1997) for material in this section.

18. Anonymous (1996).

Chapter 4: Creating Another Body

1. Harlow (1962).

2. Kolata (1991).

3. Kolata (1991). The associated quotes from ethicists also come from this source.

4. For structure-function splits of physical invention and the role of such splits for the assembly line, see Weber (1992).

5. Margulis and Sagan (1995).

6. Classified ad in *Harvard Magazine,* September-October 1998, p. 89.

7. This and the following quotes from ethicists are from Kolata (1991).

8. The material here is drawn from *Davis v. Davis* (1992).

9. Both Junior and Mary Sue Davis changed their own arguments over the course of the litigation, so I have presented their dilemma only in broad outline.

10. Strictly speaking, Dolly is an incomplete genetic copy of her mother because the mitochondrial DNA is not included in the cloning. What difference this makes is not completely clear.

11. Kolata (1997).

12. Williams (1997).

13. Wright (1997, p. 73).

14. The fecundity of the world of invention offers an early insight into how the biotechnology of self-creation may proceed. If there are n simple objects in the world (or n ideas in the mind), then in pairwise combination, the resulting number of combinations is $C(n, 2) = n(n-1)/2$, a value that far exceeds the number of simple things in the world (or ideas in the mind). Almost any artifact will embody more than two simple bound elements—and the arrangement of the chosen components must also be taken into account—so in potential the made world gives rise to a complexity of joined forms far in excess of those naturally occurring. The hand and mind of craft, invention, art, and story are just such a world. The creation of self seems to be moving into this same kind of combinatorial space. For more on this, see my previous books on physical invention (Weber, 1992a, 1992b) and also my other individual articles in References.

Chapter 5: The Connected Self

1. I am indebted to Earl Mitchell, Jr., for recounting this experience to me.

2. Vickers (1996).

3. This account is based on Witchel (1990).

4. John Jay Iselin, quoted in Witchel (1990).

5. *Hampton v. Guare* (1993).

6. Leatherman (1997).

Chapter 6: The Unitary Self

1. James (1892). This example is his, slightly modified.

2. Hofstadter and Dennett (1981, pp. 20–21).

3. Church of Bob (undated). Important concepts from the faith include: *slack*—the world needs more of it; the *subgenius*—the people for whom the faith is designed.

4. Gardner (1983).

5. It is always possible for a seemingly unrelated set of activities to have an unseen mental logic. For this reason we should be careful in attributing aimlessness to others.

6. Whitman (1892, p. 29).

Chapter 7: The Interpreting Self

1. For more on the nature of interpretation, see Bruner (1990).

2. Einstein (1949).

3. Some of these issues are addressed in Progoff (1992).

4. Bruner (1990).

5. There is, in fact, an entire discipline devoted to interpretation, known as *hermeneutics*. Typically, it deals with the art of scriptural exegesis, but it has much wider applicability. Freudian theory and psychoanalysis is another bastion of interpretation.

6. In some sense, interpretation works like Piaget's (1951) assimilation and accommodation: Experience alters existing mental structures, and those structures in turn alter experience. But the interpretive art also goes far beyond Piaget's conceptualization.

7. See also Bruner (1990) for life as a narrative.

Chapter 8: The Contracting and Expanding Self

1. James (1890, p. 144) and the self that is chosen.

2. James (1892, p. 187) actually uses *Pretensions*, not *Aspirations;* we will use the later term because it is less value laden.

3. For more on playing at the edge of ability, see Weber (1992).

4. James (1892, p. 188).

5. Frankl (1939, 1963).

6. Frankl (1939, 1963, p. 213).

7. Perry (1948) on James's idea of free will.

8. Powers (1973).

Chapter 9: The Empathizing Self

1. Gardner (1983).

2. Baron-Cohen (1997).

3. Premack and Woodruff (1978), Baron-Cohen (1997). Earlier, I noted that *theory of mind* is probably an unfortunate descriptive phrase; *mind reading* has its own problems, conjuring up palm readers and crystal balls. So we will use the more common term *empathy* and more generally speak of an *empathy system.*

4. Barnes and Thagard (1998).

5. Darwin (1965, 1872).

6. Alter (1997).

7. Gross (1997).

8. Alter (1997, p. 37).

9. Closely akin notions include animism and panpsychism. My bias is to use the best common word rather than a technical term for such ideas.

10. De Waal (1996).

11. For an extended discussion of folk psychology, see Bruner (1990).

12. Collingwood (1946). For specifics on the connection between history and empathy, see: www-phil.philengl.dundee.ac.uk/magen/uphs/framewrk.htm#background, where the notion of empathy in history draws on examples based on Keegan (1976), *The Face of Battle.*

13. From www.phil.philengl.dundee.ac.uk/magen/uphs/hermeneu.htm, based on Keegan (1976, p. 135).

14. This analysis of Hamlet is based on Barnes and Thagard (1998).

15. Hagen (1973). According to Hagen, theater people call these respective approaches to acting *representational* (imitative) and *presentational* (interior). Hagen does not like the traditional terminology because it is not really descriptive and is greatly confusing. I also find it hard to keep straight. For this reason, I use *imitative* and *interior*.

16. Hagen (1973, p. 12).

17. Hagen (1973, p. 37).

18. Hagen (1973).

19. My use of this process bears a superficial resemblance to Goffman's (1959) study of the presentation of self through varied roles in everyday life. We both use the idea of theater and acting. However, Goffman is primarily concerned with power. My concern is not power at all but how one creates a role to fit with aspiration and setting. The issue of role fit is much broader than power, for it can be centered on aesthetics, morality, or play, just to cite a few examples. Another use of "masks" is for protection, a common concern for minority people (Montoya, 1994).

Chapter 10: Wanting to Be Another Self

1. Perkins (1993, p. 107).

2. I am grateful to Earl Mitchell, Jr., for telling me this story.

3. Erikson (1968).

4. My thanks to June Skinner for telling me about mask making.

5. Turkle (1995).

Chapter 11: Creating Another Self

1. Tamagotchi (undated).

2. Lawson (1997).

3. Lawson (1997).

4. Shelley (1818, Chapter 5).

5. Segal and Adcock (1986).

6. Thurber (1983).

7. Kaplan (1988).

Chapter 12: Believing in Spirit

1. Dawkins (1992–93).

2. Interview with Richard Dawkins (1997). "Religion Is a Virus: Why God Is a Product of Natural Selection."

3. Dawkins (1991).

4. James (1897).

5. Perry (1948, p. 121).

6. Harrold (1980), Mithen (1996).

7. James (1902).

8. James (1902, p. 225).

9. Erikson (1968).

10. Hoffer (1951).

11. James (1902).

12. James (1902).

13. James (1902).

Chapter 13: Pursuing Purpose

1. James (1897, p. 27).

2. Not everyone would agree with this distinction. Alternatively, for reasons of classification, one may consider small-scale acts such as going to the post office at the very low end of purposive action: short-term, limited in scale, with little emotional or motivational significance.

3. Messner (1989).

4. Messner (1989, p. 185).

5. Messner (1989, p. 114).

Chapter 14: Finding the Sacred

1. Orians and Heerwagen (1992). Kaplan (1992). Evolutionary psychologists talk about the EEA—environment of evolutionary adaptation—attributing some semblance of uniformity to it and often evoking a savanna. Not everyone would agree. The paleontologist Ian Tattersall (1998) thinks the environments of our lineage were much more diverse than is usually supposed by

evolutionary psychologists. I suspect that he is right, but all that I need to make my point is for selected environments to trigger certain mental-emotional states, for whatever adaptive reason. These states then go on to become exaptations—that is, they take on new functions.

2. Gould (1996), Weber (1992).

3. Eliade (1958, 1996).

4. Crews (1939). The modifier "traditional" is essential because many Pueblo people are college educated and may have few ties to the beliefs of their ancestors. Others try to become a part of the modern world while keeping one foot in traditional culture.

5. This luminescent phrase is from Boorstin (1983).

6. Neihardt (1972, p. 21).

7. Neihardt (1972, p. 23).

8. Neihardt (1972, p. 27).

9. Neihardt (1972, p. 31–32).

10. Neihardt (1972, p. 33).

11. Neihardt (1972, p. 47).

12. James (1902).

13. Neihardt (1972, p. 39).

14. Neihardt (1972). Evidently, the translation process worked in this way: Black Elk spoke in Sioux, and his son translated into English. Neihardt listened, and his daughter transcribed the ongoing oral translation. There is some discrepancy between the transcription and the published version, a discrepancy that is said to be Neihardt's artistic license. This presumes that the transcription was completely accurate, Neihardt's memory contributed nothing, and the translation itself was flawless. All of these are debatable assumptions. We are left with what the Native American scholar Vine Deloria, Jr., calls "a religious classic, perhaps the only religious classic of this century . . . ," as cited in his Foreword, p. xi. I see no reason to dispute his judgment. It is a magnificent vision, whether the product of one or many minds, as is likely to be the case for any great religious document, the Bible included.

15. Zolbrod (1984).

16. Many years ago I heard the claim that Monster Slayer was the one who had killed the dinosaurs, and their blood now forms the lava beds. However, I have not been able to find any written reference to Monster Slayer as the one who actually killed the dinosaurs.

17. The essential features of the Roswell story and its aliens are available at: www.geocities.com/Area51/7595/roswell1.htm.

18. For combining events to produce an even greater sense of the sacred, it is not necessary that the effects be additive $1 + 1 = 2$. We would be well satisfied if $1 + 1$ is about $1\frac{1}{2}$.

Chapter 15: Questing for Spirit

1. Cushing (1994, originally 1883).

2. Brown (1992, p. 1).

3. Ibid. p. 21.

4. There is much more to voodoo beliefs than such practices. My apology in advance for abstracting a very small stereotypical part of a complex faith.

5. The most scientifically minded of us may find beliefs related to fetishism and voodoo difficult to entertain because they run far below the surface of rationality. Yet in their most abstract embodiment, where a model partially resembles a real or plausible form, similar beliefs also underlie scientific thinking. The use of models is an important form of thought. That they are sometimes abused and become handmaidens of gross superstition should be no more surprising than that science itself is sometimes used to create weapons instead of truth.

6. Hurston (1935, pp. 206–7).

Chapter 16: Building a Faith

1. Adler (1997).

2. Adler (1997, pp. 50–51).

3. Adler (1997).

4. Winston (1998).

5. This account of Buddism is based on Conze (1986). Because Buddism is such a large and encompassing faith, I am sure that some branches would disagree with both Conze and my own interpretation placed on top of his.

6. Conze (1986, p. 156).

7. Conze, (1986, p. 157). I have rearranged the formatting of the sentences here to more readily show a given category of characteristics.

8. The argument for the presence of arbitrariness in the made world is itself easily overstated. While there are many forms of hammer, they are often carefully specialized for a particular kind of work. Tack hammers and claw hammers fit specialized niches; they are not interchangeable. The same is true of most other artifacts—the fit of an invention and what it does is often the result of careful human thought. See Weber (1992) for more details.

9. Wilson (1993).

10. De Waal (1996).

11. Wattles (1996).

12. McFague (1987), Pagels (1995).

Chapter 17: Creating an Afterself

1. James (1898). The two quotations here are inverted in order.

2. Harrold (1980). Of course, other interpretations are also possible: Perhaps the goods of the dead one are stained by death and therefore unusable, to name but one rival interpretation. Yet we know from later burial practices, such as those of the Egyptians, that worldly goods may be interred with the dead to guide the deceased on a journey. See Harrold (1980). Mithen (1996) cites a case of the dead buried with a goat's head, one hundred thousand years ago.

3. Erman (1971), Tyldesley (1994).

4. Van Biema (1997). Does heaven exist? *Time*, 24 March 1975, 149, p. 75. Evidently, Graham no longer holds this view.

5. Smith (1991).

6. Kosko (1993).

7. Tipler (1994) presents an intellectual argument for self as information.

8. Carnegie (1933).

9. Carnegie (1933).

10. Dwight Myers, good friend, you continue to influence me.

11. This is a course that I cotaught with my colleague Em Hall.

12. James (1892, p. 191).

13. Leary (undated).

14. Leary (undated), last words from his Web site.

15. Riemer and Stampfer (1991).

16. Riemer and Stampfer (1991, p. 45–46).

17. Riemer and Stampfer (1991, p. 55).

18. Riemer and Stampfer (1991, p. 88–89).

19. Riemer and Stampfer (1991).

Conclusion: Directions of Self

1. James (1981, p. 133–134).

REFERENCES

Anonymous. "Beautiful Growth for the Cosmetics Market in Brazil." *Market Latin America,* 2 (1994).

Anonymous. "Empathy and History." Available: http://www. phil.philengl.dundee.ac.uk/magen/uphs/framewrk.htm# background. 30 October 1998. [The empathy in history notion is based on Keegan, J. (1976). *The Face of Battle.*]

Anonymous. "Hermeneutics." 30 October 1978. Available: http:// www.phil.philengl.dundee.ac.uk/magen/uphs/hermeneu.htm.

Anonymous. "Genes Linked to Baldness, Missing Teeth." *Science News,* 150 (1996): 69.

Anonymous. *Business Line,* 4 September 1997, 24.

Adler, J. "A Matter of Faith." *Newsweek,* 15 December 1996, 49–54.

Alter, J. "Genuflect Journalism." *Newsweek,* 22 September 1997, 37.

Andrews, R. C. *Under a Lucky Star.* New York: The Viking Press, 1943.

Barkow, J. H., L. Cosmides, and J. Tooby, eds. *The Adapted Mind: Evolutionary Psychology and the Generation of Culture.* New York: Oxford University Press, 1992.

Barnes, A., and P. Thagard. "Empathy and Analogy." *Dialogue: Canadian Philosophical Review,* 30 October 1998. Available: http://cogsci.uwaterloo.ca/Articles/Pages/Empathy.html.

Baron-Cohen, S. "Mindblind." *Natural History,* 106, (September 1997): 62–65.

Barron-Centers. Site: http://www.barron-centers.com/html/details.html. 27 December 1998.

Bateson, M. C. *Composing a Life.* New York: Plume, 1989.

Beeson, W. H. Site: http://www.beeson.com/index.html. 30 December 1998.

Bell, Q. *On Human Finery.* London: Hogarth Press, 1976.

Boorstin, D. *The Discoverers: A History of Man's Search to Know His World and Himself.* New York: Random House, 1983.

Booth, W. C. *The Rhetoric of Fiction.* Chicago: University of Chicago Press, 1983.

Brown, J. E. *Animals of the Soul: Sacred Animals of the Oglala Sioux.* Rockport, Mass.: Element Books, 1992.

Bruner, J. *Acts of Meaning.* Cambridge, Mass.: Harvard University Press, 1990.

Carnegie, A. *The Gospel of Wealth, and Other Timely Essays.* Garden City, N. Y.: Doubleday, Doran, 1933.

Carpenter, E. "The Tribal Terror of Self-awareness." In *Principles of Visual Anthropology,* P. Hockings, ed., 451–61. The Hague: Mouton, 1975.

Church of Bob. Site: http://www.tiac.net/users/modemac/home.html. 23 October 1998.

Coe, K. "Art: The Replicable Unit—An Inquiry into the Possible Origin of Art as a Social Behavior." *Journal of Social and Evolutionary Systems,* 15 (1993): 217–34.

Collingwood, R. G. *The Idea of History.* New York: Oxford University Press, 1946.

Conconi, C. *Washington Post,* 1 November 1988, Personalities section, E3.

Conze, E. *Buddhist Scriptures: Selected and Translated.* New York: Viking Penguin, 1986.

Cosmides, L. and J. Tooby. *Evolutionary Psychology: A Primer.* Available: http://www.psych.ucsb.edu/research/cep/primer.htm. 30 October 1998.

Crews, E. C. *Pueblo Indian Religion,* vols. 1, 2. Chicago: University of

Chicago Press, 1939, reprint, Lincoln: University of Nebraska Press, 1996.

Csikszentmihalyi, M. *The Evolving Self: A Psychology for the Third Millennium.* New York: Harper Collins, 1993.

Cushing, F. H. *Zuni Fetishes,* 1883. Reprint, Las Vegas: KC Publications, 1994.

Junior Lewis Davis v. Mary Sue Davis. 842 S.W.2d 588 (Supreme Court of Tennessee, 1992).

Darwin, C. *The Expression of the Emotions in Man and Animals,* 1872. Reprint, Chicago: University of Chicago Press, 1965.

Dawkins, R. "Viruses of the Mind," 1991. Available: http://www.physics.wisc.edu/~shalizi/Dawkins/viruses-of-the-mind.html. 30 October 1998.

———. "Is God a Computer Virus?" *New Statesman & Society,* December-January 1992–93, 42–45.

———. "Religion is a Virus: Why God is a Product of Natural Selection." Interview with Richard Dawkins, 30 October 1998. Available:http://www.motherjones.com/mother-jones/ND97/virus.html. November/December 1997.

———. "Is Science a Religion?" *The Humanist,* 57 (1997): 26.

Dennett *Brainstorms: Philosophical Essays on Mind and Psychology.* Cambridge: MIT Press, 1978.

De Waal, F. *Good Natured:The Origins of Right and Wrong in Humans and Other Animals.* Cambridge: Harvard University Press, 1996.

Diamond, J. "The Best Ways to Sell Sex." *Discovery.* (December 1996): 78–85.

Dunbar, R. *Grooming, Gossip, and the Evolution of Language.* Cambridge: Harvard University Press, 1996.

Einstein, A. "Albert Einstein: Philosopher-Scientist." In *The Library of Living Philosophers,* vol. VII, Edited by P. A. Schilpp, 3–94. Evanston, Ill.: Open Court Publishing, 1941. Available: http://www.socail.chass.ncsu.edu/~flowers/einstein/autobiog.htm.

Eliade, M. *Patterns in Comparative Religion,* 1958. Translated by R. Sheed. Lincoln, Neb.: University of Nebraska Press, 1996.

Elmer-DeWitt, P. "The (Digitized) Eye of the Beholder." *Time,* 10 February 1986, 76.

Erikson, E. *Identity: Youth and Crisis.* New York: W. W. Norton, 1968.

Erman, A. *Life in Ancient Egypt,* 1894. Reprint, New York: Dover Books, 1971.

Faulstich, P. "Pictures of the Dreaming: Aboriginal Rock Art of Australia." *Archaeology,* 39, (1986): 18-25.

Fimmel, R. O., J. Van Allen, and E. Burgess. *Pioneer: First to Jupiter, Saturn, and Beyond.* Washington, D.C.: Scientific and Technical Information Office, National Aeronautics and Space Administration, 1980.

Frankl, V. *Man's Search for Meaning,* 1939. Reprint, New York: Pocket Books, 1963.

Gallup, G. "Self-awareness and the Emergence of Mind in Primates." *American Journal of Primatology,* 2 (1982): 237–48.

Gardner, H. *Frames of Mind: The Theory of Multiple Intelligences.* New York: Basic Books, 1983.

Garner, D. "The 1997 Body Image Survey Results." *Psychology Today,* 30, (1997): 30.

Gergen, K. J. *The Saturated Self: Dilemmas of Identity in Contemporary Life.* New York: Basic Books, 1991.

Goffman, E. *The Presentation of Self in Everyday Life.* New York: Anchor Books, 1959.

Goldthwaite, J. *The Natural History of Make-Believe: A Guide to the Principal Works of Britain, Europe, and America.* New York: Oxford University Press, 1996.

Gould, S. J. "Creating the Creators." *Discover,* October 1996, 43–54.

Gross, J. "No. 1 Topic for Women in Therapy: Diana," 13 September 1997. Available: http://www.nytimes.com/library/world/diana/091397/diana-psychology.html.

Guare, J. *Six Degrees of Separation.* New York: Vintage Books, 1990.

Hagen, U. *Respect for Acting.* New York: Macmillan, 1973.

Haiken, E. *Venus Envy: A History of Cosmetic Surgery.* Baltimore: Johns Hopkins University Press, 1997.

Hampton v. Guare. 82 N.Y.2d 659 Cir.5, 14 F.3d 438, (1993).

Harlow, H. F. "The Heterosexual Affectional System in Monkeys." *American Psychologist,* 17 (1962): 1–9.

Harris, M. B. "Growing Old Gracefully: Age Concealment and Gender." *Journal of Gerontology: Psychological Sciences,* 49 (1994): 149–58.

Harrold, F. B. "A Comparative Analysis of Eurasian Paleolithic Burials." *World Archaeology,* 12 (1980): 195–211.

Harvard Magazine, September-October 1998, 89.

Hoffer, E. *The True Believer: Thoughts on the Nature of Mass Movements.* New York: New American Library, 1951.

Hofstadter, D., and D. Dennett. *The Mind's I: Fantasies and Reflections on Self & Soul.* New York: Basic Books, 1981.

Honan, C. Interview with Cindy Jackson, 19 June 1997, *(London)Daily Telegraph,* 27. WL 2318394.

Hurston, Z. N. *Mules & Men.* Bloomington: Indiana University Press, 1935.

James, W. *Principles of Psychology.* New York: Henry Holt, 1890. Reprint, Dover Publications, 1950.

———. *Psychology: Briefer Course.* New York: Henry Holt, 1892.

———. *The Will to Believe and Other Essays in Popular Philosophy.* Cambridge, Mass.: Harvard University Press, 1897.

———. *Human Immortality,* 1898. Available: http://www.people.delphi.com/vlorbik/immortal/text.html.

———. *The Varieties of Religious Experience: A Study in Human Nature.* New York: Longmans, Green, 1902. Reprint, Modern Library, 1902.

———. *Pragmatism,* 1907. Reprint, Indianapolis: Hackett Publishing, 1981.

———. *Pragmatism: A New Name for Some Old Ways of Thinking,* 1907. Reprint, Indianapolis: Hackett Publishing, 1981.

Johnson, V. Site: http://www.psych.nmsu.edu/vic/faceprints.

Johnson, V. S., and M. Franklin. "Is Beauty in the Eye of the Beholder?" *Ethnology and Sociobiology,* 14 (1993): 183–99.

Kaplan, J. A. *Unexpected Journeys: The Art and Life of Remedios Varo.* New York: Abbeville Press, 1988.

Kaplan, S. "Environmental Preference in a Knowledge-seeking, Knowledge-using Organism. In *The Adapted Mind: Evolutionary Psychology and the Generation of Culture.* Edited by J. H. Barkow, L. Cosmides, and J. Tooby. New York: Oxford University Press, 1992.

Keegan, J. *The Face of Battle.* New York: Viking Press, 1976.

Kiernan, V. "Cosmetic Uses of Genetic Engineering May Soon Be a Reality." *The Chronicle of Higher Education,* 3 October 1997, A 17.

Kolata, G. "When Grandmother Is the Mother, Until Birth." *New York Times,* 5 August 1991, A7.

———. "On Cloning Humans, 'Never' Turns Swiftly into 'Why Not' " *New York Times,* 2 December 1997, A1.

Kosko, B. *Fuzzy Thinking: The New Science of Fuzzy Logic.* New York: Hyperion, 1993.

Kotre, J. *White gloves: How we create ourselves through memory.* New York: Free Press, 1995.

Lawson, C. "A Toy That Steals Hearts Only to Break Them." *New York Times,* 22 May 1997, B7.

Leary, T. Site: http://www.leary.com. 27 December 1998.

Leatherman, C. "Numerous Academics Have Been Duped by a Scam Using Names of Prominent Scholars." *The Chronicle of Higher Education,* 23 May 1997: A10–11.

McArdle, S. "Overview of the U.S. Cosmetics and Toiletries Market." *Drug & Cosmetic Industry,* 160 (June 1997): 28.

Margulis, L., and D. Sagan. *What Is Life?* New York: Simon & Schuster, 1995.

McFague, S. *Models of God: Theology for an Ecological, Nuclear Age.* Philadelphia: Fortress Press, 1987.

Messner, R. *Free spirit: A Climber's Life.* Seattle: The Mountaineers, 1989.

Mithen, S. *The Prehistory of the Mind: The Cognitive Origins of Art, Religion and Science.* London: Thames and Hudson, 1996.

Montoya, M. "*Mascaras, Trenzas, y Grenas:* Un/masking the Self While Un/braiding Latina Stories with Legal Discourse." *Chicano-Latino L. Rev,* 15, 1994, 1–37.

Myers, G. E. *William James: His Life and Thought.* New Haven: Yale University Press, 1986.

Neihardt, J. G. *Black Elk Speaks: Being the Life Story of a Holy Man of the Oglala Sioux as Told Through John G. Neihardt,* 1932. Reprint, Lincoln: University of Nebraska Press, 1972.

Niebuhr, G. "Is Satan a Real Being? Most Americans Think Not." *New York Times,* 10 May 1997, Y8.

Orians, G. H., and J. H. Heerwagen. "Evolved Responses to Landscapes." In *The Adapted Mind: Evolutionary Psychology and the Generation of Culture.* Edited by J. H. Barkow, L.Cosmides, and J. Tooby. New York: Oxford University Press, 1992.

Otto, R. *The Idea of the Holy,* second edition. New York: Oxford University Press, 1958.

Pagels, E. H. *The Origin of Satan.* New York: Random House, 1995.

Penis Power Quarterly. Site: http://www.best.com/~wking/ppq.html. 27 December 1998.

Perkins, D. N. "Person-plus: A Distributed View of Thinking and Learning. In *Distributed Cognitions: Psychological and Educational Considerations.* Edited by G. Salmon. New York: Cambridge University Press, 1993, 88–110.

Perry, R. B. *The Thought and Character of William James.* Cambridge, Mass: Harvard University Press, 1948. Reprint, Nashville: Vanderbilt University Press, 1996.

Piaget, J. *Play, Dreams, and Imitation in childhood.* New York: W. W. Norton, 1951.

Pinker, S. *How the Mind Works.* New York: W. W. Norton, 1997.

Povinelli, D. J., and C. G. Prince. "When Self Met Other." In *Self-awareness: Its Nature and Development.* Edited by M. Ferari and R. J. Sternberg, 37–107. New York: Guilford, 1998.

Powers, W. T. *Behavior: The Control of Perception.* Chicago: Aldine, 1973.

Premack, D., and Woodruff, G. "Does the Chimpanzee Have a Theory of Mind?" *Behavioral and Brain Sciences,* 1 (1978): 525–6.

Progoff, I. *At a Journal Workshop: Writing to Access the Power of the Unconscious and Evoke Creative Ability.* New York: Putnam, 1992.

Quindlen, A. "Barbie at 35." *New York Times,* 10 September 1994, Y15.

Riemer, J., and Stampfer, N., eds. *So That Your Values Live On: Ethical Wills and How to Prepare Them.* Woodstock, Vt.: Jewish Lights Publishing, 1991.

Roberts, A. F. "Tabwa Tegumetary Inscription." In *Marks of Civilization: Artistic Transformations of the Human Body.* Edited by A. Rubin. Los Angeles: Museum of Cultural History, University of California, 1988.

Rubin, A., ed. *Marks of Civilization: Artistic Transformations of the Human Body.* Los Angeles: Museum of Cultural History, University of California, 1988.

Schneider, D. S., S. Levitt, D. Morton, P. Yoo, S. Skolnik, A. Brooks, R. Jones, R. Arias, L. McNeil, J. Sugden, D. Sider, M. Salcines, B. Sandler, and M. Nelson. "Mission Impossible Deluged by Images from TV, Movies and Magazines, Teenage Girls Do Battle with an Increasingly Unrealistic Standard of Beauty—and Pay a Price." *People,* 45 (3 June 1996): 64.

Segal, M., and D. Adcock. *Your Child at Play: Three to Five Years.* New York: Newmarket Press, 1986.

Shelley, M. *Frankenstein; or The Modern Prometheus,* 1818. Reprint, New York: E. P. Dutton, 1933.

Singer, D. G., and J. L. Singer. *The House of Make-believe: Children's Play and the Developing Imagination.* Cambridge, Mass.: Harvard University Press, 1990.

Singh, D. "Adaptive Significance of Female Physical Attractiveness: Role of Waist-to-Hip Ratio." *Journal of Personality and Social Psychology,* 65 (1993): 293–307.

Smith, H. *The World's Great Religions: Our Great Wisdom Traditions.* New York: HarperCollins, 1991.

Smith, J. "The U.S. Cosmetics and Toiletries Sector in 1995." *Drug & Cosmetic Industry,* 158 (1996): 28.

Spindler, A. "It's a Face-lifted, Tummy-tucked Jungle Out There. *New York Times,* 9 June 1996, F1.

Spindler, K. *The Man in the Ice.* New York: Harmony Books/Crown, 1994.

Tamagotchi. Site: http://www.geocities.com/Tokyo/Temple/ 8772/main.htm. 1 December 1997.

Tattersall, I. *Becoming Human: Evolution and Human Uniqueness.* New York: Harcourt Brace, 1998.

Thurber, J. "The Secret Life of Walter Mitty." In *My World and Welcome to It.* New York: Harcourt Brace, 1942. Reprint, Mankato, Minn.: Creative Education, 1983.

Tipler, F. *The Physics of Immortality: Modern Cosmology, God and the Resurrection of the Dead.* New York: Doubleday, 1994.

Time 142, no. 21 (fall 1993): cover photo.

Tooby, J., and L. Cosmides, "The Psychological Foundations of Culture." In *The Adapted Mind: Evolutionary Psychology and the Generation of Culture.* Edited by J. H. Barkow, L. Cosmides, and J. Tooby. New York: Oxford University Press, 1992.

Turkle, S. *Life on the Screen: Identity in the Age of the Internet.* New York: Simon & Schuster, 1995.

Turner, M. *The Literary Mind.* New York: Oxford University Press, 1996.

Tyldesley, J. *Daughters of Isis: Women of Ancient Egypt.* London: Penguin, 1994.

Tylor, E. B. *Religion in Primitive Culture.* Gloucester, Mass.: Peter Smith, 1970.

Van Biema, D. "Does Heaven Exist?" *Time,* 24 March 1997, 149, 70–78.

Vickers, M. "Stop, Thief! And Give Me Back My Name." *New York Times,* 28 January 1996, F1.

Watkins, E. "Technology At Your Service: Lodging Technology Isn't Much Good If It Doesn't Enhance Guest Service Levels." *Lodging Hospitality,* 46 (1990): 141.

Wattles, J. *The Golden Rule.* New York: Oxford University Press, 1996.

Weber, R. J. *Forks, Phonographs, and Hot Air Balloons: A Field Guide to Inventive Thinking.* New York: Oxford University Press, 1992.

Weber, R. J., S. Dixon, and A. M. Llorente. "Studying Invention: The Hand Tool As a Model System." *Science, Technology, & Human Values,* 18 (1993): 480–505.

Weber, R. J., and D. N. Perkins., eds. *Inventive Minds: Creativity in Technology.* Oxford University Press, 1992.

Whitman, W. *Leaves of Grass.* Philadelphia: McKay, 1918. Available: http://www.jefferson.village.virginia.edu/whitman/works/leaves/1891/text/frameset/html. 23 October 1998.

Williams, G. C. *Adaptation and Natural Selection: A Critique of Some Current Evolutionary Thought.* Princeton, N.J.: Princeton University Press, 1996.

———. *The Pony Fish's Glow.* New York: Basic Books, 1997.

Williams, G. C., and R. M. Nesse. "The Dawn of Darwinian Medicine." *The Quarterly Review of Biology,* 66 (1991): 1–22.

Wilson, E. O. *Consilience: The Unity of Knowledge.* New York: Knopf, 1998.

Wilmut, I., A. E. Schnieke, J. McWhir, A. J. Kind, and K. H. S. Campbell. "Viable Offspring Derived from Fetal and Adult Mammalian Cells." *Nature,* 385 (1997) 810–13.

Wilson, J. Q. *The Moral Sense.* New York: Free Press, 1993.

Windschutle, K. *The Killing of History: How Literary Critics and Social Theorists Are Murdering Our Past.* New York: Free Press, 1996.

Winston, D. "Campuses Are a Bellwether for Society's Religious Revival." *The Chronicle of Higher Education,* 16 January 1998, A60.

Witchel, A. The Delusions That Gave Life to 'Six Degrees.'" *New York Times,* 21 June 1990, B1.

Wright, R. *Time,* 10 March 1997, 73.

Zolbrod, P. *Dine Bahane: The Navajo Creation Story.* Albuquerque: University of New Mexico Press, 1984.

INDEX